My Big Red Machine

My Big Red Machine

The Tales, Drama, And Revelations Of A Fan Turned Journalist Covering Baseball's Greatest Team

TERENCE MOORE

Copyright © 2025 by Terence Moore.
All rights reserved.

No part of this publication or the information in it may be quoted from or reproduced in any form by means such as printing, scanning, photocopying or otherwise without prior written permission of the copyright holder.

Library of Congress Cataloging-in-Publication Data

Names: Moore, Terence (Sports journalist), author
Title: My big red machine: the tales, drama, and revelations of a fan turned journalist covering baseball's greatest team/Terence Moore
Summary: This book gives the journey of a young fan who grew up to become a professional sports journalist covering his baseball heroes.
Identifiers: LCCN 2025917737 | ISBN (hardcover) 9798999371119 | ISBN (paperback) 9798999371102 | ISBN (e-book) 9798999371126 | ISBN (audio) 9798999371133
Subjects: LCSH: Baseball—Cincinnati Reds—Pete Rose— Joe Morgan — Sparky Anderson. | History—Sports journalism—The Cincinnati Enquirer — San Francisco Examiner. | SPORTS & RECREATION/ General

Dedication

To the eternal memory of Sam and Annie Moore who always were proud of Terence, Dennis, and Darrell, their sports-loving sons who followed after their parents.

Contents

Foreword by Marty Brennaman xi

Introduction xv

1. Black Tuesday (and Wednesday) 1
2. Go Irish and Cubbies 27
3. Is This Heaven? 43
4. The First Red Machine 59
5. The New Red Machine 79
6. An Almost Dynasty 101
7. The Real Dynasty 133
8. The Transition 153
9. Goodbye, Machine 175
10. Pete and Joe 195
11. The Call 219

Epilogue 235

Acknowledgments 241

FOREWORD

Marty Brennaman,
MLB Hall of Fame Broadcaster

When I think back over my 46 years with the Reds as an announcer and when I go back to those early years of the 1970s, I remember how I was blessed to have come to Cincinnati in 1974, and then to have the Big Red Machine all of a sudden take baseball by storm and win back-to-back world championships in 1975 and 1976. I look back on those years, and I think more about the people I knew more so than anything else, because I crossed paths with some very, very talented individuals, and they obviously were players, managers, baseball executives and what not. But I also encountered some talented individuals covering this ball club, and they were journalists for a living, and one young man stood out back then.

He's not so young today, but the one young man who stood out back then was a fellow by the name of Terence Moore. He was working for *The Cincinnati Enquirer*, and doing Reds stories was one of the early positions he held, because he was a graduate of Miami University in Oxford, Ohio, and he was fortunate enough to get a job right out of college in what essentially was his hometown. He covered those Reds, and he did it with incredible aplomb and with incredible ability to resonate with veteran ballplayers, many of whom would someday go into the Baseball Hall of Fame, and Terence did it like falling out of bed.

I was amazed by Terence's willingness to write tough pieces when necessary, because there were veteran writers who by that time had begun to hold this club in awe, and with good reason, because of the success it had had in general and because of the great individual talent that was such a vital part of that ball club. But Terence Moore never had a problem with walking up to a player and talking to him and asking him very insightful questions, and I think that drew instantaneous respect from the veteran guys he was talking to. They realized this guy isn't cut out of the same cloth as a lot of these other writers.

The reason Terence made such a memorable impression on me is because I loved to watch guys who had this innate ability that I believe they were born with to go into the writing business and make a difference as far as the people back then who opened the paper every day and read what guys wrote. Very quickly, those people formed a habit of reading Terence Moore, because they could see that this young man had the talent, so they were going to read him and read him religiously. He operated as a pure journalist from the start. After he did his reporting and his interviewing of those stars and others associated with the Big Red Machine, he waded through his material, picked out what was important and chucked aside what wasn't. That's why — and I can say this as somebody who has followed Terence closely through the years — he was able to rise so quickly in this profession to a position of very, very big-time prominence.

So the fact that the young man out of Miami Ohio I met way back in the late 1970s is writing this book today is not surprising to me. In fact, I would say to Terence Moore: "What the hell took you so long? I mean, you've lived this. You saw this team. As a fan, you saw what it did to the Red Sox in seven games in 1975, and as a fan, you saw what this team did in 1976 in making short order of Billy Martin's New York Yankees in four games. Then as a journalist, you saw the great players and manager Sparky Anderson up close and what they meant to this team. You also saw as a journalist the various pieces of the ball club begin to depart as the Big Red Machine was dismantled."

Nobody is more qualified to write this book than the young man I first met way back in the 1970s on his way to becoming the accomplished veteran that he is now. I think you're going to find as you go to Page 1 after reading this foreword and then the introduction and then begin to read what he writes and what his impressions were and what was impactful to him — you're going to find that this book is going to become second nature for you, and you won't be able to put it down.

You'll automatically find yourself telling your relatives and your friends, "If you want to read a great baseball book about the Big Red Machine back in the 1970s and learn things you never knew before, this is the book to read."

I recommend it highly, because I know what Terence's talents were then, and I know what his talents are today, and I would say very concisely: Do yourself a favor, because after you read this book by Terence Moore, you will be absolutely amazed.

Photo Credit: The Cincinnati Enquirer.

Author's note: *Never has there been a sportscaster more outspoken and more respected than Marty Brennaman, a master at announcing, not only baseball, but football and basketball over the decades after growing up in his native Virginia. In addition to his Cooperstown induction, he was named Ohio Sportscaster of the Year 16 times and Virginia Sportscaster of the Year four times, and he is in the National Sportscasters and Sportswriters Association Hall of Fame as well as the National Radio Hall of Fame.*

Bigger than that, Marty Brennaman and Joe Nuxhall, his broadcast partner for the first 30 of his 46 years as the radio voice of the Cincinnati Reds, were more than announcers. They were family to me and to anybody else who followed the team in those days.

Introduction

James Brown!!! So, would standing up close and personal someday to Johnny Bench, Joe Morgan, Tony Perez, and, Oh, my God, Pete Rose, along with the rest of my Big Red Machine guys from the Cincinnati Reds, match a brief yet private audience involving my two brothers and me with The Godfather of Soul?

Yes.

Well, no.

Both situations were complicated.

Those Reds players of the late 1960s through the 1970s filled my childhood with magic, which brings this to mind: They say you should never meet your heroes. Unlike other fans, I got a chance, not only to meet them during their prime as athletes, but to cover them as a journalist. I also developed life-long relationships with some of them. Along with the thrill on Friday, May 14, 1976, of walking into that home clubhouse for the first time at Riverfront Stadium in Cincinnati at age 20, I was also terrified: *What if these players don't live up to my expectations? What if getting to know them ruins everything?*

It didn't ruin everything. But it did.

I told you it was complicated.

There also was the race factor. I grew up in a family of Jackie Robinsons, starting with my dad, Sam Moore, who went from a janitor at Indiana Bell in South Bend during the early 1950s to the first African American supervisor in the history of AT&T during the 1960s, when he was transferred to Cincinnati. The family joined him, of course. He later became one of AT&T's first African American managers after a series of transfers that took us to Milwaukee after a brief stop in Chicago. My mom, Annie Moore, was the first African American employee of Associates Savings and Loan, which was based in South Bend, and she later became the first African American supervisor for the Federal Reserve Bank in Milwaukee. My brothers, Dennis and Darrell, and I were close to our parents. They gave us the foundation for handling racial issues that we would experience, and they were omniscient.

I was on my way to becoming the Jackie Robinson of many things, especially regarding sports journalism. Among my "firsts," I was the first African American sportswriter in the history of *The Cincinnati Enquirer* when I joined the paper in May 1978. Days, weeks and months later, I soon became only the second African American reporter ever to spend a significant amount of time writing about a Major League Baseball team for a major metropolitan newspaper. As fate would have it, my assignments involved the Big Red Machine, the greatest baseball team of all time.

Covering these future Hall of Famers would be enough of a big deal for any young journalist, but it was more than that to me. Those Cincinnati Reds were my heroes of the sport while growing up.

I balanced fandom with professionalism.

It was difficult, but it wasn't.

OK, it was.

Did I mention this was complicated?

In addition to back-to-back World Series titles in 1975 and 1976, those Reds won more games during the decade than anybody in baseball. The solar system focused on the Machine's every move. So, I had that pressure as a 22-year-old reporter, along with the Black thing, especially since I began working for the Enquirer a week after I graduated from Miami University in Oxford, Ohio, just 35 miles north of Cincinnati.

It all led to nearly 50 years for me as a professional journalist.

My future assignments included those powerful Oakland Raiders and San Francisco 49ers teams of the 1980s when I worked for the *San Francisco Examiner*. There were also my 25 years as a newspaper columnist for the *Atlanta Journal-Constitution* before I transitioned to a combination of internet columnist and TV commentator. I've covered more than 30 Super Bowls, multiple Final Fours, numerous Olympic, World Series and

Introduction

college football bowl games, major prize fights, golf tournaments and other sporting events.

And yet nothing topped those years going from fan to journalist with my Big Red Machine. I developed a strong connection with several of those cogs. There was Joe Morgan, for one. He was baseball's greatest second baseman ever on baseball's greatest team ever, and he was African American.

Over the years, as Morgan went from Hall of Fame player to Emmy-winning broadcaster, I became his most trusted confidant among journalists regarding his thoughts on racism. He always was blunt and passionate on the subject, which I will share in this book. For one, he joined baseball great Hank Aaron in telling me during the early 1980s that those who ran the game feared there were too many successful African American players. In fact, both Morgan and Aaron told me back then that, by design, there would be a minuscule number of African American players in the Major Leagues by the 21st century.

They were correct.

As you can tell, this is not just another Big Red Machine book, and there have been many. Take it from Marty Brennaman, who kept saying, "Wow. I've never heard *that* before," on the other end of the phone as I relayed to him several of the things I was putting in the book. This is the same Marty Brennaman who knew the pulse of the Reds better than anybody as their play-by-play radio announcer for 46 years through the 2019 season.

Marty and I became friends during the early part of his Reds career, and our phone call regarding my book was the first time I heard the gifted Baseball Hall of Fame broadcaster nearly speechless.

I provided Marty details of the most riveting interview ever given by Bob Howsam, the Big Red Machine architect who bore his baseball soul to me at 87 in January of 2006 (which was two years before his death).

Marty's reaction?

"I have to be honest with you," Marty said. "He told you a lot of stuff I had no knowledge of, and I thought I heard everything about those Reds teams, but I would say 70 percent of what Bob Howsam said to you, I have never heard before. He may have not only told anybody but you all that stuff. I'm serious. I found it fascinating. This will add to the interest, I will promise you that, and it's not just me. You've got stuff that nobody has ever heard before."

Along with Howsam and Morgan, I have such "stuff" from George Foster, Tony Perez, Sparky Anderson, and other integral members of the Big Red Machine. Then there is Rose, baseball's all-time hits leader and my all-time favorite player, and our conversations often went deeper than deep. They happened throughout the nearly half century after I first met him during my initial trip to the Reds clubhouse at Riverfront Stadium.

I was overwhelmed that day.

On Friday, May 14, 1976, I was 20, and it was nearly two years to the day before I would officially leave college to become a professional journalist. I saw my future as a fan-turned-journalist and didn't know it.

Rose and the rest of his Reds teammates were like family to me, both during and after their playing days. When Dad was transferred by AT&T during the fall of 1968 to Cincinnati, the foundation for the Big Red Machine began that next year. The walls and the roof followed in 1970 when I began to devour all things Reds through the radio airways or in person at Crosley Field and later at Riverfront Stadium.

Even with more AT&T transfers for my dad to Chicago and then Milwaukee, I couldn't get enough of those Reds, especially as they grew during the decade into a dynasty that nevertheless produced some of the most agonizing moments ever for a baseball franchise and for a loyal fan like me.

Those Reds were charismatic, too.

Later, when I became a professional sports journalist, I had the chance to separate fact from fiction involving my Big Red Machine as an eyewitness from the press box, in the locker room, around the dugout, and by the batting cage, and the fiction was minimal while the facts were extraordinary. I was trusted enough by several of the Machine's players to learn amazing things, even beyond their glorious run, and I've shared them in this book.

Introduction

I got chills while typing.

So about meeting James Brown.

When we moved from South Bend to Cincinnati in November 1968, my dad bought our house from Tom Hankerson, a noted program director and radio voice for WCIN, the local African American station. He was close to Brown, who recorded his songs at the time at King Records in town.

In 1969, Hankerson gave a group of backstage passes to our family and to our next-door neighbors to see Brown perform at Cincinnati Gardens. We were already huge fans. In 1967, when we still lived in South Bend, the pompadour-wearing singer, who had just debuted the hit single "Cold Sweat" for our already mighty collection of his records, kept us and everybody else standing and screaming at Morris Civic Auditorium.

Two years later in Cincinnati Gardens, we were standing and screaming again for the same guy, but this was different. This time we had a chance to meet James Brown face-to-face behind the curtains.

It wasn't what we expected.

Yeah, his fancy hairdo was just inches away from us. Yeah, we could reach out and touch his colorful outfit and his Cuban-heeled boots with the pointy toes. Yeah, his Famous Flames were right there.

We kept thinking, wow.

Look how short he is.

In contrast, despite going from fan to journalist, my Big Red Machine folks remained bigger than life, especially Pete Rose.

I hope you enjoy reading the stories about my life and the Big Red Machine.

Chapter 1

Black Tuesday (and Wednesday)

The last time I saw Pete Rose was by accident. During the fall of 2015, he sat there, looking comfortable enough to order lunch and maybe dinner and breakfast later from his lounge chair before a handful of students in a conference room at Miami University in Oxford, Ohio.

I was mesmerized by the sight.

Then again, this was Peter Edward Rose, my all-time favorite baseball player as a youth, and he also became my all-time favorite athlete during my career as a professional sports reporter of nearly five decades. He sat there, chatting across the way, clad in his standard attire during the latter innings of his life. He wore a white cap with a "C" in the same color. His oversized button-up white dress shirt with gray stripes had the words "Hit King" on one of the collars, and below his dark slacks, his white boots looked ready for the revival of disco.

Rose resembled Rose, but he owned more weight around his head and his waist than I had ever seen before. He sounded the same, with his distinctive baritone voice that occasionally made grammarians cringe. He was delivering parts of his considerable life story in this cozy setting at my alma mater, where I served as a visiting professor in the Media, Journalism and Film department. I did so between working in Atlanta as a national sports columnist for internet sites and as a commentator on local and national television.

I whispered to somebody nearby, "Why is he here?" I was told that my guy, otherwise known as "Pete" and "Charlie Hustle" during his 23 Major League Baseball seasons – mostly as a star player for the Cincinnati Reds, located 35 miles to the south –was attending this little event in the afternoon before his big lecture that evening. The latter was titled "Winning is Everything: The Hit King Talks Ethics in Sport."

Yeah, this was my guy, but Pete Rose?

Ethics in sports?

Ohhhkayyyy.

I had no idea about any of this. While taking a break from grading papers, I just happened to peek into this room at the student center, and after seeing a 74-year-old man I had first met exactly 39 years, four months and seven days before, I tried not to interrupt his flow. I slipped into a seat in the distance.

Next thing I knew, I heard that voice.

"There's Terry. That's Terry Moore. He and I go back a long way," said that voice, coming from Rose, pointing and smiling like it was Friday, May 14, 1976, when we first met in the Reds clubhouse at Riverfront Stadium. He still had those sparkling eyes. I saw them way back then during my maiden journey inside the living quarters of a professional sports team, and that particular clubhouse belonged to my Big Red Machine.

Those Reds were part of my body, mind, and soul, mostly for the good, but there were ghastly times, too. I already knew about extreme passion as a sports fan. I was born and raised through adolescence in South Bend, Indiana, home of the University of Notre Dame, where Knute Rockne, Touchdown Jesus, and The Golden Dome made college football famous. From birth, I bled the Blue and the Gold of the Fighting Irish, and I was higher than high for the grandest of their victories, and lower than low for any of their losses, especially the infamous ones. Believe it or not, there were many.

I still cringe over the words "Anthony Davis."

In November 1974, Notre Dame moved closer to a second consecutive national championship with a 24-0 lead at the Los Angeles Coliseum, but Southern Cal scored 55 unanswered points, and Davis stomped on the Irish's grave with four touchdowns.

I've yet to recover.

The same goes for every postseason loss involving the Big Red Machine during my youth when eating and sleeping became optional for me in the aftermath.

Then I got to cover those Reds up close and personal working for *The Cincinnati Enquirer* during the late 1970s as a sports journalist, and the first rule you learn in the profession is NO CHEERING IN THE PRESS BOX. I didn't. Even so, I developed a strong relationship over the decades with many of those Reds, especially Rose, who did so much to trigger my obsession as a youth for the Big Red Machine.

They say you shouldn't meet your heroes. Well, I did, and then I went further. I dealt with them on a consistent basis as a double oddity. First, I was in my early 20s when the average age of the majority of the journalists writing frequently about the Big Red Machine ranged between twice my age and slightly shy of deceased.

Second, I was the only one darker than a baseball.

Until I was a 1977 summer intern with the *Enquirer* – which was before I became a full-time employee at the paper the next spring – there never had been an African American as part of the media contingent for the Reds, and they became baseball's first professional team in 1869. In fact, I was only the second full-time African American writer in the history of the paper, the first African American intern, and the first African American ever in the sports department.

I also joined Larry Whiteside of the *Boston Globe* back then as the only African Americans in the universe working for major metropolitan newspapers and writing about baseball beyond a story here and there.

Oh, and for me, this was the Big Red Machine. It also was my Big Red Machine, the team I cherished so much, but the team that would cause my professional demise in a flash if I forgot for a moment I wasn't a fan anymore, you know, especially with all those eyes on an extremely young journalist who happened to be Black.

Talk about pressure.

This added to it: The Big Red Machine reigned when newspapers were king, so since the Reds of southwestern Ohio drew from a tri-state area of Ohio, Indiana, and Kentucky, their media contingent in the 1970s was competitive and huge. On a regular basis, it involved the two major dailies in both Cincinnati and Dayton, the Hamilton, Ohio, paper, and then there were frequent visits from the *The Columbus Dispatch* and the *The Courier-Journal* in Louisville.

I had supporters among my peers, but there also were the detractors, and they mostly struck from the shadows. It didn't matter either way. Since I grew up in a family of Jackie Robinsons, courtesy of my parents who were "the first" at several things, I wasn't allowed to feel sorry for myself, and I wasn't going to fail.

"No matter what. Don't let anybody get inside your head," Sam Moore used to say as the combination of our dad and the former Army sergeant who became the first African American supervisor and later manager in the history of AT&T. He consistently matched his actions with his words for me and my younger brothers Dennis and Darrell. The same was true of Annie Moore, our mother who did extraordinary things as well: "Never forget that the only person who can put limits on what you can do in life is yourself," she would say.

So, regarding my days of writing about the Big Red Machine, along with my decades afterward working as a professional journalist in San Francisco and later Atlanta, those days were about surviving, advancing, and prospering.

Haters were just momentary distractions.

Forget them.

Even during my early years as a professional journalist, I did that, and I did so enough to break stories along the way … and nothing changed into the 21st century.

While researching this book, I discovered an interview I did with Bob Howsam, the architect of those Reds as general manager, and our lengthy chat occurred slightly less than two years before his death in February 2008. According to Baseball Hall of Fame broadcaster Marty Brennaman, who was the radio voice of the Reds for 46 years through the Big Red Machine era, "70%" of what I got from Howsam was brand new.

When Howsam wasn't making me gasp by telling the true reason the Reds let my guy Pete Rose leave the Reds as a free agent after the 1978 season for the Philadelphia Phillies, Howsam was explaining why he tried to make a significant move after the Reds lost the 1970 World Series that would have kept the famous Joe Morgan trade of 1972 from happening.

There was so much more from that interview.

But during the Big Red Machine days, Howsam gave the public nothing.

The bottom line: Howsam remembered my professional reporting skills at *The Cincinnati Enquirer*, which meant I conquered (or at least controlled) that fandom thing while covering my Big Red Machine. But through it all, Pete Rose remained my guy. Fate kept it that way, even beyond our chance meeting in 2015 at Miami University.

- I was there during much of Rose's National League-record 44-game hitting streak through the summer of 1978.
- I was there in Philadelphia in October 1980 after Rose helped to secure a World Series victory for his Phillies in the ninth inning against the Kansas City Royals, when catcher Bob Boone dropped a foul pop-up but Charlie Hustle, rushing over from first, made the catch before the ball hit the ground.
- I was there in Chicago when Rose tied Ty Cobb's all-time hits record at Wrigley in September 1985, and I was there in Cincinnati three days later when he broke the record at Riverfront Stadium.
- I was there in Plant City, Florida, during the spring of 1989 when Rose told me during a one-on-one conversation that he huddled with Baseball Commissioner Bart Giamatti the previous day but that it wasn't about his gambling habits, even though it was.
- I was there in Cincinnati during the fall of 1989, sitting in the front row in a back room of Riverfront Stadium, where Rose stared into local and national TV cameras and said, "I did not bet on baseball."

So here was fate bringing Rose and I together again in 2015, and of all places, it happened in Oxford, Ohio, home of my university, featuring a gorgeous array of red brick buildings amongst manicured grounds less than an hour's drive north of Rose's old MLB stomping grounds along the Ohio River. While Pete, good, ole Pete, delivered his familiar gestures and smiles in the distance to his young audience, the old memories surrounding my guy and my Big Red Machine began surfacing in my mind like line drives.

For instance . . .

Despite everything great about the Big Red Machine, its horror of horrors (and there were significant ones) never left my soul.

Thanks, Carlton Fisk.

He's otherwise known as That Guy to those of us into mom, "Gilligan's Island" reruns, and all things Big Red Machine, baseball's greatest team (sorry, 1927 New York Yankees). That Guy used the 30 ounces of his 34-inch Louisville Slugger to produce the most agonizing moment for the Machine. It happened at 12:33 a.m. on Wednesday, Oct. 22, 1975, at Fenway Park in Boston to place an exclamation point besides my worst experience as a sports fan.

That's when Fisk homered in the bottom of the 12th inning, and the Red Sox took Game 6 of the 1975 World Series over the Reds, but you know what?

The Reds won Game 7.

The Reds won the 1975 World Series!

They really did. Instead, nobody cares outside Cincinnati or within the memories of those who prefer truth to fantasy. As for fantasy, baseball historians have combined with much of the national media to make the Fisk homer bigger than the Reds winning it all, and it happened as soon as his blast hit Fenway's left-field pole.

I couldn't stand That Guy, and here is another example of how life often works as a fan turned journalist. Fifteen years after the Red Sox didn't win the 1975 World Series, Fisk played elsewhere in the Major Leagues. He caught for the Chicago White Sox during the summer of 1990. As a columnist for *The Atlanta-Journal Constitution*, I was in the

Windy City writing about the last days of Comiskey Park, and for the best piece, I knew I had to speak to That Guy since his All-Star Game trips were in double digits, and since he was the elder statesman of the White Sox, and since he ranked among the wisemen of baseball.

Which brings me to confessions: No matter how long you've been a professional sports journalist, your emotions from your fan days never leave you. They might be dormant in your memory, but they can surface out of nowhere by something like the sight of That Guy. When that happens, you must control yourself, or at least try.

Even though we had never met before, Fisk was so nice. His answers had depth, and his body language suggested he would talk as long as I needed him.

At the end of our discussion at Fisk's locker in the White Sox's crumbling home, I said, "Thank you," and he said with a smile, "You're welcome," but I still wanted to clench my teeth. I wanted so badly to shout while pointing at That Guy, *The Reds won the 1975 World Series!* Then I reminded myself that I made the transition years ago from diehard fan to seasoned journalist, and I thought also about this: After the horror of horrors of That Guy on Wednesday, Oct. 22, 1975, at 12:33 a.m., I should forgive That Guy since everything came together in the aftermath for my Big Red Machine, and it was awesome.

Let's stay there, but we'll return to That Guy.

During the 1970s, the Reds steamrolled their way to more victories than anybody in the decade. They grabbed back-to-back world championships in 1975 and 1976, four National League pennants, and six division titles. They did that, because they were baseball gods, which is why I lost my mind over these guys while living in Cincinnati. They had Cooperstown folks at catcher in Johnny Bench, at first base in Tony Perez, at second base in Joe Morgan and at manager in Sparky Anderson. They had the career hits leader in third baseman Pete Rose, and even with his gambling issues, he should be in the Baseball Hall of Fame, especially since the game has become an authorized haven for oddsmakers and betting slips.

Johnny, Tony, Joe, Sparky, Pete.

Just those Big Red Machine cogs made this a glorious team for the ages, but they were complemented by left fielder George Foster who won a couple of National League home run titles and a National League Most Valuable Player award.

There was shortstop Dave Concepcion, who owned five Gold Gloves and nine trips to the All-Star Game, and he should have a Cooperstown plaque. There was center fielder Cesar Geronimo who was so elite at his position that he combined with Bench, Morgan, and Concepcion to give the Reds four Gold Glovers in the middle of their defense. There was right fielder Ken Griffey Sr., who proved through his career batting average of .296 that he was more than just the father of Ken Griffey Jr., his Baseball Hall of Fame son.

Beyond those sluggers, the Big Red Machine had a couple of starting pitching aces. Flame-thrower Don Gullett began torching Major League hitters as a teenager, and he continued as an adult. The postseason-clutch Jack Billingham owned an 0.36 ERA over 25.1 innings after three trips to the World Series. Those Reds also had baseball's best bullpen ever, which is why "Captain Hook" became Anderson's nickname since he hadn't a problem leaving the dugout early during games (while always skipping over the chalky foul line to avoid bad luck) to choose from his collection of gifted relievers, spanning from Wayne Granger and Pedro Borbon to Clay Carroll and Rawly Eastwick.

It wasn't until I discovered through a conversation with Tony Perez decades later that such dominance for those Reds placed them in dangerous situations during the 1970s whenever the Big Red Machine rolled into town.

"Because of us, baseball had to change how players walked from the ballpark on road trips to get on the team bus, and now they pull the bus close to the gate, and you just get in it," said Perez in his always charming Cuban dialect. "Before, it used to be we would have to walk across the street between fans to get to the bus, but they changed that in Chicago, because so many fans wanted to attack Pete. They didn't like how hard he played. It happened in Los Angeles, too, and it even got to the point where they started driving the bus right onto the field at Dodger Stadium to get our whole team. Then everybody in baseball started doing that because of us, but, well, what would you expect? We beat a lot of people, and they got angry."

Did I mention those Reds were a machine? They were an efficient one, a spectacular one, a charismatic one, a BIG one, and thanks to the sporting gods, I had three different lives with them over six decades.

Life No. 1: I built my youth around everything they did: meals, outings, sleeping, and just existing. For whole seasons, I documented every plate appearance and pitching move of those Reds and of their opponents in a scorebook. For wins, I agonized over how they did it, and for losses, well, you don't want to know. During the playoffs, which often showcased the Big Red Machine, let's just say I was a mess.

Life No. 2: No more fandom for me, which meant no more turning those Reds into something beyond mythical. Well, such was the goal. I became a rarity since I got the chance to see what my sporting heroes were really like beyond just the images in my mind. That happened during the late 1970s after I became a professional sports journalist a week out of college for *The Cincinnati Enquirer*. The Big Red Machine became part of my duties on a frequent basis, and it was otherworldly, but it didn't surpass what happened next.

Life No. 3: I went from writing the first story ever about some 8-year-old kid named Ken Griffey Jr. when he was just the son of the right fielder for the Big Red Machine, to developing ties forever with several of those Reds.

Joe Morgan and Pete Rose topped that list.

While Morgan and I hadn't a problem huddling for more than an hour in person or over the phone to discuss everything from the intricacies of the "hit and run" to the true reasons for the decline of African American players in Major League Baseball, Rose was my guy, period. He entered my heart after one moment, probably two, when I saw the Cincinnati native play live for the first time. It was at the Reds' old home of coziness called Crosley Field, and it was during the summer of 1969. Then I met Rose seven years later, when he approached me out of baseball heaven one day with a handshake and a smile, and from there, fate had its way, even bringing us together at my college alma mater in 2015.

The legacy of the Big Red Machine – well, my Big Red Machine – was incredible, but as a fan and as a journalist, there always was that agony.

It was because of That Guy.

We're back to Carlton Fisk and the horror of horrors. For somebody like me who squeezed the Big Red Machine tighter than tight, those horrors wouldn't stop during Game 6 of the 1975 World Series at Fenway Park in Boston during the night of Tuesday, Oct. 21, 1975. Worse, they climaxed in the cruelest way during the early morning of Wednesday, Oct. 22, 1975. That Guy swung, then leaped, and then waved, and then clapped his way around the bases for his Red Sox after he hit the foul pole in left field at 12:33 a.m.

The ball kept drifting, drifting, drifting farther to the left, but unfortunately for those of us blessed by the baseball gods (you know, those who enjoyed everything about the Big Red Machine), the ball didn't keep drifting out of play.

Surely this was the devil's work. The drifting ended with the ball slamming against the left-field foul pole to become the game-winning hit that forced Game 7. With one swing from That Guy, my whole world turned from red – as in those Reds who were just a victory away from solidifying their preeminence by winning their first world championship as The Big Red Machine – to black, as in the darkest moment during my 19 years on earth up to that point as the most diehard of fans involving a supposedly invincible team.

I almost couldn't breathe, which is why I couldn't speak, but it wasn't as if I had something to say anyway to anybody for the rest of my life.

As a sophomore at the same Miami University that would place Rose and me together again 40 years later, I watched those horrors from Oxford, Ohio, with fellow Reds fan Chip Grobmyer on the portable TV set in our dorm room. Before That Guy even touched home plate after his dagger to the heart in the bottom of the 12th inning, I ignored the numbness throughout my body, I rose from my desk that had unread notes for an Econ test the next morning, and I headed to the door for a journey toward nowhere in particular.

I wandered around my red-brick surroundings. As beautiful as they were – poet Robert Frost called Miami "The most beautiful campus that ever there was" – all I could see was a ball ricocheting off a foul pole 891 miles to the northeast.

Eventually, with the early morning getting later, I found myself uptown on a bench under the rusty water tower that was half a century old.

Why, why, why? Why did the greatest team of that era – and likely of all time, but only potentially up to that point – keep having awful things happen to it? I'm talking about evil things, and as the minutes became hours underneath that water tower, I sat there, staring into the distance and agonizing over every one of those "almost" moments for those Reds. OK, they still were my Reds.

In 1969, they were right there.

There were a bunch of "firsts" that year involving the Reds as well as the Moores of Sam and Annie. As for us, that was our first baseball season in Cincinnati after AT&T transferred Dad to southwestern Ohio from our native South Bend, Indiana. As for the Reds, that was the first year of division play for Major League Baseball, so the National and American Leagues were split into west and east divisions, and the Reds were in the NL West.

There were two Big Red Machines, by the way. That was the first season of the two versions since Johnny Bench made his first start on Opening Day as the Reds' catcher. Rose and Perez joined Bench on that first Big Red Machine, and so did Lee May, nicknamed the Big Bopper from Birmingham, who played first base with Tony Perez at third base during those days. Tommy Helms was at second base. Elsewhere that season, Joe Morgan operated in obscurity with the Houston Astros. (By the way, he likely would have remained a decent but not great player away from the Big Red Machine if Reds general manager Bob Howsam worked the trade he wanted after the 1970 World Series, but I digress for the moment.)

With two weeks left during that 1969 season, the Reds were two games behind the division-leading San Francsico Giants who led the Los Angeles Dodgers and the Atlanta Braves by a half game. The Reds were surging, though. But despite leading the Major Leagues in just about every offensive category, they finished four games back.

Bummer.

Then again, the 1969 Reds couldn't pitch. Their team ERA was 4.11, the sixth-worst mark below the MLB average of 3.61.

In 1970, oh, 1970.

That's when I really fell in love with these guys.

You had speedy center fielder Bobby Tolan joining holdovers Bench, Perez, May, and Helms among the key regulars, and the first Big Red Machine was in full swing (literally) that season after slugging its way to 70 victories in its first 100 games. Those Reds won the NL West by 14 ½ games, they swept the Pittsburgh Pirates of Willie Stargell and Roberto Clemente in the NL Championship Series, and then they faced the Baltimore Orioles in the World Series from the inferior American League.

No problem.

Oh, no.

Brooks Robinson, Brooks Robinson, Brooks Robinson.

The dude was everywhere, diving and jumping and twisting to make ridiculous plays around third base, but only when he wasn't ripping a clutch hit just about every time he strolled to the plate. In the best-of-seven World Series, the Baltimore Robinsons dismantled the Big Red Machine in five games.

The Baltimore Robinsons?

Well, in addition to Brooks Robinson for those Baltimore Orioles, you had Frank Robinson, the former Reds star for a decade. He was traded to the Orioles after the 1965 season since management said he was "an old 30." He nevertheless won the AL Triple Crown during his first year in Baltimore, and then the supposedly senior citizen by Reds management standards went nuts during the 1970 World Series.

In 1971, play baseball, not basketball.

Somebody should have shouted that to Bobby Tolan (PLAY BASEBALL, NOT BASKETBALL) before he spent the winter after the 1970 season perhaps daydreaming of a dual role with the Reds and the Royals, the former NBA team in Cincinnati. This almost was as brutal for the Reds as the Baltimore Robinsons.

During a pickup basketball game, Tolan damaged his Achilles tendon along with the Reds' chances of returning to the World Series.

Reds officials fumed, almost as much as I did.

Tolan's injury came after he ignored a clause in his contract that outlawed Reds players from participating in such activities, but he did it anyway.

With Tolan and his speed gone for the 1971 season, it signaled bad things to come for the first Big Red Machine since it couldn't run, and at least for that year, it also couldn't do the main thing that it always had done, and that was hit.

The nearly team-wide slump sent the Reds to a fourth-place finish in the NL West, and that season had me wondering if I would ever sleep again.

In 1972, who is Joe Rudi?

Who is Gene Tenace, for that matter, or any of these other guys for the Oakland A's in the World Series?

That's what I kept thinking to myself in October 1972 after the Reds somehow couldn't beat those guys for a world championship. The ugly memories of Rudi, always Rudi doing *something*, and Tenace returned three years later as I sat underneath the water tower recalling how little about those A's made you take them seriously, especially if you were a National League chauvinist like me.

I also was a baseball traditionalist, which meant I looked at those A's as weirdos. They wore mustaches and softball uniforms of green and gold with white spikes (yeah, white instead of black ones like everybody else), and just from the baseball side of things as they headed into the World Series to face my Big Red Machine, they had a microscopic team batting average during the regular season, and they didn't have Reggie Jackson, their future Hall of Famer who was injured.

No worries.

The 1972 Reds had everything, including black spikes.

After the Reds rebounded during that regular season from no Bobby Tolan, no offense and no clue the previous year, they rolled into their second World Series in three seasons as the New Red Machine, which was the second Big Red Machine. They had Joe Morgan bringing his stolen bases, his Gold Glove, his timely bat, and his leadership skills to the Reds following an off-season trade of magnificence with the Houston Astros. So the New Red Machine was supposed to crush the A's.

Instead, the A's could pitch, and Rudi and Tenace played out of their minds, and the World Series reached a decisive seventh game, which the Reds lost. At home. With my guy, Pete Rose, ripping a drive to the Riverfront Stadium warning track in left field, where Joe Rudi (who else?) made the catch.

They are cursed.

Yeah, a group of voodoo doctors have dolls of my Big Red Machine folks, and they're jabbing away with needles, trying to please the ghosts of the 1927 Yankees.

In 1973, I mean, puhleeze.

As my stomach did more flips under the water tower, I recalled how nobody in baseball finished the 1973 regular season with more victories than the Reds' total of 99, and when they reached the NL Championship Series as winners of the National League West, they faced a New York Mets team from the National League East that set a Major League Baseball record for the worst winning percentage (.509) ever for a division winner.

The Reds had Rose, Bench, Perez, Morgan, and their other shining stars, and the Mets had nobody worth mentioning outside Baseball Hall of Fame pitcher Tom Seaver and a couple of other solid hurlers.

Somehow, that NL Championship Series reached a fifth and decisive game.

Somehow, the Reds didn't win.

In 1974, sooooo close.

The Reds battled the Los Angeles Dodgers into the last week of the 1974 regular season while attempting to grab a fourth NL West title in five years. At the end, the Big Red Machine won 98 games, which was more than anybody in baseball – except for the Dodgers, who had Jimmy Wynn doing explosive things in the batter's box and Mike Marshall staying untouchable on the pitcher's mound.

The Dodgers won 102.

Where are those witch doctors?

Somebody has to find those witch doctors!

Now here were the 1975 Reds, and they were an absolute dream, but under the water tower, they were forcing me into a lifetime of nightmares.

In addition to the usual suspects that season of Rose, Bench, Perez, and Morgan, Dave Concepcion and Ken Griffey Sr. became superstars. George Foster used his bat to terrorize pitchers, often when needed the most. From center field, Cesar Geronimo turned spectacular catches for others into routine ones for himself, and he was one of baseball's best hitters at the bottom of a lineup. The starting and relief pitching was Captain Hook perfect for manager Sparky Anderson, and nobody in baseball came close during the regular season to the Reds' 108 victories. They flattened the Pirates in the NL Championship Series, and after a bunch of thrillers during the opening five games of the World Series, they traveled to Boston on Tuesday, Oct. 21, 1975, needing just a Game 6 victory for two things: to avoid a decisive Game 7 at Fenway Park, and to capture their first world championship in 35 years.

I was geeked, and then I wasn't.

This was long before That Guy strolled to home plate hours later, because those horrors were already happening.

Fred Lynn gave the Red Sox a 3-0 lead in the first inning after he blasted a three-run homer, but that was good and bad, along with the Big Red Machine blowing spark plugs during its inability to score for the opening four innings. The bad part of that scenario was obvious, but here was the good part: With the Red Sox threatening a blowout, I loved that I could start preparing mentally for another "almost" moment in Big Red Machine history (see 1969, 1970, 1971, 1972, 1973, and 1974), and this time, I didn't have to suffer from drama.

I even contemplated grabbing my Econ notes for that next day's exam and bolting my dorm room for the trip across campus to study in the library.

I convinced myself Game 6 was over right there.

Red Sox rout, which means they'll win Game 7 with ease at Fenway. Eh, I don't like it, but at least I can study, get some sleep and maybe ace that Econ test in the morning.

So much for fantasy. I stayed put, and then everything began to happen on our TV screen, where the thrills (or I should say horrors, in my case) kept coming in massive waves, and they wouldn't stop until 12:33 a.m. the following day.

It was great for me, but only in spurts.

The Reds tied things at 3-3 in the fifth inning, and after two runs in the top of the seventh and another one in the eighth, they were up 6-3 heading to the bottom of the inning. My Big Red Machine was six outs away from capturing one of the most exciting World Series ever. Well, those were the universal thoughts at the time. By the end of that night and the early, early, early morning of Wednesday, Oct. 22, 1975, baseball historians were rubbing their eyes over what they were labeling the greatest World Series ever with much help from Game 6, which they ranked as the greatest World Series game ever.

Maybe that was true, but I couldn't tell you. I was miserable, starting with the first of those many horrors from Game 6, and it happened in the bottom of the eighth.

With the Reds holding that 6-3 lead, and with two outs in the inning, Red Sox pinch hitter Bernie Carbo headed to the plate, which was interesting. He began his baseball career with the Reds. In fact, they made this left-handed hitting outfielder the 16th overall pick of the 1965 Major League Baseball Draft. That was 20 spots higher than the next player selected by the Reds, and that was Johnny Bench, who became the greatest catcher in baseball history, and Carbo became one of the game's biggest flakes.

When Carbo finally joined the Reds as a rookie in 1970, I saw him play often at Crosley Field and later Riverfront Stadium. He platooned in left field with the right-handed hitting Hal McRae, and the results were wonderful. Carbo's .310 batting average with 21 home runs and 63 RBIs in 125 games earned him Sporting News Rookie of the Year honors, but he vanished at the plate during the next two years. The Reds shipped Carbo to the St. Louis Cardinals before the 1973 season, and then he was off to the Red Sox in 1974, and he brought his nutty ways with him. Among other things, the guy known as "The Clown" and "The Idiot" by teammates traveled with a stuffed gorilla that he nicknamed "Mighty Joe Young."

Even so, I was there as a fan at Riverfront Stadium in Cincinnati for Game 3 of this same 1975 World Series when Carbo ripped a pinch-hit homer against his old team. The Reds still won in 10 innings, and now they were four outs away from a world championship in Game 6 at Fenway Park with that 6-3 lead and with two outs in the bottom of the eighth.

To me, it didn't matter the Red Sox had runners at first and second. I also shrugged when Sparky Anderson did something he never had done before during his six seasons managing the Reds. He ignored the percentages. He was into analytics decades before it became a thing, but not in this situation. If this were like those other times, with the left-handed hitting Carbo as a pinch hitter and representing the tying run, Anderson would have gone with left-handed relief specialist Will McEnaney to face Carbo 99.9999% of the time.

This was that .0001% for Anderson, but watching from my dorm room, I didn't question the move, and I didn't flinch. Not only were the Reds up by three runs in the eighth, but this was Splendid Sparky, the king of the Big Red Machine, and he later told reporters that he stayed with the right-handed Rawley Eastwick on the pitcher's mound, because he was convinced if he signaled for McEnaney, Red Sox manager Darrell Johnson would have switched from Carbo to Jaun Beniquez, Johnson's right-handed-swinging designated hitter.

King Sparky looked omniscient since Carbo resembled a T-ball player against Eastwick during most of his seven-pitch at bat. He responded with a couple of clueless swings for two strikes. On a 2-2 count, he fouled off a couple of pitches, and he barely got a piece of the second one to stay alive at the plate.

Then came Eastwick's next pitch, and I'm still dazed. Carbo bashed Eastwick's fastball high and deep to center field and beyond the head of Cesar Geronimo and over the farthest barrier for a three-run homer. Game 6 was knotted at 6-6, and while the screams of despair were deafening throughout the rest of Hepburn Hall since we were deep in Reds country around southwestern Ohio, I was too stunned to make a sound.

I couldn't move.

Bernie Carbo?

Imagine how I would have felt back then if I had known the rest of the story involving the start of the Game 6 horrors for the Reds, triggered by their former bench player. Decades later, Carbo told The Boston Globe that he wasn't just a cartoon character in the minds of his teammates. He said he was an abuser of drugs and alcohol throughout his Major League career, and before Game 6, he told the newspaper, "I probably smoked two joints, drank about three or four beers, got to the ballpark, took some (amphetamines), took a pain pill, drank a cup of coffee, chewed some tobacco, had a cigarette and got up to the plate and hit."

Lovely.

And the Game 6 horrors continued.

With the 6-6 tie still in place, and with the bases loaded for the Red Sox in the bottom of the ninth, and with no outs, and with Fenway Park growing louder, the Sox were on the verge of snatching a World Series game from my Big Red Machine in a spectacular way. I tried not to look, but you know what they say about car crashes, particularly ugly ones, and here were my thoughts: *It's over, and after screaming at the top of my lungs in the middle of Cook Field on campus, I'll go study for that exam. As for the Reds, after this Game 6 meltdown and an inevitable victory for the Red Sox at home in Game 7, something else will happen regarding the Red Sox's first world championship since Babe Ruth was their star pitcher in 1918 before turning Yankee legend with a bat. Their defeat of both the Reds and The Curse of the Bambino will provide more reasons for the East Coast media to keep duping America into thinking the Red Sox really are God's gift to baseball.*

Sorry, East Coast media, but the Red Sox were Reds wannabes. With the bottom of the ninth looking more hopeless by the moment, I thought about how the Reds became baseball's first professional baseball team in 1869. I thought about how they always embraced their status as the smallest market in the Major Leagues by treating every Opening Day in Cincinnati as a national holiday, highlighted by a citywide parade and the closing of schools and businesses. I thought about how they eventually were blessed with a Big Red Machine, and how the 1975 Red Sox of Carl Yastrzemski, Luis Tiant, Fred Lynn, and the Green Monster couldn't match the star power of their Cincinnati counterparts of Rose, Morgan, Bench, Perez, and others during the World Series.

So the Reds were the favorites to win the 1975 World Series comfortably, but the Big Red Machine was sputtering again. No, choking. The bottom of the ninth kept going from awful to worse for the Reds, and the Red Sox were on the verge of smashing away the 6-6 tie with the bases loaded and nobody out. I kept wondering: How did the Reds blow that three-run lead in the bottom of the eighth inning, and *Bernie Carbo*?

I was hurting, and up next to the plate for the Red Sox was Fred Lynn, Mr. Perfect, who was on his way to winning American League honors for Rookie of the Year and Most Valuable Player, and he got a Gold Glove for his play in center field. The left-handed Lynn was batting against the same left-handed Will McEnaney who had a 99.9999 % chance of facing the left-handed Carbo in the previous ending. That said, there was a 0.0000% chance of the Reds getting out of this situation, and then Lynn swung and lifted a flyball deep and the opposite way toward the narrow spaces down the left-field line of Fenway Park.

Uh-oh.

The Reds' left fielder was George Foster who was gifted with his bat, but not so much with his glove or his arm. Several years later, when I covered a Reds game at Riverfront Stadium for *The Cincinnati Enquirer*,

Foster misplayed a ball near the wall, or maybe he didn't. Whatever the case, he told reporters, "I don't do things that aren't necessary."

But back to the bottom of the ninth in Game 6 of the 1975 World Series. With Lynn's flyball threatening to become the game-clincher for the Red Sox around that left-field corner, I stood up from the chair at the desk in my dorm room, and I thought about a couple of things within milliseconds. Instead of stopping to do all of that yelling and screaming in the middle of Cook Field along the way to the library, I could just start walking now, and maybe I might finish under the water tower or something. I knew the deal, even without channeling the future me on George Foster's thoughts about chasing flyballs toward walls.

No way George Foster – *George Foster!* – was going to catch that ball, and even if he did, Denny Doyle would tag up from third base and score with the greatest of ease.

Back-to-back miracles followed.

First, Foster raced toward the foul line, reached above his head, and made the catch within inches of crashing into the wall near the slither of foul territory in that part of Fenway from the grandstands. Then as Doyle left third base within a flash after the catch and sprinted toward home faster than he had ever run before, Foster made the throw of his life. It was a laser on line for a one bouncer to Bench who grabbed the thing like an infielder as he stood in fair territory before making the swipe tag of Doyle sliding headfirst.

I refused to enjoy the moment. Even after The Catch, The Throw, and The Tag, the Red Sox still had runners on first and third, but Rico Petrocelli grounded out to end the ninth. I still didn't exhale. Something just told me another horror was about to leap from the Fenway shadows.

This time, it began with a tease.

In the top of the 11th, with Ken Griffey Sr. at first base and one out, Joe Morgan decided enough was enough. As soon as the ball left his bat for a rising journey to right field after he twisted his quick wrists, I joined my roommate, the rest of Hepburn Hall, and those around the tri-state area of Ohio, Indiana, and Kentucky with cheers headed for Mars and then Jupiter. We knew that left-handed swing. It helped Morgan become the 1975 National League Most Valuable Player with a .327 batting average, 94 RBIs, and 67 stolen bases. Despite playing second base – which traditionally was the position of what baseball old-timers called Punch-and-Judy hitters for their lack of power – Morgan also ripped 17 homers, and most were huge.

This one was huge. Then it wasn't.

Morgan's homer never happened.

Somehow, Red Sox right fielder Dwight Evans ran just shy of forever toward the short fence in right field to make a one-handed catch after he leaped toward the stars as his body fell toward the stands. Not only did he rob Morgan, but he recovered from his acrobatics enough to fire the ball toward first base. He picked off Griffey who was so sure Morgan's drive was at least a double that he already was rounding the bases.

Those horrors continued in the top of the 12th when the Reds stranded two runners. Then That Guy led off the bottom of the inning against Reds reliever Pat Darcy, whose sinker didn't sink enough, and his pitch bounced off the left-field foul pole at 12:33 a.m.

So 39 years later, I talked to George Foster about life in retirement, which included some of his charitable work around Goodyear, Arizona, where the Reds held spring training at the time, and he told me something that was unknown by the public until then. He explained what happened after Fisk's blast sent me to under the water tower.

"The ball dropped straight down," Foster said. "Since I was over there, looking up to try to determine whether it was going to go fair or foul, it just dropped, and I didn't really have to move that far. It came right down toward me, so I just caught it and just took it right into the clubhouse."

Now think about this: Foster could have given the ball to a batboy while heading to the dugout, or he could have lobbed the thing into a bucket with other balls. He also could have tossed that piece of living baseball history into the outstretched hand of a Red Sox fan nearby in the left-field stands or anywhere along his trip to the visiting dugout at Fenway. But he never contemplated any of those options, particularly the latter, which would have made somebody happy and rich. Historic baseballs generate big bucks, and even beyond that, Foster still could have tossed the Fisk ball to a fan out of habit. "Well, we weren't allowed to do that back then," Foster said of what became a common practice, but of what got players fined during the 1970s by Major Leagues cops. "And besides, since the game finished so late, there was hardly anybody there in the stands to give it to."

Then Foster sort of forgot about the ball.

"It was in your glove, so you put your glove in your locker, take off your uniform and go take a shower," Foster said, because in his mind, it was just another ball that bounced off a foul pole at 12:33 a.m. to win a World Series game in the bottom of the 12th inning. He added, "There wasn't any thought about that ball being that important."

Foster put the ball in his duffel bag, which he suggested was a perfunctory move. It stayed in that bag through Game 7 the next day and during the Reds' trip back to Cincinnati from Boston. In fact, the ball remained in that bag during his journey home to California for the winter and through the rest of his life until around the turn of the 21st century. That was when he said "somebody" asked him in 1999 for a souvenir from the 1975 World Series, and the famously gracious Foster found his old duffel bag, pulled out the ball and handed it to the person. Eventually, the ball hit by That Guy made its way to various sports auction places through the years. By the summer of 2022, the ball belonged to the folks at Just Collect, a company that specialized in vintage sports cards and memorabilia, and they estimated the ball's value back then at $280,000.

And Foster just gave it away.

"You're just punishing yourself if you worry about those types of things, because there is nothing you can do about them," Foster told me, shrugging over the whole situation before adding, "It's like water under the bridge."

It's also like this: Contrary to those who still believe the 1975 World Series ended with That Guy and his homer in Game 6, there was a Game 7 at Fenway Park. So the way that Fall Classic kept ebbing and flowing, I knew there was more drama to come. Sure enough, the Red Sox took another early 3-0 lead through five innings before Tony Perez sent a Bill Lee blooper pitch over the Green Monster in left for a two-run homer in the sixth. The Reds tied things at 3-3 with another run in seventh. Then, during the top of the ninth, Ken Griffey Sr. scored from third on a Joe Morgan single to shallow center field to give the Reds a 4-3 lead.

When Red Sox legend Carl Yastrzemski ended the bottom of the ninth inning and the World Series by lifting a flyball that fell gently into the glove of Cesar Geronimo in center, those splendid cogs for the Big Red Machine were world champions.

Not that anybody cared.

OK, I'm exaggerating, but only a little. I cared. Still, I was so exhausted from my trip to the water tower until nearly sunrise after Game 6 that my reaction to the Reds surviving Game 7 was more relief than glee.

As for everybody else, especially those in charge of documenting for posterity what happened during this most classic of Fall Classics, something was apparent from the start. To them, Game 7 of the 1975 World Series didn't matter. To them, yeah, The Big Red Machine returned to the World Series the following year to sweep the Yankees for back-to-back world championships. But to them, it was "theoretically" back-to-back world championships for the Reds, because to them, the 1975 one never happened.

I'm back to Game 6 and That Guy.

"I hear it over and over again, and it's ridiculous," Ken Griffey Sr. told me decades later before adding more of the truth. "Carlton Fisk and that home run. It's like nothing else took place during that World Series, and it's insulting to us."

Joe Morgan often told me similar things, saying between expletives, usually with arms waving and eyes flashing, "What do they show whenever they talk about the 1975 World Series? They don't show me knocking in Griff from third base with the winning run. They don't show us celebrating after the last out at Fenway Park. They show the ball hitting the foul pole in left field and Carlton Fisk trying to wave the ball fair while jumping up and down and running to first base. When you ask people at random, 'Who won the 1975 World Series?' They will say the Red Sox, because they only keep showing that home run."

I agreed with Foster, Morgan, and others who didn't believe the earth was flat. As THE Big Red Machine disciple, the glorification of That Guy and Game 6 of the 1975 World Series was unseemly to me, then it got worse. I took my first trip to the Baseball Hall of Fame in Cooperstown, New York during the summer of 2024. I wanted to see every bit of the place, but nothing surpassed my desire to visit all things Big Red Machine.

My Big Red Machine.

I saw the Hall of Fame plaques for Joe Morgan, Johnny Bench, Tony Perez, and Sparky Anderson, and I was mesmerized. Unlike the others in bronze, Sparky didn't look like Sparky, but he was in Cooperstown, so who cared? There were statuettes of Reds announcers Marty Brennaman and Joe Nuxhall sitting behind a desk with microphones in their hands. I couldn't stop smiling and remembering. Courtesy of my transistor radio, "Marty and Joe" were the dominant voices in my head during much of the 1970s.

Elsewhere, there was a display case featuring a can of Pete Rose's soft drink called "Pete" along with his No. 14 home jersey for the Reds, and my goosebumps exploded over a memory I'll share later. The exhibit also had Morgan's glove, Bench's catcher's mitt, Perez's 1976 baseball card, and George Foster's black bat. On the front of the glass enclosure was a yellow card, and underneath the title of "The Big Red Machine," it read: "A dominant force in the National League for much of the 1970s, Cincinnati's Big Red Machine reached the postseason six times during the decade with four trips to the World Series when the club captured back-to-back championships in 1975 and 1976."

That was nice, but this wasn't.

Less than a giant step from that Big Red Machine exhibit, the Baseball Hall of Fame had a whole display case in commemoration of Game 6 and That Guy from the 1975 World Series. There was the bat from that moment (but not the ball, of course), and in contrast to the Big Red Machine exhibit, this one had a video that ran on a continuous loop. I began feeling old feelings again, and not in a good way. The video showed That Guy swinging, and then waving, and then leaping, and then clapping as the ball hit the foul pole screen at Fenway Park in Boston at 12:33 a.m. on Wednesday, Oct. 22, 1975, and that wasn't all.

In another section of the Baseball Hall of Fame, there was a black-and-white photo of That Guy, dropping his bat and looking toward the foul pole with Bench behind the plate and Darcy on the mound facing the same direction.

That still wasn't all.

In another part of the Baseball Hall of Fame, there was *another* photo of That Guy and his moment. This one showed That Guy halfway to first base, still studying the flight of the ball toward the Green Monster, and everything was frozen in time – his wide-open mouth, his arms attempting to wave the ball fair and his feet off the ground during one of his leaps. In contrast, as I kept running into a multitude of stuff about That Guy and Game 6, this was happening in real time: The look of disgust on my face.

That was opposed to my look of shock with my guy Pete Rose, sitting there at Miami University in Oxford, Ohio, smiling and acknowledging me before a generation of students who likely hadn't a clue about the depth of his fame, or infamy, according to some. But I wasn't among the "some," which I will discuss at length in the upcoming chapters. I also will tell you later what happened near the end of Rose's trip to my alma mater.

The Terry-Pete connection was destined by the sporting gods, and fate also led me to other things. For instance: Throughout my life as an African American loving sports as well as journalism, I experienced an epidemic of "firsts," but that was inevitable since I grew up in a household dominated by Jackie Robinsons.

CHAPTER 2

Go Irish and Cubbies

It took a while for me to discover something. Along my earthly journey, blessed by the sporting gods in so many ways, the Big Red Machine was Notre Dame football, and Notre Dame football was the Big Red Machine.

It made perfect sense ... after a while.

I saw something else in hindsight. Soon after my birth, my parents as Jackie Robinsons in our household – as well as an environment filled with encouragers and also power, not from Johnny Bench, Tony Perez, and George Foster, but from The Holy Trinity of the Father, The Son, and the Holy Spirit – helped me develop the tools for a smooth transition toward handling two things: my move from fan to journalist in a flash, and my ability to baffle haters as an African American involved with a lot of "firsts."

Life was mostly carefree for me in the beginning. My road to the Big Red Machine began 245 miles to the north of Cincinnati in South Bend, Indiana, where I was born during the mid-1950s in St. Joseph Hospital. Oh, and here's some trivia: University of Notre Dame football legend George Gipp died at the same medical facility 35 years earlier of strep throat and pneumonia. So my ties to the hometown Fighting Irish began with the "Let's win one for The Gipper" guy after I took my first breath.

We lived just a few punts away from Touchdown Jesus, which stretches toward the heavens from that campus of the world's most famous college football team.

I loved Notre Dame.

The Grotto of Our Lady of Lourdes, where you could light candles for miracles. The Victory March played by the nation's first university marching band. The Collegiate Gothic buildings that outdated even Irish sainted coach Knute Rockne who first named his splendid running back of the 1920s "The Gipper." No doubt, I worshipped everything involving Irish football, and the same went for my two brothers Dennis and Darrell, both younger than I by 11 months and three years, respectively.

Since we grew up in the household of Sam and Annie Moore, we became sports fans in general, just like our parents. They were addicted to competition. It spanned from Dad and Mom spending weekends rolling bowling balls around town for trophies to battling other couples across a card table in multiple games of Bid Whist or Spades.

They cheered for sports involving Washington High School, which was their alma mater on our west side of town, and through us boys watching our parents, we learned to enjoy nearly anything featuring running, jumping, leaping, rolling, shooting, dribbling, passing, hitting, fielding, tackling, putting, and chipping.

As a family as well as a community, our daily existence involved Notre Dame, Notre Dame, and more Notre Dame, and we enjoyed it. The Irish *were* South Bend during my youth. They held that distinction despite a slew of other nationally known entities and individuals in this northern Indiana city, with its St. Joseph River joining the Nile in Egypt as one of the few rivers to flow north instead of south. There were barely 102,000 South Bend citizens back then, but they were enough to create a highly productive environment even beyond the global reach of Notre Dame and its Golden Dome.

The cars of the Studebaker brothers rivaled those of Ford and General Motors around the country, and Studebaker Corporation was based in South Bend with Singer Sewing Machine Co., peerless in the world for the making of sewing machine cabinets, built from the local black walnut trees. Bendix Corporation surfaced in town during the early 1920s. Among other things, it supplied most of the hydraulic systems for American bombers during World War II, and Bendix continued through the decades as a leading maker of automotive brake shoes and later computers, radio, and televisions. The South Bend Range Company built commercial ovens and ranges for hotels and restaurants everywhere. There also were the manhole covers from sea to shining sea with the words "South Bend" on the front of the cast iron mixed with concrete, and the combination was made at the South Bend Foundry Company.

That was the short list.

Which tied into this: Many of those jobs in South Bend belonged to my relatives who could fill much of Notre Dame Stadium. I joked with sports journalist friends heading to cover Irish home football games that virtually all of the African Americans they encountered would be related to me. While my dad had nine brothers and sisters, my mom had eight. Throughout the 1970s, only two of those siblings lived away from South Bend. Both sets of grandparents were in town, and so were great aunts and great uncles, the overwhelming majority of my 42 first cousins and numerous second cousins.

Years later, my dad told me after shaking his head, "I can't name more than a couple of people who were unemployed back then. There were so many jobs available throughout the city, and people had a strong work ethic."

Take Samuel Lee Moore, for instance.

He began as a janitor at Indiana Bell in South Bend during the mid-1950s when he got an honorable discharge from the U.S. Army at the end of the Korean War. He was a sergeant first class among paratroopers, and after returning to town, he worked his way up from janitor to electronical engineer to the first Black supervisor in the history of AT&T. He later became one of the company's first Black managers.

During our South Bend days, Dad turned our garage into an electronics shop. It was his side business that involved fixing TVs, radios, and just about anything else that plugged into an outlet. If you added his work ethic to his athletic prowess – which included his ability to shoot and sink baskets with either hand since he was ambidextrous, along with his expertise with a golf club, a bowling ball, and a billiard stick – he was our local celebrity.

Annie Mae Moore also fit that category. Years after she was the first and only African American on the award-winning marching band at Washington High School as the lead trombone player, she was the first and only African American employee at Associates, a national savings and loans company based in South Bend. She went from custodian to filing clerk despite multiple rejections of her applications for both positions.

The rejections were race-related, and Dad had similar issues. But they urged the three of us boys to follow their lead, which involved fighting on without flinching and without "having somebody convince you that you can't do something," as Mom used to say. Between working at Associates and serving as the perfect mother – who cooked and sewed and planted flowers and attended PTA meetings and helped with homework – she grabbed her share of bowling trophies to solidify her superstar status with us.

Beyond our household, there were all of those nationally known superstars with South Bend connections, and they didn't fit a pattern.

My mom grew up next door to Junior Walker, the leader and the saxophonist for Junior Walker & the All-Stars, which was a Motown group that won three Grammy Awards. She also was a classmate of Lloyd Haynes, or Mr. Dixon from the popular TV show of the 1960s called "Room 222," where Haynes played a high school history teacher. Both Mom and Dad were South Bend friends with the parents of Vivica A. Fox, who became an actress, producer, and TV host. There also was my Uncle Charlie. He joined other graduates of Central High School in South Bend to smile even more whenever their school's old English teacher and basketball coach moved toward one of his 10 national championships at UCLA.

Some guy named John Wooden.

Even so, nobody or anything topped Notre Dame football. I was wonderfully spoiled by my Irish teams. I grew up in South Bend during the 1960s, when Ara Parseghian became a Notre Dame icon on the sidelines in the manner of Knute Rockne (three national championships) and Frank Leahy, who won four national titles.

Not surprisingly, Mom dressed my brothers and me in only certain types of Notre Dame sweatshirts because, she explained, "These are the ones Ara wears during games," which meant they were good enough for her boys. Since Notre Dame rarely lost under Parseghian, we were proud to emulate the leader of a program that routinely smashed opponents to become a perennial contender for national championships. The Irish won it all twice under Parseghian during his 11 seasons as head coach, and they were close two other times while finishing fifth or better in the final Associated Press or Coaches Poll eight times.

Notre Dame football became my obsession, which meant Notre Dame football was foreshadowing things to come with my Big Red Machine.

I knew every word to the Victory March before I could cite the Pledge of Allegiance, and there was other Notre Dame-related stuff. During our neighborhood pickup games (which involved tackling, not tagging, and without helmets, shoulder pads, or other football gear as we played on grass as well as on the concrete of the streets), I pretended I was Terry Hanratty or Nick Eddy on offense or Alan Page on defense.

They were among the Irish studs of the 1960s.

My brothers and I spent the early hours before Notre Dame home football games with some of our cousins on Eddy Street at the house of Uncle Ed Lee and Aunt Henrietta. Among relatives and friends, they lived the closest to campus. Their front yard gave us the best vantage point to count the number of out-of-town license plates on cars moving in slow motion to the tailgate sections. For huge games, the Goodyear Blimp regularly flew into town, and after the ABC cameras showed it nationally on air, we sprinted outside to look skyward to catch the thing right there above us.

When the football action began, we watched mostly to see how badly the Irish would crush whoever they were playing. We also studied the sidelines to see if we were, indeed, wearing the same Notre Dame sweatshirt as Ara.

Notre Dame football wasn't our only thing.

There was golf.

My dad helped to integrate the courses in South Bend during the late 1950s, and with a 7-handicap into his 80s, he was known as "Fairway Sam" on his way to three holes-in-one and at least 30 trophies for winning various tournaments. My mom was only an occasional golfer, but she enjoyed the sport, and she joined my dad as a prolific bowler. They rolled their way to awards both singularly and collectively around South Bend alleys, and the whole family spent Saturday mornings turning to televised bowling events as one of the warmups during the fall before Notre Dame football games. We watched golf, too, and every Memorial Day weekend, we followed the exploits of drivers such as A.J. Foyt and Mario Andretti in the Indianapolis 500. ABC's Wide World of Sports was must-see weekly television, along with the huge sport in Indiana of high school basketball and anything else featuring athletes.

Our professional sports teams were 85 miles to the west in Chicago, home to the Blackhawks of the National Hockey League, the Bulls of the National Basketball Association, the Bears of the National Football League, and two Major League Baseball teams in the White Sox and the Cubs. Just as nearly everybody in South Bend wrapped their arms around the Irish, the same was true of the Bears, even though they were barely bearable to watch during the 1960s beyond the extraordinary likes of Gayle Sayers on offense and Dick Butkus on defense. The Blackhawks and the Bulls also had universal appeal in South Bend.

Then there were the White Sox and the Cubs. During the bulk of the 1960s, they were shaky on their best days, but they had significant fan bases in South Bend, where zero-to-few folks claimed loyalty to both teams.

We were Cubs folks.

Well, that was our immediate family.

If you polled the other relatives, who were nearly all African Americans, they would choose the White Sox since they were considered more minority friendly. While future Baseball Hall of Famer Ernie Banks became the first Black player for the Cubs in September 1953, the White Sox had Cuban outfielder Minnie Minoso in their starting lineup more than two years earlier. That was enough for Aunt Inez, Uncle Edgar, and the rest. They made frequent trips from South Bend to Comiskey Park, not so much to see the White Sox, but to make sure their eyes weren't deceiving them with the sight of Minoso, who actually was somebody darker than Ted Williams inside a Major League Baseball uniform.

Our family preferred Billy Williams, Ron Santo, and Banks, the dominant stars of the Cubs during the early 1960s. They were future Baseball Hall of Famers with pitcher Ferguson Jenkins, who came along in the middle of the decade.

Fergie was joined by one of the game's all-time best double-play combinations in shortstop Don Kessinger and second baseman Glenn Beckert, and Baseball Hall of Fame manager Leo Durocher arrived about that time. The Cubs went from awful during most of my early youth to promising by 1966, and they trended toward better than that by the end of the decade. So our family shrugged when Aunt Inez, Uncle Edgar, and the rest continued to fond over just the mention of Minoso, who retired in 1964 before he returned to the White Sox for cameo appearances during the late 1970s and early 1980s.

We had those Cubs, and in contrast to those White Sox of just Minoso in the minority department on their roster, those Cubs had at least three players who looked like us in Banks, Williams, and Jenkins.

We never went to Wrigley Field, the ivy-filled home of the Cubs, but we often brought the Cubs into our house in South Bend, and that was some trick. As an electronics whiz, my dad perfected that trick, which involved climbing onto the roof of our house and planting a large chunk of aluminum that stretched toward the sky. It was an antenna, and courtesy of my dad, it did more than just catch signals from the three local television stations in South Bend. When he climbed the roof to twist the antenna the right way (you know, between the times he had to grab the thing off the ground or the rooftop due to high winds or heavy snow), he could capture WGN in Chicago, which allowed us to watch everything from "Bozo's Circus" and classic movies to "Garfield Goose" and one of the season-long Cubs games on air.

The WGN signal was better deep at night or early in the morning. Since the Cubs played home games only during the afternoon back then, we spent most of our time sitting before our black and white TV screen in the living room, trying to separate Ferguson Jenkins from Don Kessinger through a snowy background. It didn't help that the distinctive voice of Cubs announcer Jack Brickhouse wasn't so distinctive since it kept fading in and out, but we still stayed glued to whatever we were seeing in front of us.

We even watched some of the White Sox games carried by WGN, and Brickhouse also did those games, but it wasn't the same. Since we were Cubs fans, we were heavily into the National League, which meant we often saw the Chicago North Siders in the 1960s against the Reds. Even so, I had no memory of specific Cincinnati players during those times – not even of my future guy, Pete Rose – and that was because our focus remained totally on those rising Cubs players.

Well, that was the case, unless the Cubs faced a team with bigger-than-life African American megastars such as Hank Aaron and Willie Mays. I knew them. When they played the Cubs, my dad often got lucky enough after climbing to the roof to make the right tweaks for us to see Aaron's quick wrists and Mays' overall flash.

Decades later, when I was a veteran writer instead of a young fan, I *really* knew Aaron and Mays, starting with Aaron, owner of 755 home runs and a reputation as one of the most inspiring Americans ever by the time of his death in January 2021.

No journalist was closer to Aaron than I was. For nearly 40 years, we discussed everything involved with his past and present. I even conducted his last interview when he shared never-before-told stories about his life in the winter of 2020. He discussed his fears with the Atlanta Braves during the weeks and the months prior to breaking Babe Ruth's all-time home run record of 714 on April 8, 1974. at home against the Los Angeles Dodgers.

Among other things, Aaron said he spent road trips during his Ruth chase barricading himself in hotel rooms due to death threats and racist letters.

"I get disgusted, yes, because I think this (didn't happen) to anybody else," Aaron said to me, just two months before his death. "I think about

Pete Rose (in 1985) when he was going through his chase of Ty Cobb's (career hits) record, and he was having the time of his life. Nobody said anything; nobody did anything. He did what he wanted to do, and I couldn't do one damn thing. I was not blessed to even go out to have lunch or dinner. If it hadn't been for teammates of mine (Dusty Baker and Ralph Garr) bringing me lunch or dinner, I mean, if we played a night game, they would bring me a sandwich to my room. If it weren't for them, I would have starved to death. That's the kind of stuff that people don't really understand. No, no, they don't understand it because they'll say right quick, 'Oh, that never happened.'"

Then there was Mays, the iconic slugger and center fielder of mostly the New York and San Francisco Giants. I encountered "The Say Hey Kid" often during my *San Francisco Examiner* days of the 1980s, and then off and on for years after that.

By then, my fandom was yesterday's news, so I shrugged when I discovered Mays often was surly with reporters. Sometimes, you got the Good Willie who was polite and engaging, but mostly not. During a phone call in the early 2000s, I got the good Willie. He told me about his relationship through the decades with his godson – you know, Barry Bonds, baseball's all-time home run leader with 762. Mays told me, "When Barry was 5, Pat, his mother, used to bring him to the ballpark, and, oh, just about every day, he would stay in my locker mostly all the time. Barry would be chewing gum and all of that kind of junk and seeing what kind of glove I had. He would mess around with me just daily."

With that Mays conversation, and with many of the others I've had involving other famous sports personalities, I occasionally drifted here in my mind: *To think, as that young fan in South Bend, Indiana during the 1960s, that I would have such interactions with such people, that wouldn't even have been a figment of my imagination.*

Neither was cable television.

Beyond the antenna thing on roofs to catch WGN for the Cubbies or White Sox, there were few options to watch Major League Baseball games in South Bend. That said, the big three networks of ABC, CBS, and NBC spent various stretches during the 1950s and 1960s broadcasting national games on Saturdays, Sundays, or both.

My brothers and I made frequent visits to our maternal grandparents' house. They lived on the street behind us, along with Uncle Larry, the world's biggest New York Yankees fan. To his delight, the networks loved his Bronx Bombers, and he required us to spend those times in silence. He didn't wish to miss anything said over the air while he devoured his cases of Pepsi, and we followed his wishes – until we got restless around the middle of the first inning. To keep from getting smacked in the back of the head by Uncle Larry for speaking above a whisper, we were off to the kitchen for Grandma's cookies or outside away from Uncle Larry's First Commandment: Thou shalt not move during any baseball game, and if the Yanks are involved, don't even think about it.

Uncle Larry cherished the Yankees the most during the 1961 season, which led to my first clear memory of knowing Major League Baseball was actually a thing. That's because Uncle Larry spent that summer calling my brother Dennis "Mickey," as in Mickey Mantle, and me "Roger," as in Roger Maris.

"Yeah, you're going to be just like Mickey," Uncle Larry kept telling Dennis, who always responded with a smile across his 4-year-old face. Then, not to leave me out of the conversation as the older brother by slightly less than a year, Uncle Larry would say with his hand on the top of my head, "And you, you're going to be another Roger."

We hadn't a clue who those people were.

We barely knew our ABCs.

Nevertheless, Uncle Larry used to grab one of the baseball bats in his room, take us outside and show us how Mickey and Roger swung for – who else? – the Yankees. "No, no. You put your elbow like this, and you wrap your fingers over here," he said, and we nodded, and then we returned to the rest of our lives of cartoons and coloring books.

We discovered – either through Uncle Larry or just by the passage of time – that Mantle and Maris spent 1961 chasing the single-season home run record of Babe Ruth, who slammed 60 for the Yankees in 1927 over a 154-game schedule. Mantle and Maris battled neck-and-neck that summer during the first year of MLB's 162-game schedule, and Uncle Larry joined others in pulling for one of those Yankees to surpass Ruth's 60 within 154 games. It would keep Major League Baseball from adding an asterisk to the record-breaker due to the extra games, but there was an asterisk. While Mantle finished with 54 homers, Maris ripped his record 61st on the last day of that new 162-game season.

The main thing Uncle Larry cared about in 1961 was that New York rebounded from losing the 1960 World Series in seven games to the Pittsburgh Pirates. This time, the Yankees lived up to their Bronx Bombers nickname by grabbing the world championship in five games against their overmatched foes from the National League.

The Reds.

Just weeks from turning 6, I hadn't a clue about the Reds. I was too busy trying to figure out what it meant being Uncle Larry's Roger Maris, and think about this: Despite all of those years watching (sort of) the Cubs on our TV screen after my dad performed his hocus-pocus on the roof, and despite Uncle Larry's anointing of Dennis and me as miniature versions of his favorite guys in pinstripes, it wasn't until seven years after that 1961 season that Major League Baseball was on the verge of sharing part of my heart with Notre Dame football.

That was 1968, and like everybody else who lived back then, the infamous moments of that year torched my soul, starting with the political assassinations of Dr. Martin Luther King Jr. that April and Robert F. Kennedy two months later. In fact, when Kennedy announced he was running for president during the spring, he campaigned in South Bend, and I stood along a street near our house to touch his fingertips as his motorcade drove by.

After my mom woke us up in the middle of that June night to rush to the TV set, I saw RFK in a pool of blood on the floor of a Los Angeles hotel room, and it felt like a death in the family. I mean, I touched his fingertips. There were race riots everywhere that summer, including in South Bend, and Vietnam protesters dominated streets across the country. Violence followed that fall in nearby Chicago during the

Democratic Convention, and on live television, there was police brutality inside and outside the proceedings.

As traumatic as all of that was for me and others, 1968 affected my psyche forever for another reason: Baseball, and this was a two-part thing.

First, my brothers and I were in our second year of playing Little League, and we were coached both seasons by our dad. It was a family affair since our mom was the secretary of the whole Little League operation on that side of town, and she joined my dad in going way beyond their designated roles. Since several of our teammates were from shaky home situations, my dad made the rounds of picking up players in our Chevrolet Impala station wagon before practices and games. The trip to and from baseball diamonds featured arms, legs, and heads dangling out of our car windows. At the start of that first Little League season, some of our teammates wore their dirty uniforms from the previous game to the next game. My mom sensed what was happening, and she asked those players to bring a change of clothes with them. Then after games, my mom would clean their uniforms in our washing machine and have the fresh ones ready for them by the time the station wagon was ready to roll again.

Our opening year of Little League in 1967 was nothing more than a novelty, a fleeting activity, something to do until Notre Dame began playing again, at least for me. The same was true of baseball in general. I liked watching the Cubs on that snowy screen (well, sometimes I liked it), and I recalled a few batting lessons from Uncle Larry (OK, not really), but since I didn't mind my label from my brothers and my cousins as a "bookworm" for my glowing report cards, I could take or leave this Little League thing. It showed. Even with my dad as the coach, I spent that first year batting last and playing right field, and that meant I was the worst player on the team, or somewhere in the vicinity.

Then came 1968.

Actually, the baseball significance of that year for me began during the previous winter when I decided after my disastrous first year of Little League that I could remain a bookworm while also becoming decent with a bat and a glove. It was my secret desire, but I needed to take action. With my allowance money, I went to our local Kmart to buy a whiffle ball and plastic bat. I tied the whiffle ball to one end of a rope, and I wrapped the other part of the rope to one of the poles on our clothesline in the backyard. From there, I practiced whacking at the ball with my plastic bat for the longest time, and that remained my routine several days a week through the spring of 1968. I also bought a rubber ball, and I threw it against our garage to simulate either groundballs or fly balls. It allowed me to practice defense, and through it all, my brothers, cousins, and neighborhood pals responded with giggles.

Those giggles turned into gawking after I spent that 1968 Little League season batting first and playing center field, among baseball's glamour positions. I was named the most improved player of our whole Little League, and with the overall success that season of my dad-coached Tigers team, I was hooked on baseball, even beyond those snowy images on our television screen of Wrigley Field, or was that Forbes Field, or maybe it was a photo of the lunar surface from one of those Apollo space missions?

Who knew?

I knew one thing for sure.

I knew another team called the Tigers was doing well in 1968, and they were in Major League Baseball. That was around the time I discovered radio also could bring you games after I heard Vince Lloyd and Lou Boudreau sounding even more passionate than Jack Brickhouse during their Cubs broadcasts for WGN Radio. Then, while flipping around the dial one day, I stumbled upon KMOX from St. Louis with Harry Caray and Jack Buck giving their spirited analysis of the Cardinals. Just like their counterparts on WGN Radio, I could hear Caray and Buck speaking clearly in South Bend, but mostly at night. I had a similar experience with WJR, where I found Ernie Harwell, the radio voice of the Detroit Tigers. I was intrigued by Harwell and those other Tigers, even though they were in the American League, unlike the Cardinals and the Cubs' other opponents during those non-interleague days.

Something was up with those Cardinals and Tigers. During the summer of 1968, I began seeing them on the NBC Game of the Week with veteran lead announcer Curt Gowdy and Brooklyn Dodgers legend Pee Wee Reese. Before long, the Cardinals and the Tigers were winning the pennants of their respective leagues, and then they were meeting in the World Series with players who already felt enchanted to me.

Leading the way, you had Al Kaline, Willie Horton, Bill Freehan, Denny McLain, and Mickey Lolich for the Tigers. Then you had Bob Gibson for the Cardinals, along with Lou Brock, Curt Flood, Steve Carlton, and Uncle Larry's former Yankees guy, Roger Maris, who was with the Cardinals by then. There also was a reserve outfielder for the Cardinals named Bobby Tolan, and little did I know in 1968, he would become one of the players I would worship within the next couple of years for my Big Red Machine.

I was in the seventh grade at Benjamin Harrison Elementary School in South Bend, and my group of friends since kindergarten did certain things together. If we weren't inventing paper decoders to use between ourselves like spies on the television drama "The Man from U.N.C.L.E," we were taking turns every Monday night visiting each other's homes to watch "The Monkees" TV show and at least the start of "Rowan & Martin's Laugh-In" before we rushed out the door to finish homework before bedtime.

That October of 1968, we created a new thing, which actually was an old thing in the history of young baseball fans. We smuggled transistor radios into our classes to hear the World Series. We hadn't a choice. The first night World Series game wouldn't be until 1971, so if you were a baseball fan in 1968, with all of those wonderful names in the latest World Series for the Tigers and the Cardinals, and if you were forced to leave your house to learn about reading, writing, and arithmetic, you had to do what you had to do. The teachers knew what was going on, but they didn't care. They also wanted to know the World Series score of the moment. For the decisive Game 7 in St. Louis on a Thursday afternoon, one of my Benjamin Harrison teachers even rolled a TV into the room from the school's audio and video department for us to watch parts of the action until the bell rung for us to change classes.

I didn't want to leave, but at least I had my transistor radio.

Inning after inning, Bob Gibson blew fastballs past Detroit hitters to finish with eight strikeouts during his complete game for the day, and he owned a record 35 Ks for the World Series. The problem for Gibson and the Cardinals was that Mickey Lolich did something better than Gibson to become the World Series Most Valuable Player. He also had a complete game, but the only run he allowed for the Cardinals was a homer in the ninth.

In contrast, the Tigers managed three runs off Gibson in the seventh and another one in the ninth for a 4-1 victory.

I was addicted to baseball.

Actually, It happened earlier in 1968, and not only because of my renaissance season in Little League. With our parents out of town, my brothers and I spent a few days at the home of Aunt Inez and Uncle Edgar, the White Sox fans who lived in South Bend near a complex filled with American Legion games on summer evenings. We would devour Aunt Inez's soul food with glee each night, followed by scoops of ice cream, and then Uncle Edgar would drop us off at the tree-lined ballpark. "No rush," he would say, as we got ready to dash toward the stands while he headed back to his Studebaker Lark. "Take your time. Just enjoy the games. I'll be here sitting in the car until y'all are ready to go."

Sometimes, that was more than a couple of hours, but Uncle Edgar didn't care. He was deep into his senior years. When he wasn't playing cards or working in his garden or making wine from his grapevine, his favorite pastime was to sleep, and our insatiable baseball fever just gave him more time to catch a few more winks after pulling the lever to lean back (way, way back) in the driver's seat of his vehicle.

After I enjoyed a heavy dose of those American Legion games, an inspiring Little League season, and that thrilling 1968 World Series, Notre Dame football was loaded again that fall with a promising quarterback named Joe Theismann. My joy didn't end there. I joined those friends since kindergarten in inventing more fun things to do. High school was near at Washington, where basketball reigned and where my parents attended with other relatives. Then, with Aunt Flossie's legendary rolls and Aunt Janie's chocolate cakes, and with Mom taking us on more autumn trips to the St. Joseph River to enjoy the changing colors on the Indiana maple trees, life in South Bend was good, and it was sprinting toward great.

Then Dad came home with some news.

We were moving.

Moving?

Yeah, Dad said he was getting transferred by AT&T, and before he continued, I had a bunch of thoughts at once.

Wait. What? Oh, that's right. Dad told us during the spring of 1968 that AT&T was moving us to Indianapolis, but the promotion fell through. So now AT&T is back to say we really are headed to Indianapolis. I know some things about the 500, but it looks like I'll have to brush up on the intricacies of Gasoline Alley. Instead of Notre Dame football, the folks around Indianapolis are more into Indiana basketball. I'll still catch the Irish on the radio, and Lindsey Nelson does national TV recaps of Notre Dame football games every Sunday. As for Aunt Flossie's legendary rolls and Aunt Janie's chocolate cakes, our South Bend relatives and friends will be only a 2 ½ hour drive to the north on US 31.

Then Dad spoke again.

The AT&T transfer wasn't to Indianapolis.

It was to Cincinnati.

Where's Cincinnati?

CHAPTER 3

Is This Heaven?

After spending most of my 12 years on earth in northern Indiana, it was tough during early November of 1968 saying goodbye to relatives (tons of them) and friends. We were preparing for our new life in southwestern Ohio. Actually, I did well with my emotions on my last day at Benjamin Harrison Elementary School, where my parents once attended along with aunts, uncles, and cousins, but then I saw friends I'd known since kindergarten. They were crying all around me at their desks.

Why are they crying?

Oh.

For the first time since Dad told us in late October that AT&T was transferring him to Cincinnati to become a supervisor, it hit me. I wanted to shed tears, too. I did, but only until I finished making the half-mile walk home from Harrison to pack the rest of my stuff not going on the moving van into our 1966 Ford Galaxie 500 sedan of black and gray.

With Dad driving, Mom in the front seat and brothers Dennis and Darrell joining me in the rear, we were off to the unknown. We headed straight south out of South Bend through the familiar cornfields and flat roads we had often viewed when Dad took us on Sunday trips after dinner. Three hours later, we maneuvered through Indianapolis, where AT&T nearly sent Dad earlier in the year as a supervisor before his bosses reneged on the deal. Then we kept going south while moving slightly to the east on I-74, and the closer we got to the Indiana/Ohio state line, the more I began noticing something.

The world wasn't flat anymore. Whereas northern Indiana was about streets and highways that were perpendicular and parallel and level and predictable, southwestern Ohio was about dips and curves and hills and adventure.

I loved it already.

Then, after we officially crossed into Ohio, with Cincinnati right there, looking so much like its nickname of the Queen City, courtesy of its physical beauty through an endless range of mountains instead of hills to my young eyes, I loved it more. This was before we had even driven downtown, where many of the office buildings made the Golden Dome on Notre Dame's campus resemble something like a statuette.

As we headed for our new home in the northern Cincinnati suburbs, we hadn't even seen the official seven hills that comprise the city. We hadn't even seen those classic bridges across the Ohio River into Kentucky, including the John A. Roebling Suspension Bridge that was the largest suspension bridge in the world until Roebling built the Brooklyn Bridge about a couple of decades later. We hadn't even seen the Delta Queen, the steam-powered riverboat that continued its role since the early 20th century of taking as many as 170 passengers up and down the Ohio River. We hadn't even seen the construction of the new Riverfront Stadium, where the American Football League expansion team called the Bengals would play some day with the Reds, and where the Bengals would join the NFL in two years after the merger. We hadn't even seen the massive layout for Procter & Gamble, headquartered in the city and makers of, well, nearly everything (toilet paper, potato chips, batteries, diapers, cereal, detergent, etc). We hadn't even seen Skyline Chili, the local delicacy of spaghetti topped with meat sauce that contains cinnamon, cloves, nutmeg – maybe chocolate, too? – and then covered with a mound of shredded cheddar cheese (you can also add kidney beans and/or chopped onions).

We also hadn't even seen Cincinnati Gardens, where the Royals played as an NBA franchise, or Crosley Field, Cincinnati's version of Wrigley Field for the Reds.

Is This Heaven?

Those times were coming, but for the moment along I-74, we had our new house to find on the outskirts of Mount Healthy, a name that replaced "Mount Pleasant" in 1850 after its citizens were among the few in southwestern Ohio to survive a cholera epidemic. Mount Healthy was a 20-minute drive north of the Carew Tower, the distinctive building shown with the rest of the Cincinnati skyline at the beginning of several popular TV soap operas during the 1960s. That was because many of those shows were sponsored by Procter & Gamble, which sat on our bucket list of local places to visit.

Our new house was a recently built tri-level, and just beyond the backyard was a park with a baseball diamond. In other words, the theme continued: I loved it. We all loved it. The neighborhood was filled with kids our age who enjoyed playing baseball. The youth baseball system called Knothole League filled up parks everywhere. Near our park, you had the greatest ice cream shop on earth called the Mount Healthy Dairy Bar. Oh, and compared to South Bend, the Cincinnati area was warmer with less snow, which gave us more time to play baseball with kids in the neighborhood on that baseball diamond behind our house.

The previous owner of our house was Tom Hankerson, a noted personality on WCIN, Cincinnati's Black radio station, and he was close to some performer named James Brown who had his record-producing studio in town. A year or so after we settled into Hankerson's old place, he got us back-stage tickets to meet The Godfather of Soul himself following one of his concerts. My brothers and I were stunned. Not so much by shaking Brown's hand, but by his height of 5-foot-6, if you included part of his processed hair.

Nevertheless, it was *James Brown*.

Did I say we all loved that Cincinnati?

It did take time getting used to the red clay of southwestern Ohio compared to the rich black soil of northern Indiana, but here was the biggest adjustment: When it came to college football, the kids in the neighborhood and throughout school were obsessed with the Ohio State Buckeyes of Woody Hayes and couldn't care less about Notre Dame.

Where is this Notre Dame?

And who's Ara?

Those folks were serious. Then it got worse. In 1968, which was our first college football season in Cincinnati, archrival Purdue upset Notre Dame back in South Bend, and the Irish lost again a few games later at Michigan State before they ended their regular season with a tie at intrastate rival Southern Cal. Even worse, Ohio State went undefeated to win the Big Ten and the national championship.

Neither the love nor even the like of Ohio State was going to happen for us, but we adopted the other sports teams of southwestern Ohio. It began with the Royals. South Bend lacked an NBA team, and the one in Cincinnati had Oscar Robertson, the Indiana native from Indianapolis and already one of the game's all-time greatest players. We were frequent visitors to Cincinnati Gardens during the winter of 1968 and the spring of 1969, and the Big O perfected the triple-double before our very eyes. As a whole, the Royals were average, but they were entertaining since Robinson's teammates included "Jumpin'" Johnny Green, who played above his 6-foot-5 frame, and Jerry Lucas, a seven-time NBA All-Star.

We had this system for every game. After our parents bought cheap seats in the upper deck, we did what kids regularly did back then. We hustled down to the box seats during the fourth quarter to watch the rest of the game as the ushers winked and nodded while walking the other way.

With much help from the Royals during our opening months in town, our Cincinnati stay already was a winner. In contrast, the Bengals were mostly losers during that 1968 season, their first as an AFL team along the way to the NFL. Even though we didn't attend any Bengals games that year at their makeshift home of Nippert Stadium at the University of Cincinnati, we watched from afar. We saw hints of future success after they upset the Denver Broncos and the Buffalo Bills in consecutive weeks at home, and Pro Football Hall of Famer Paul Brown led the Bengals as coach, general manager, and owner. We also went to high school football and basketball games, and we saw the Cincinnati Bearcats play hoops at their quaint little Armory Fieldhouse, which was Oscar

Robertson's college home as the nation's three-time leader in scoring before he joined the Royals.

For our first Christmas in Cincinnati, we already had our collective gift, which was Cincinnati. We also thought beyond the snowflakes. My dad scratched his golf itch by guiding balls into his putting machine in the living room, and both parents found places around town for rolling bowling balls. My two brothers played basketball, and I returned to the whiffle ball, the plastic bat, and the rubber ball to prepare for the next baseball season. In fact, all three of us couldn't wait to grace the diamond behind our house from sunrise to sunset, which we eventually did throughout our stay in Cincinnati.

Baseball, baseball, baseball. What ignited our already sizzling inferno even more for the national pastime after we settled into southwestern Ohio was that something became apparent whenever we turned on the TV, flipped through the radio channels, read either of the two local newspapers, or talked sports with just anybody beyond "Hello."

The city was Reds hot.

Especially approaching the new decade of the '70s.

Once, during one of the Royals games we attended, we saw nearly half of the kids at Cincinnati Gardens rushing toward a section of box seats before the fourth quarter. My brothers and I didn't go, but we got the insight scoop from somebody who did. There was a Pete Rose sighting, but it was a false alarm, and I started thinking, Pete Rose? Well, OK.

We kept hearing everywhere during our first winter in town about Johnny Bench, fresh off his 21st birthday. They said he already might be the best catcher in Major League history, and they mentioned how he spent the previous season with the Reds at 20 doing so many spectacular things with his glove and his arm that he won a Gold Glove as a rookie. They said his hands were massive, because they were. They said he was confident – actually, cocky, because he was. They said he could hit, too. He finished the 1968 season with a .275 batting average, 15 home runs. and 82 RBIs, which weren't good numbers for a catcher. Those were extraordinary ones, and he grabbed National League Rookie of the Year honors. They also said he already had one foot in the Baseball Hall of Fame, and they said the other one would get there by the end of the 1969 season or by the end of 1970 for sure.

Who were "they," by the way? They were anybody with common sense. They saw this rock of a player at 6-foot-1 and 197 pounds from Binger, Oklahoma, and they said he was not only a Cooperstown guy in waiting, but a solid piece for a Cincinnati team that already had hometown star Pete Rose (yeah, *that* Pete Rose who supposedly was at that Royals game) hustling to fame, sluggers Tony Perez and Lee May and a bunch of other studs in the starting lineup to form something like a machine someday.

A big one.

It definitely would be a red one.

Going into that 1969 season, the Reds already were peerless at the plate. They spent the previous year leading the Major Leagues in team batting average at .273 and runs scored with 690. They also set a National League record with 5,767 plate appearances, which meant they had a bunch of extra whacks throughout the season to keep pitchers jittery on the mound. Speaking of pitchers, the 1968 Reds had none, at least not enough good ones. Their team ERA of 3.56 was the second-worst mark in the Major Leagues, and that was during "The Year of the Pitcher," when Bob Gibson burned through hitters toward his ridiculous 1.12 ERA. Gibson was among the reasons MLB officials decided to lower the mound, and he was the primary reason the 1968 Cardinals won the pennant. The Reds finished 14 games behind St. Louis at 83-79 in the NL before divisions, and even though Bench couldn't pitch, he gave them hope for a 1969 breakthrough.

Well, that was what "they" kept saying during the Hot Stove League, the name for baseball talk from the end of the season to February when pitchers and catchers reported to Florida and Arizona.

When spring arrived faster than I expected – since we discovered the snow in southwestern Ohio didn't stay as long as the lingering white carpet on the ground in northern Indiana – I had three paths to baseball euphoria. First, we had that diamond beyond our backyard. If there was just the hint of daylight, and if the grass didn't resemble a swamp, we were playing, which meant my brothers and I were participating in endless games with the multitude of boys around our age in the neighborhood. Between the real games, we invented little ones such as "rundown," where Dennis and I took our places at bases sitting the standard 90 feet apart. Then our younger brother Darrell would try to beat our throws to either bag as a baserunner during our simulated version of a rundown. About a decade later in 1977, Darrell became the first African American baseball player ever for the University of Wisconsin, and he was a leadoff hitter noted for his base-stealing skills, setting the season record at 31 steals in 1981.

He thanked his older brothers.

My second path to baseball euphoria during the spring and summer of 1969 involved the Knothole League, Cincinnati's advanced version of Little League. Ours was in Mount Healthy, about a block away from the Mount Healthy Dairy Bar, which often came into play a couple of years later when Dennis and I played for the Aardvarks. Coach Oren Miller paid the whole Mount Healthy Dairy Bar bill for ice cream orders from our players after games, but only if we won.

We won a lot.

Those Mount Healthy diamonds were packed with players, relatives, and spectators during the spring and summer of 1969 and beyond. I also landed my first job with a steady paycheck through Knothole. I became an umpire for games of the younger players in the league, and the job required more than just standing behind the catcher and calling balls and strikes. Since Knothole baseball in Cincinnati was serious stuff, I needed to join others during training sessions with the umpire supervisor of the league. There also was an exam afterward involving the rule book, which had its Knothole League tweaks. After I passed, I received umpiring gear, including a silver clicker for balls, strikes, and outs, and it became my constant companion beyond umpiring.

The $10 per game was superb, especially for a 13-year-old baseball player, always looking to purchase more items for either his Knothole games, his high school career on the horizon, and those backyard pickup games.

Then came my third path to baseball euphoria in 1969, and it involved everything surrounding the Reds. Before long, I wondered, "Where have these guys, this team, and this city been all of my life?" As a family, we discovered something in a hurry as that date of Monday, April 7, 1969, moved closer on the calendar. Around Cincinnati, that date was like the arrival of Saint Nicholas or The Ball dropping in Time Square or the Easter Bunny delivering his colored eggs or Mardi Gras on steroids.

That date was our first Opening Day in Cincinnati.

Wow.

We didn't see this coming.

Our first Opening Day in Cincinnati (and for others afterward) had the intensity of a national holiday, complete with the closing of streets, businesses, and schools. The early highlight always is the Findlay Market Parade, which started in 1920, and for every Opening Day, the parade begins on the northwest side of the city at Findlay Market, Ohio's oldest continuously operated market that opened in 1852.

For this Opening Day, there were marching bands, floats, elephants, Clydesdales, and celebrities, both local and national. The parade passed the heart of downtown: Fountain Square, with "The Genius of Water" statue showcasing a woman with water pouring from the palm over her hands, and city officials turned off the fountain during the winter months. They let the water flow again on Opening Day, which only made sense. The parade finished its nearly two-mile journey after reaching the Reds' ancient home of Crosley Field, where the bands, the elephants, and the rest of the group took a trip around the diamond before the packed house. Then the parade left the premises beyond an outfield gate to allow the Reds to do their thing.

The entire event was shown live on local television, and why not? In Cincinnati, nothing else mattered on Monday, April 7, 1969.

Such things happen when your city is noted for producing the first professional baseball team, and that was the Cincinnati Red Stockings in 1869, which meant 1969 was the 100th anniversary of the franchise. For the longest time, Major League Baseball officials honored the city for its pioneering ways through Cincinnati's Opening Day. Not only were the Reds given the first game every season in the majors, but they were allowed to begin at home during the afternoon while their peers were off until at least the following day. By the end of the 20th century, MLB officials had other thoughts. They chipped away so much at Cincinnati's Opening Day tradition that it became pebbles on the floor of history.

The demolition started one season when the Reds had their normal afternoon game on Opening Day, but MLB officials added other games that night while stressing the Reds still had the first pitch of the season. Soon after that, MLB officials spent a year scheduling American League games at the same time as the Reds' afternoon game on Opening Day, but MLB officials said the Reds still had the National League opener. Once the 21st century arrived, there were games not involving the Reds to begin the season in foreign countries, and Cincinnati's Opening Day tradition had become no tradition in the minds of MLB officials.

Despite it all, we had Opening Day in its purest form on Monday, April 7, 1969, but the Los Angeles Dodgers were party poopers. They won 3-2 with their pitching combination of Don Drysdale and Bill Singer holding our supposedly machine-like team to four hits, including two for the Reds in the bottom of the first inning.

I watched on TV, but I listened to the radio.

During the summer of 1968, when we still lived in South Bend, I discovered radio was a splendid way to follow Major League Baseball, but you needed the right voices. It began for me with Vince Lloyd and Lou Boudreau doing Cubs games on WGN in Chicago. Later, I heard Harry Caray and Jack Buck on KMOX in St. Louis with the Cardinals and Ernie Harwell on WJR in Detroit with the Tigers. In Cincinnati, I found two other announcers to quench my baseball thirst in Jim McIntyre and Joe Nuxhall of WLW. McIntyre delivered play-by-play with energy and pleasantness. Nuxhall was the color man who let you know what he was without saying so directly, and the former Reds pitcher was more than this: He was a native of nearby Hamilton, the favorite uncle for those listening, the team's biggest fan – and the youngest player ever to appear in an MLB game at 15 years old.

Due to a shortage of Major League baseball players during World War II, Nuxhall was called up from the Minor Leagues by the Reds. He took the mound on June 10, 1944. He returned to the Reds in 1952 for the start of two more stints with the team, and when the second one ended after the 1966 season, he joined McIntyre in the broadcasting booth. Nuxhall became a significant figure in my professional sports journalism career – helping to propel it from the ground toward the sky with a couple of gracious moves that came out of nowhere – but long before that, there was Monday, April 7, 1969, when I was 13 and listening to "Jim and Joe on the radio" as Cincinnati folks liked to say.

You needed a Jim and a Joe back then as a Major League Baseball fan. Outside a few gigantic markets that televised the bulk of the home team's games (like WGN in Chicago for the Cubs), radio was your best bet to follow your team on a regular basis. It also became your favorite bet if you had a Jim and a Joe versus whoever was in the broadcasting booth for one of the few locally televised games of your boys. During our first Opening Day in Cincinnati, I had that TV screen in front of me, but I also had that radio in hand, when Pete Rose led off the bottom of the first inning against Drysdale with no score.

Then it was 1-0 Reds.

With the switch-hitting Rose batting left-handed against Drysdale, who routinely threw flames from his right arm, Rose sent the first pitch he saw the opposite way, and it kept drifting high and deep until it reached the screen above the left-field wall for the first home run by anybody during the 1969 season. McIntyre described the moment, with his voice rising as much as Rose's ball, and Nuxhall provided the same background noise that was his signature during those situations.

"Get outta here."

"Get outta here!!!"

Now that was fun, and so was this: The next batter. It was Bobby Tolan, and I saw and heard him play the previous year with the 1968 St. Louis Cardinals during the World Series before he joined the Reds weeks later. He followed Rose to the left side of home plate, and he crushed a Drysdale pitch into the right-field bleachers. The Reds' offense vanished in the aftermath, and all the Dodgers needed was a run in the second and two more in third to seal victory.

That was just one game, though. The Reds proved as much 13 days later when Jim Maloney unleashed his assortment of fastballs to throw a no-hitter against the Houston Astros, and it happened at Crosley Field, among the most hitter-friendly ballparks ever made. Complementing Maloney's gem, the Reds feasted at the plate for a 10-0 victory, but then came the next day. The Astros' Don Wilson threw a no-hitter against the Reds, and that was only the second time no-hitters were exchanged in successive Major League games.

Except for Maloney, the 1969 Reds remained pitching challenged, but who cared? I didn't, at least not that season, which was our first summer as a family to say we had a Major League team in our hometown. The Reds kept things lively with all kinds of sluggers to combine with proficient line-drive hitters. That group featured Tony Perez, Johnny Bench, Lee May, Alex Johnson, Rose, and Tolan, and even though the Reds were losing about as many 8-7 games as they were winning, they were captivating. They also kept hovering near the top of the National League West during that first year of baseball's new format. Before the 1969 season, MLB officials separated both leagues into divisions of east and west, and the winners would play each other for the pennant and entry into the World Series.

That's when something occurred to me after the Reds won five straight games in mid-July to sit 2 ½ games from first place in the NL West.

While the Reds were in that division, the Cubs were in the NL East. *They could meet during the NL Championship Series!*

That's right. Our first Major League Baseball team – which we struggled to see in South Bend, Indiana, on a snowy TV screen after my dad climbed to the roof for an adjustment of the antenna toward WGN in Chicago – *that* team was in a different division than these Reds who had quickly become my team.

As for the Cubs, we spent our years in South Bend watching Ernie Banks, Billy Williams, Ron Santo, Ferguson Jenkins, Don Kessinger, Glenn Beckert, and Randy Hundley when they had only promise as a team, but this was different. Now they were streaking toward the playoffs during the prime of their careers. Around that same time in July, the Cubs were up in the NL East by five games. They led the division by as much as nine games a month earlier, but they still raced toward becoming the first Cubs team to make the postseason since its 1945 forefathers reached the World Series, and I pulled for the Cubbies.

Except when they played the Reds.

Here was when I knew my transition from Banks to Bench was complete: My new boys faced the old one for the first time on June 13, 1969. The wind was blowing out of Wrigley Field in Chicago, and with the home crowd going bonkers through the speaker of my transistor radio, the Cubs outslugged the Reds 14-8, and I was sick.

I needed to get used to that feeling. For whatever reason, the Reds rarely could beat that generation of Cubs, even during the rise of the Big Red Machine, and I had my theories, but they came years later.

As for 1969, the Reds were competitive against nearly everybody not named the Cubs to stay in a wild NL West chase. It involved the Reds battling the San Francisco Giants, the Atlanta Braves, and the Dodgers. I watched during the few times the Reds were on local or national TV, but I listened all the time to Jim and Joe. Literally. My strongest desire that summer of 1969 was to attend a game inside the Reds' distinctive-looking home we often passed in the distance from I-75 as it sat in the middle of a neighborhood on the west side of town. There were so many factors keeping us away. At 13, I couldn't drive, and since my brothers were younger, well, they weren't headed behind the wheel anytime soon. Even if any of us had a driver's license, we were part of a one-car family, and both parents worked.

We also had Knothole League baseball games to play, and I had other ones to umpire. Then there was our location. We lived in Mount Healthy, which wasn't exactly a few fungoes away from Crosley Field, so riding our bikes across the city's numerous hills and curves to the right-field bleachers wasn't an option. It also wasn't an easy bus ride with a couple of transfers from our northern suburb to that part of Cincinnati.

Even so, Dad promised that we would go to our first Reds game that summer when everybody's schedules aligned, but that didn't happen until fall.

We weren't disappointed.

The Reds played the Cubs.

I had three Major League Baseball games smothered with pixie dust during my years as a fan, and this was the first one.

On the mostly rainy night of Tuesday, Sept. 2, 1969, the magic began after the whole family climbed into the same 1966 Ford Galaxie that brought us to Cincinnati less than a year before. Storm or no storm, we were going to this game. The closer we got to Findlay Street, Western Avenue, Dalton Avenue, York Street, and McLean Avenue – otherwise known as the five streets bordering the Reds' quirky ballpark – the clearer the sky became. We parked and walked toward what was a 58-year-old structure, and it looked amazingly spry with its white paint that seemed brand new and the majestic red (what else?) words "Crosley Field" on the wall behind the right-field bleachers. The rain stopped, and there were only stars. That applied to above, where the hint of a rainbow was forming, and to below, where the Reds and the Cubs prepared to thrill us just by existing.

Even before we entered, Crosley Field had this smell. It consisted of buttered popcorn, roasted peanuts, perfectly cooked hot dogs, and freshly cut grass. There also were other things making my nose wish to smile, but I couldn't determine what they were.

Whatever they were, I wanted to inhale the mixture as long as possible. I knew my senses would never feel that way again. Well, not until I returned to this place from the loveliest part of my imagination. After we moved through the turnstiles of the two-decked ballpark with spotless everything and a capacity of maybe 29,000, my first thought was to drop to my knees. My second thought was to paraphrase a line from a baseball movie still two decades away, but the sporting gods helped me go back to the future with the words.

Is this heaven?
No, it's Crosley Field.

Here were all of those Crosley Field things I heard about from Jim and Joe, as well as from what I saw on TV screens. You had the little hill of 15 degrees that was the warning track against the left-field wall. Officially, it was called The Terrace, but to clumsy outfielders, it was The Terror or The Terrible. You had the gigantic scoreboard that was in center field, stretching from the ground to nearly as tall as the upper grandstands. The scoreboard gave the results of other games, along with balls, strikes, outs, and even the batting average of the hitter of the moment. The scoreboard also had a large and square Longines clock at the top, and ads for locally brewed Hudepohl Beer and Webber's Sausage were displayed among its four billboards in every corner. You had the rightfield bleachers, called the Sun Deck during day games and the Moon Deck during night games. You had that grass, that perfectly cut baseball lawn, and it annually earned the praises of groundskeepers around the majors.

We took our seats along the right-field line in the upper grandstands, and the view was spectacular, especially with the bright lights showcasing that greenest of grass, and something else caught our attention without trying.

Ernie Banks' shoes.

"Look. *Look*. I can't believe how shiny they are," said Dennis, pointing toward first base as the rest of us turned away from those other Crosley Field things to stare with my brother at the black spikes of Banks, the Cubs' future Baseball Hall of Famer. Prior to this, we saw the man known as Mr. Cub mostly on that snowy TV screen in South Bend, Indiana. He inspired the Moore boys that night to a lifetime of the cleanest footwear possible when playing sports. The spikes of the other players also were Army clean, but nobody was on the level of Banks who ranked as a five-star general in that area to a bunch of corporals.

The Cubs starting lineup had our old gang. Banks, Williams, Santo, Kessinger, Beckert, and Hundley, and while Leo Durocher still was in the dugout as manager, the starting pitcher was Ferguson Jenkins, another future Baseball Hall of Famer with Williams, Santos, and Banks. There also was fresh blood for the Cubs in Oscar Gamble, their 19-year-old rookie outfielder with the biggest Afro in sports. During batting practice for the Cubs, my brothers and I left the upper grandstands to join the other kids dangling our scorecards from the railing along the box seats, and I got Gamble's autograph.

Then it got better.

I saw my new sports heroes in the flesh.

Oh. My. Goodness.

Bench, Perez, May, Tolan. There was Alex Johnson, who often stumbled up and down that little hill in left, but who could hit shots in the gaps at will. There was Tommy Helms. Even though he had the weakest bat on the team, he was the quickest second baseman ever at delivering the ball from his glove to first on double plays. There also were others, and I loved them all. That was before everything changed forever when I went from having several favorite players on the Reds to one. It began when somebody for the Cubs sent a sinking flyball across the way from us toward shallow right field. With cap flying off, the guy playing out there for the Reds sprinted forward like his hair was full of wasps. He made the catch after a belly-first slide as mud splattered against his face from the grass still moist from the rain.

It was Pete Rose.

It was Cincinnati's own Pete Rose, and he got a standing ovation as he raced back into position after wiping himself off.

"What a hotdog," somebody said in the row behind us, speaking in a conversational tone to a person either to his left or to his right, or maybe it was to everybody. I didn't turn around, but my ears were wide open as the guy added, "I went to high school with Pete over at Western Hills, and that's so typical of him. He's nothing but a hotdog."

I was confused. After I glanced at Rose, crouched in the distance for the next pitch, I leaned over to my dad, sitting to my right, and I said just above whispering, "The guy behind us said Pete Rose is nothing but a hotdog. What's a hotdog?"

My dad leaned over and said, "Show off."

I wanted to ask, "What's a show off?"

Instead, I studied Rose in right field. I noticed how he turned his body toward center field or the right-field line or home plate, depending on the hitter, likely to help the eventual 1969 Gold Glove winner get a better jump at the crack of the bat.

When the inning ended, Rose sprinted to the dugout while everybody else jogged. He continued moving toward his second consecutive National League batting title with three hits against the mighty Jenkins, and he would lead baseball with a batting average of .348. Even though he was thrown out at second base by Cubs right fielder Jim Hickman after he tried to stretch a single into a double, at least he was aggressive. He played that game as if it was the seventh game of the World Series, and whether he was a "hotdog" or a "show off," I shrugged.

Just like that, Peter Edward Rose was my guy, but once again, neither he nor his teammates could keep that generation of Cubs from doing what it often did, and that is beat the Reds by any means necessary. This time, Jenkins dominated everybody not named Pete Rose for nine innings, Gamble pounded the Reds' pitching, and the Cubs managed an 8-2 blowout during an otherwise fairytale trip for me to baseball wonderland.

The season ended a month later for both teams. While the Reds just missed catching the Braves for the NL West title, the Cubs and their collection of future Hall of Famers suffered one of the worst implosions in sports history when they finished eight games behind the New York Mets in the NL East after leading them by nine games in mid-August.

Major League Baseball rocked for me, though.

During the 1969 season, with the Reds greasing their cogs for a machine, I found paradise on earth among ballparks, and my player for the ages kept hustling inside it.

CHAPTER 4

The First Red Machine

Six days after the end of the greatest Major League Baseball season of my life (or so I thought at the time), something crazy happened on Oct. 8, 1969.

The Cincinnati Reds fired manager Dave Bristol.

Uh . . . *what?*

Moments after that shocker, the Reds had another one. They said they had already signed their new manager, and since those were the pre-internet days, sports journalists went scrambling with phone calls, morgue visits (the old newsroom term for searching the paper's library) and knocks on doors to see if anybody knew anything about George Lee Anderson, otherwise known as Sparky. He was a feisty Minor League player. He later excelled as a Minor League coach with four pennant winners in four years with four different teams. His Major League experience was one year, and that was the previous season of 1969 for the expansion franchise in San Diego, where he was the third-base coach for the Padres.

Now, at 35, Anderson had become the youngest manager in the Major Leagues with a starting lineup so loaded with power that Bob Hertzel of *The Cincinnati Enquirer* wrote on July 4, 1969, that it was the Big Red Machine.

We're back to the sporting gods, or I should say the newspaper gods in this case. Eight years after Hertzel's "Big Red Machine" reference, I worked at the *Enquirer* as an intern, and I often encountered him at the office or at the ballpark.

I used to read this guy every day after we moved to Cincinnati, I thought whenever I saw Hertzel, while trying to hide my wide eyes in his presence.

Just like the other veteran writers I encountered during my early years as a professional journalist, I studied everything about Hertzel, a mostly jovial guy who nevertheless was extremely protective of his beat. For some reason, he reminded me of Buddy Hackett, the comedian. I watched the way he asked questions, took notes, did interviews, and he could write. He could really write, and he did so faster than anybody I've ever seen. He also was peerless on deadline, and his copy always was clean and clever.

As for Hertzel's first use of "Big Red Machine," it took barely weeks into the 1970 season before his words became the official name for baseball dominance along the Ohio River, and I wondered the same thing as everybody else: Since Dave Bristol was a huge part of the Reds' rise, why would they get rid of him?

About a decade later, I stopped wondering. That's when I worked for the *San Francisco Examiner* covering the Giants, and the players spent the 1980 season calling their manager "Sergeant Carter" behind his back.

Not in a good way.

Yep, I'm talking about Dave Bristol, managing his fourth and last Major League team by then, and "Sergeant Carter" was the overbearing character in the 1960s TV sitcom called "Gomer Pyle." There is more to that Bristol-Sergeant Carter story, and it involved me (also not in a good way), but all I knew in October 1969 was that the Reds just whacked the guy who had the team on the rise. He had moved from coach to manager of the Reds in the middle of the 1966 season when their fate already had been sealed. They finished that year 18 games behind the Los Angeles Dodgers, winners of the National League pennant before division play, but Bristol's Reds improved over the next three seasons.

They went from 76 to 87 victories in 1967.

Then, after the Reds ended that season and the following one 14 ½ and 14 games, respectively, behind the St. Louis Cardinals, they nearly reached the 1969 playoffs before they fell four games shy of the Atlanta Braves in the National League West.

Bristol had lots of help since he inherited many of the guys he managed during the nine years he coached in the Minor Leagues for the Reds. He had Tony Perez, Tommy Helms, Lee May, and my guy Pete Rose. Another one of Bristol's players from his Reds farm system days joined the others later, and he was Johnny Bench.

But the Reds fired Bristol for Sparky who?

I'm back to the baseball and the newspaper gods.

After my transformation from fan to reporter, those gods gave me close interactions with both managers.

Years after Anderson went from "Sparky who?" to a manager in the Baseball Hall of Fame after earning two World Series rings with the Reds and another one with the Detroit Tigers, he stunned me during a poolside conversation at a hotel in Oakland, California. He told me when he thought his Cincinnati bosses needed to dismantle the Big Red Machine. The more he delivered what I didn't wish to hear, the more I wanted to cover my ears, and the more I realized I hadn't fully evolved from fan to reporter.

The Sparky of Cooperstown wasn't the guy I saw entering the 1970 season to lead the Reds with what I considered a nothing resumé.

I kept thinking Bristol got robbed, but only until I met Bristol.

Here's the rest of that Bristol-Sergeant Carter story. When I began covering the 1980 Giants for the *San Francisco Examiner*, they were in turmoil on the field, where they faded quickly in the National League West, and in the clubhouse, where there was drama by the moment. Bristol was the common denominator. In June, he exchanged punches in his office after a game with John Montefusco when the starting pitcher complained the manager pulled him off the mound too early in the ninth inning. After they were separated by other players and coaches, they both emerged with black eyes.

What was *that* all about?

"I didn't want to hear that, so I told him to get out of my office," Bristol said later, shouting even louder than Sergeant Carter while answering our questions among the San Francisco media contingent regarding Montefusco. "When he wouldn't go, I pushed him out. I stood up to him because I'm the manager."

Oh, boy.

Montefusco said, "Bristol provoked it. He didn't like what I was saying, and he told me to get out of his office. I was backing up, and he kept pushing and pushing. I told him, 'You better stop it, or I'll deck you.' He kept pushing me, at least 10 times, before he sucker-punched me."

Then came July in St. Louis, where Bristol didn't slug me, but he grabbed me in a rage in the visiting clubhouse at old Busch Stadium.

With the Giants reeling again, slugger Jack Clark told me before a game against the Cardinals that the old-school Bristol wasn't communicating with the modern-day Giants. "If a player doesn't do the job one day out there, then he really comes down hard on you," Clark said, sitting at his locker in the cramped visiting clubhouse with the manager's office three or four steps away. "It's too long of a season for that, and a manager can't think that he's too far above his players. He just can't sit in his office."

Since I first learned from Mrs. Griesbach as a sophomore working for my high school newspaper in Milwaukee that you must get both sides of a story, I told Clark I was going to relay his words to Bristol. "Go ahead," Clark said, pointing toward the visiting manager's office as I took those three or four steps before entering the open door. The more I delivered Clark's words to Bristol, the more his face turned redder than one of his old Reds caps. "I know damn well I do communicate with the players," Bristol said, and then Sergeant Carter returned to go from loud to louder, standing and screaming, "Who told you that?"

Jack Clark.

With Bristol's head just shy of exploding, he rushed from behind his desk, grabbed my right arm and pulled me into the clubhouse over to Clark's locker. Other Giants players and coaches watched with bemusement and horror. They couldn't believe what they were seeing. Neither could I, especially after Bristol stood over Clark, while yelling with arms waving, "Tell him I communicate with the players. Tell him, Jack. *Tell him.*"

I looked to my left, where Vida Blue stood at his locker, just out of Bristol's view, and the former Cy Young pitcher with the mischievous smile kept throwing up his arms to mimic the manager's tirade.

Even though Bristol was signed to manage the Giants through 1982, owner Bob Lurie decided Sergeant Carter had to go at the end of that 1980 season. So Bristol was fired, just as he had been by the Atlanta Braves after the 1977 season, and by the Milwaukee Brewers after the 1972 season, and by the Reds after the 1969 season.

Throughout my 1980 dealings with Sergeant Carter, well, Bristol, I kept drifting back to my time as fan while thinking, "My Big Red Machine just missed blowing its transmission on that one, and maybe Bob Howsam knew from the start what he was doing by replacing the explosive Bristol with the cerebral Anderson."

Bob Howsam.

Who's this Bob Howsam?

That's what I thought more than a decade earlier as a Reds fan. On WLW radio and in the Cincinnati papers, I kept discovering that *Bob Howsam* made the decision to replace Bristol with Sparky. Howsam joined the Reds in January 1967 as general manager after he served in that same role with the St. Louis Cardinals along the way to three pennants during the decade and two world championships. He hired this Sparky guy for coaching jobs in the Minor Leagues with the Cardinals and later for the Reds. Years later, as a professional sports journalist, I had the last extended interview with Bob Howsam before his death in early 2008, and he was shockingly blunt about his role in constructing (and deconstructing) the Big Red Machine. But 40 years earlier, all I knew before the 1970 season as a Reds fan – when I finally sensed something wonderfully unique was happening to Cincinnati baseball – was that Bristol was gone, and this Sparky guy was in charge.

This Sparky guy delivered great vibes. He grew up in southern California, but for those of us from the Midwest, he was your next-door neighbor. You could imagine him fixing your flat tire while urging you to go inside and rest. He spoke plainly, and probably too much so for your average English teacher. He embraced double negatives when he wasn't splitting verb infinitives, not that he knew what any of that meant. Then there was his appearance. For the youngest manager in baseball, he looked old, but it was a distinguished old. Even though the top of his head was dark, both sides were gray, and by the start of the 1971 season, his head was as white as it would be for the rest of his life.

He went by Sparky, too. You had to like that, and throughout his slight frame of 5-foot-9 and maybe 170 pounds, he flashed no signs of having a "Sergeant Carter" anywhere surrounding his bones. That was splendid news for his players who were mostly self-starters, and they included Tony, Tommy, Bobby, Johnny, Lee, and my guy Pete. They approached the early part of their prime with a heavy amount of charisma and a mightier dose of slugging, and even though they needed more pitching, I couldn't care less.

Boy, could they slug.

This was my team.

The feeling intensified as I moved through the winter and the spring toward the 1970 season with Cincinnati things contributing to my glee. Take those live local TV shows, for instance. They aired every weekday, and they were as unique to the city as the natives saying "please?" instead of "pardon me?" when they didn't understand your question. Each of those shows had elements of their national counterparts of that era such as "The Jackie Gleason Show," "The Tonight Show with Johnny Carson," "The Carol Burnett Show," "The Ed Sullivan Show," "The Sonny and Cher Variety Hour," "The Dean Martin Show," and the Bob Hope specials.

Those live local TV shows in Cincinnati had singing, dancing, and cooking, along with discussions among guests about movies, politics, gardening, and everything in between. There also were comedy skits and standup routines, just like those national shows, but there was a significant difference.

Except for "The Tonight Show" with Johnny Carson and the Bob Hope specials that aired only periodically, those national shows were once a week and generally an hour long. Those Cincinnati shows were live Monday through Friday for 90 minutes in the cases of Paul Dixon and Bob Braun, the heavy hitters on WLW, the NBC affiliate. One day, you might flip to Dixon's show and see Robert F. Kennedy or Imogene Coca or even the wedding between two rubber chickens (which happened). Then if you stayed for "Bob Braun's 50-50 Club," you might find somebody in one of his chairs such as Phyllis Diller, Red Skelton, Dick Clark, or Bob Hope, among Braun's closest friends.

If you switched to WCPO, Cincinnati's CBS affiliate at the time, you saw Nick Clooney, that station's Paul Dixon and Bob Braun, but Clooney's show lasted just an hour each day. He had his built-in Hollywood connections. They came through Rosemary Clooney, his sister who was an acclaimed singer and actress for more than five decades with ties to Bing Crosby, Hope, and others. This was the same Nick Clooney whose son George Clooney became a Hollywood star.

Yeah, those shows were captivating, but here was the primary reason I enjoyed them, and it began with the 1970 Major League Baseball season. Unless I had to do something like go to school, those shows were must-see events for Reds fans, and everybody in Cincinnati back then was a Reds fan. It became your civic duty to flip the dial to see which member of the Big Red Machine might stroll from behind the curtains for a segment or three.

Those Reds lived in my head. With spring training approaching, I daydreamed at Mount Healthy South Junior High School about the Big Red Machine by writing or drawing something related to the team on the front and back cover of the notebook for whatever class I had. I added to the writings and the drawings all season. If I had enough room for only a geometry formula or Woody Woodward's offensive numbers for 1969, well, so much for the basic quantities describing a sphere and those variables.

In one notebook, I listed my batting order for the Reds, and in another, I scribbled a different one. I drew my version of the team's logo with "Reds" in white letters against a red background, and like the real thing, my thing was surrounded by a white buffer against the red border composing the wishbone C. I drew half-serious and half-cartoonish looks of Reds players, coaches, and Sparky, but my best work came on the front inside cover of the notebooks. That's where I drew the Big Red Machine as the vehicle I saw in my imagination.

How I remained near straight A's on all of my report cards during that 1969-1970 academic school year for the eighth grade, I'll never know.

OK, I know.

It went back to the Reds.

Years later, Los Angeles Dodgers manager Tommy Lasorda would talk about the Big Blue Dodger In The Sky, but I discovered there was a Gracious Red Of The Reds In The Sky. At least for me, because back then, the Reds delivered a pitch down the middle of the plate in my direction called their "Straight A" program. All students who got straight A's on their report card during the winter semester of 1969 could submit a copy of that report card to the Reds and receive two free tickets to three games during the 1970 regular season.

Despite the daydreaming, I got straight A's.

Maybe it was the Gracious Red Of The Reds In The Sky, but this was for sure: As the definitive Big Red Machine fan, I wanted to see as many games as possible during what my gut kept saying would be an epic baseball season in Cincinnati.

Even with those straight A's in hand, I kept telling myself, "No way. This is way too good to be true. Surely Reds officials aren't going to give a bunch of kids two free tickets to each of three games this season to watch the best team in baseball?" I just knew something would go wrong, but I went through the motions. I filled out the application as if I were handling nitroglycerin, and then I put it in an envelope with a copy of my report card and the required signatures from school administrators and parents. After that, I waited, and then I waited some more. I kept thinking to myself, "Did it get lost at the post office?" Every day, I checked the mailbox for something on the outside of an envelope containing the wishbone C that I had been drawing throughout the winter.

One day, probably sooner than reasonably could have been expected, there it was. The congratulatory letter arrived to give me the option to pick three games out of the 30 or so offered on the home schedule, and the Reds needed my decision several weeks before Opening Day. I dissected the pros and the cons of attending each game on the list, and then I made my choices after two or three days of deliberation. In hindsight, the Gracious Red Of The Reds In The Sky was with me, and so was Pure Luck.

My first choice involved the Dodgers, and why not? I thought, "You never can go wrong seeing one of the consistently best teams in the National League, and it's on June 20, a Saturday afternoon game at Crosley Field, scheduled to close sometime during the summer after six decades." My next choice involved Hank Aaron, my all-time favorite player not associated with the Cubs in the old days or the Reds of the moment. His Atlanta Braves were among the options, so I picked Wednesday, July 1, just because it had a nice ring to it, and "Who knows?" I thought. "I could see Hank jack one." By then, the Reds could be in their new Riverfront Stadium, complete with artificial surface instead of the natural grass of Crosley Field and with all the modern things for baseball of the latter 20th century. Finally, I checked Saturday, July 25, because it was the St. Louis Cardinals of Bob Gibson and Lou Brock. I still got chills recalling them against the Detroit Tigers during the 1968 World Series, when I smuggled a transistor radio into my Benjamin Harrison Elementary School classes in South Bend, Indiana. "To see Gibson, Brock, and the rest in the flesh, wow," I thought.

I was enlightened with all three picks. We would go to other Reds games during that 1970 season as a family or just as brothers, but for me as the ultimate Big Red Machine fan, those picks were on a different level.

Long before the first pitch of those games, it was spring, and the Reds were finishing up in Tampa, Florida, which became their home back then from January through March. The Gracious Red Of Reds In The Sky (along with my love of writing and reading) already was foreshadowing my life to come. I had this growing fascination with sports media, especially if the subject involved Notre Dame football or the Big Red Machine.

That spring, it was Reds, Reds, and more Reds for me. During much of spring training, I devoured everything over the WLW radio airways from Jim McIntyre and Joe Nuxhall, including the pregame and postgame shows and the games themselves. That remained my routine during the season, because I couldn't get enough of those guys. They led me to discover the joy of keeping a scorebook. For most Reds games during that 1970 season, I charted what happened after every pitch, and I did so through the words of Jim and Joe. I even wrote them a letter during the summer to tell them how much I enjoyed their broadcasts, and McIntyre shocked me with a handwritten note of thanks.

Then there was *The Cincinnati Enquirer*, which came to our doorstep every morning. I read every word from Bob Hertzel, that Reds beat writer who first coined the term "Big Red Machine."

In the spring of 1970, I also began buying sports magazines like crazy. Sports Illustrated, Sport magazine, Super Sports, Inside Sports, Baseball Digest, and Street & Smith's Official Baseball Yearbook were musts. Those magazines and others regularly had Reds folks on the cover, including my guy Pete Rose, which is why the friendly paycheck I got from umpiring Knothole League games came in handy.

As Opening Day arrived on Monday, April 6, 1970, I couldn't get a particular song out of my head. It summed up the status of the Reds, the mood throughout a region burning with baseball fever, and a 14-year-old native of South Bend, Indiana, latching onto his new city and sports team like they were his from birth. The song was written by Larry Vincent for the 1961 Reds along their way to the National League pennant, but nine years later, the song kept surfacing inside me as the Big Red Machine anthem of the moment.

The whole town's batty about Cincinnati,
What a team, what a team, what a team.
Each man and lady from one to eighty,
How they scream, how they scream, how they scream.
Keep on rooting, every inning,
And they'll do their best to keep on winning.
You can tell your Aunt Hattie,

This year in Cincinnati,
What a team, what team, what a team.
I was pumped.

Those live TV shows in Cincinnati were Reds hot, and during what would be the last Opening Day at Crosley Field, the Findlay Market parade never was more spectacular to start a season, and the same went for the Reds.

This was the First Red Machine. There were two of them, and whereas the second one did everything – literally – this one was about pounding opponents to death and then stomping on their graves. In fact, after the Reds spent the previous two seasons leading the Major Leagues in most of the top team offensive categories, this one was expected to do the same in 1970, but only more dramatically, and it did. Sparky Anderson put the primary cogs of the First Red Machine in his starting lineup to open the season, and they each had their own ways of making this a terrific team for fans and a terrifying one for foes.

Johnny Bench stood peerless among catchers, and he crushed pitches, too. Even though Tony Perez was an error machine at third base, he joined Bench in making pitchers miserable. And let's just say first baseman Lee May wasn't called "The Big Bopper from Birmingham" for nothing. Tommy Helms at second and Woody Woodward at shortstop were the only offensively challenged folks on the roster. Even so, with those bombers in front of them, they just needed to do what they did, and that is, they were wizards at turning double plays. Bobby Tolan operated a smooth center field, and he was a prolific line-drive hitter and base stealer. The Reds platooned two rookies in left field in the left-handed-hitting Bernie Carbo, who eventually was named National League Rookie of the Year by The Sporting News, and right-handed-hitting Hal McRae, who later became a standout designated hitter in the American League.

Then there was my guy Pete Rose, moving toward his second consecutive Gold Glove in right field, and the Cincinnati native already owned the previous two NL batting titles while edging closer to more hits than anybody, you know, like in baseball history.

Pitching? Don't ask.

Well, Jim Maloney owned a fastball that made him the right-handed Sandy Koufax with three no-hitters, but he ruptured a tendon in his toe during spring training and basically was done for his career at 29. Wayne Simpson became a baseball sensation as a rookie starter through the 1970 All-Star break, but his rotator cuff wouldn't cooperate after that.

The other starters were OK, but the Reds did have extraordinary relievers in Wayne Granger and Clay Carroll, and did I mention the Big Red Machine could slug like crazy?

That overwhelming power gave the Reds a 10-game lead in the NL West on Saturday, June 20, when my dad dropped off my brother Dennis and me at the Crosley Field parking lot. As a fan, this was the start of the second of the three games of my life smothered with pixie dust. The first happened the previous year when the whole family went to Crosley Field on Tuesday, Sept. 2, 1969, which was slightly less than a year after we moved to Cincinnati from South Bend. My two brothers and I had never been to a Major League Baseball ballpark, and the experience was astounding. The Reds played back then with those sluggers on the rise, and that already was enough, but they faced the same Cubs team that we spent the 1960s trying to see through the cloudy picture on our TV screen since the antenna on top of our roof mostly struggled to capture the signal from WGN in Chicago.

That first game of pixie dust was at night, but this one against the Dodgers featured sunshine without a cloud in the sky or a care in the world, and it had to be that way.

This was the perfect day.

Who is that elderly Black guy with a silk stovepipe hat? And why is he wearing tuxedo tails, a dark frock coat, and a bowtie for a baseball game? We didn't see him during our other times at Crosley Field.

He was "Peanut Jim" Shelton, and Dennis and I moved closer to hear his tradition since the early 1930s of singing, "Wanna bag of peanuts?" outside Crosley Field while roasting his wares in the coals on his pushcart. As we walked toward the ballpark – which always looked young, with its seemingly fresh coat of white paint every game instead of old, with its birth certificate that says it was born at the corner of Findlay Street and Dalton Avenue in 1912, there was that smell again. We hadn't a clue what it was, although freshly cut grass and buttered popcorn figured heavily into the mix.

Whatever it was, it was Crosley Field.

We loved that little hill of a warning track against the left-field wall. We loved the screen above that wall where homers went to die. We loved the sun deck on this bright afternoon to house those in the bleachers. We loved the gigantic scoreboard that was center field. We loved the multiple measurements from home plate to different parts of the outfield walls. We loved seeing the cozy stands that made you feel you could reach out and touch anybody on the field from anywhere you were sitting.

So why are the Reds leaving paradise again to go to Riverfront Stadium?

There also was that lovely matter of the visiting and home clubhouses. They weren't in the ballpark. To the delight of fans, everybody from both teams had to exit Crosley through a tunnel on the third base side. Then they walked through the crowd to reach the clubhouses in a separate building along the left-field line.

As a baseball historian, I kept glancing around Crosley Field, and I kept envisioning a bunch of things. The first MLB night game happened here in May 1935, and President Franklin Roosevelt flipped the switch from the White House. Two years later, somebody snapped that photo of two Reds pitchers rowing a boat over the centerfield wall after Mill Creek flooded this West End neighborhood, including the ballpark. The Reds' Johnny Vander Meer hurled the first of his consecutive no-hitters from that mound in June 1938. The Beatles held a concert at Crosley Field in August of 1966 around second base.

Now Dennis and I sat in the lower grandstands of this sacred place along the third-base side with my straight-A tickets. We had only sun against the bluest of skies. We had Ronnie Dale still making pretty sounds with his organ keys. We had the distinctive voice of Paul Sommerkamp as the public address announcer gracing the air. In addition, between partaking in our hot dogs, Cracker Jack, and sodas, we watched the soaring Reds against the Dodgers of Maury Wills, Willie Davis, and all of their Cooperstown stars of the past.

It was the NBC Game of the Week.

We never wanted to leave.

Then the perfect day got better. Johnny Bench blistered a pitch for a homer, and Tony Perez did the same, and so did Lee May. To make things grander, my guy Pete Rose unleashed the dandiest of throws from right field to nail the Dodgers' Jim Lefebvre trying to slide home. Eventually, the Reds won 5-4, and then we rushed to the edge of the railing of the box seats like the other youngsters with our scorecards in search of autographs. After I grabbed more than a few, Bench stood at home plate with the sun even brighter during a live national TV interview with NBC's Tony Kubek. When Bench finished, he turned for a dash to the tunnel and the clubhouse. "Johnny, can you sign this?" I shouted, and he looked at me, saying, "Wait right there, and I'll be back after I go to the clubhouse."

I'm not sure why I believed him.

Moments later, ushers cleared us out of the area, but we were allowed to move with the other kids to the railing along the tunnel near third base. It led to the clubhouses. While my brother and I waited for Bench's return, we dangled our scorecards over the railing for others to sign, but it didn't matter to me. I already had the signatures of Bobby Tolan, Tommy Helms, and batting coach Ted Kluszewski, the former Reds slugger of the 1950s. Then came the last person through the tunnel, and it was Reds reliever Wayne Granger, the guy who just collected his Major League-leading 15th save of the year. *Oh, why not get Granger?* So I had my scorecard positioned for him to do the good thing or the bad thing.

He did the worst thing. With an angry stare, he knocked the scorecard out of my hands for it to meet a grimy fate on the floor of the tunnel.

Whether Bench ever returned, we never knew. This was before cellphones, and we had to rush out of Crosley Field to meet our dad at a designated spot a few blocks away, but our perfect day remained perfect.

Not even Wayne Granger could ruin it.

Thirty-seven years later, when I was deep into my career as a sports columnist, the phone rang at my desk for the *Atlanta Journal-Constitution*. No, it wasn't Wayne Granger. It was an elderly woman, and she said she read a couple of my pieces on my affection for the Big Red Machine. She mentioned the death of her husband. She added she was selling some of his sports memorabilia to end the clutter in her house. "We used to live in Cincinnati, so maybe there's something here you might help me get rid of," she said with a sweet voice. I agreed to stop by, expecting to find little of interest for me, and I was correct.

Well, that was until she led me to the corner of the basement before she pointed at a sturdy reddish chair with a wooden back and seat. It was supported by steel legs, the kind that lasted forever at old Major League ballparks.

There was a faded label on the front of the chair's back with the words: "June 24, 1970, from the last game at Crosley Field."

How much do you want for this?

She shrugged, saying, "$50?"

Sold.

Since I got the bargain of a sports collector's lifetime, I hustled toward the door. I moved as fast as I could with a ballpark chair that was much heavier than it looked, just in case she said something like, "Oh, I meant $500."

Dennis or I could have sat in that chair on June 20, 1970, the last Saturday game ever at Crosley Field. According to its label, the chair was still there four days later, when I listened with my heart pounding to Jim and Joe on the radio delivering vivid pictures throughout their broadcast of Crosley's final game ever. Bench ripped the game-tying homer that night against the San Francisco Giants in the bottom of the eighth inning, and May followed with what became the game-winning homer for a 5-4 victory. Then the Reds left for Houston before they returned for the first game at Riverfront Stadium on Monday, June 30, 1970, against the Braves. Hank Aaron did the expected by crushing the first homer ever at the new place, and his Braves won an 8-2 rout, but then came the next day of Tuesday, July 1, 1970.

Remember? The Gracious Red Of The Reds In The Sky helped me choose that game before the season from my straight-A options. This time, I took my brother Darrell, and we watched Tommy Helms, not only the weakest hitter in the Reds' lineup, but maybe in the Major Leagues, lift a high fly down the left-field line in the sixth inning to rise just above the fence to kiss the yellow screen for the first homer by a Reds player at Riverfront. It also spurred their first victory at the place when they crushed the Braves 9-2.

Riverfront was no Crosley. The Reds went from the best grass field in baseball to the first MLB team with an all-artificial surface, except for sliding pits around the bases and dirt areas around the pitcher's mound and home plate. The flying saucer of a stadium was as geometrically simple as the old place was beautifully complex, but Peanut Jim made the trip from Queensgate to that part of the Ohio River. So did Ronnie Dale, Paul Sommerkamp, and every member of the First Red Machine.

The smell stayed behind.

Too bad.

Then again, all was well for me with the senses regarding the last of my three straight-A games from the Reds. It was as memorable as the other two. On Saturday, July 25, at Riverfront Stadium, the St. Louis Cardinals were in town. Bob Gibson didn't pitch, and Lou Brock never got a chance to test his speed against Bench's rifle arm. But the Reds won, and that's all that mattered. Speaking of Bench, he went 3 for 4 with a homer, and he was just warming up for the following day when I listened to Jim and Joe on the radio describe his game of the year, and it was against Steve Carlton of the Cardinals. It matched future Hall of Fame catcher against future Hall of Fame pitcher, and Bench conquered the spotlight. He homered not once, not twice, but three times against Carlton, and courtesy of Bench's four hits, seven RBIs and 13 total bases for the game, the Big Red Machine was officially the Big Red Machine with a 12-5 clubbing of their pitching-rich opponent.

This was even more striking: With that victory, the Reds had 70 victories in their first 100 games of the 1970 season.

The only thing that paused the Reds' dominance was the Baseball All-Star Game. It occurred 11 days before that July 25 game at Riverfront Stadium, where the National League won 5-4 in the bottom of the 12th inning when my guy Pete Rose ran over Cleveland Indians catcher Ray Fosse at home plate with the clinching run. I expected nothing less from Charlie Hustle, and I had another All-Star Game moment as thrilling as that one. The day before Rose's play, my dad as an AT&T supervisor took a break from his job downtown to get autographs from the lobby of the hotel for All-Star Game celebrities. His signatures on the back of a cardboard notebook ranged from Roberto Clemente and Danny Kaye to Bowie Kuhn to Richie Allen. As a family, we also saw President Richard Nixon waving to the crowd outside his hotel in downtown Cincinnati, and he eventually threw out the ceremonial first pitch of the All-Star Game.

What a baseball summer.

Our Knothole League play continued to go strong with Coach Miller's Aardvarks team spending a lot of time at the Mount Healthy Dairy Bar, and we still had game after game on the diamond behind our backyard, but only until the Reds game started.

Before long, it was autumn, and the Reds ended the regular season with a record of 102-60 that could have been better. Once again, they couldn't beat that generation of Cubs with Ernie Banks, Billy Williams, Ron Santo, Ferguson Jenkins, and the rest. I knew I had made the full transition from the old guys from our South Bend days to the Big Red Machine, because even though every Reds loss knocked the air out of body for a while, let's just say it took much longer for normalcy to return if the Cubbies were involved. The 1970 Reds dropped the season series to only two teams that year: those Cubs and the San Diego Padres, who joined the Montreal Expos back then as expansion teams in their second year.

Here's what the Cubs and the Padres had in common: They owned pitchers who perfected the off-speed pitch. The dirty little secret on how to beat the First Red Machine was to stay away from fastballs.

That was my story, and I kept it quiet.

Neither the Cubs nor the Padres were in the playoffs, so I felt wonderful about October. I was more giddy after the Reds demolished the Pittsburgh Pirates during the National League Championship Series in a sweep. Then came the World Series and the Baltimore Orioles, but there was nothing to see there. When you grew up in a National League city back then, you were taught the American League was inferior, and that's because it was.

To be fair, there was the "out of sight, out of mind" thing in 1970 when interleague play wasn't close to happening that century. Unless you lived in New York, Chicago, the Los Angeles area, or the San Francisco Bay area, you saw that other league only in the All-Star Game and the World Series, which supported the mindset of NL superiority. The 1970 All-Star Game sent the NL to an eighth consecutive victory, and the AL won only once during the previous 13 games. That was when the players in both leagues took the Mid-Summer Classic seriously. For verification, see Pete Rose playing linebacker against Ray Fosse.

As for the World Series, the 1969 Orioles took their baseball high of 109 victories against a New York Mets team that only slipped into the playoffs after all of those Baseball Hall of Famers of the Cubs choked. Even though both the Mets and the Orioles swept their league championship series, Las Vegas gave the Mets 100-1 odds to beat the Orioles.

So much for odds and the AL.

The Mets flattened the Orioles in five games during the best-of-seven World Series, and the next season, those same Orioles were in the Fall Classic facing an NL opponent significantly stronger than the one of Tom Seaver and a bunch of obscure dudes from New York's Major League team not named the Yankees.

Everything went as planned by the Gracious Red Of The Reds In The Sky with Games 1 and 2 of the 1970 World Series in Cincinnati. The Reds exploded to a 3-0 lead in the opener, and I wondered if the Big Red Machine would ever lose again? Then Orioles third baseman Brook Robinson brought some of us back from Jupiter to Planet Earth, and he would do that often. First, the Orioles chipped away at the Reds' lead with two runs in the fourth inning and another one in the fifth for a tie game. The sixth followed, and the Orioles hinted of ugliness to come for the Reds after Lee May sent a grounder down the third-base line. Somehow, Robinson ignored the fact he was playing on an all-artificial surface for the first time in his life at 33, rushed over to backhand the ball, and while his momentum carried him toward the third-base seats, he spun to deliver a no-look throw to Boog Powell at first.

Lee May was slow, but he wasn't *that* slow.

Robinson's one-bounce prayer beat May to first base, and it wasn't replay worthy, even if there was replay back then, which there wasn't.

During that same inning, the Reds suffered from the worst call in the history of the World Series, and likely of pro sports during the postseason. They had Bernie Carbo at third base with the potential go-ahead run, and he rushed home when Ty Cline hit a chopper in front of the plate that Orioles catcher Elrod Hendricks grabbed in fair territory and reached back for Carbo. The problem was, Hendricks tagged Carbo with an empty mitt. A photo on the cover of Sports Illustrated that week showed Hendricks holding the ball in his bare hand, and the photo showed something even worse.

As the play developed, home plate umpire Ken Burkhart was knocked out of position, and he made the call while looking over his right shoulder with his back to the plate. He hadn't a clue what was happening, but he still called Carbo out.

Granted, Carbo didn't touch home plate, but that was the first time. Even though he returned seconds later to score accidentally while arguing the call with a screaming Sparky Anderson, whose dark hair turned white right there, Burkhart's blunder stood.

I wasn't pleased. Then Robinson (who else?) slammed a solo homer in the seventh for the go-ahead run for the Orioles that became their winning run, and my dislike for Burkhart's blunder turned from anger to pain.

Burkhart had nothing to do with Game 2.

This time, the Reds held a 4-0 lead through the third inning at Riverfront Stadium, but they collapsed again. And, of course, Robinson (who else?) contributed to the Orioles' rally to go ahead in the fifth with an RBI single. That was a microcosm for the rest of the 1970 World Series that featured the Reds winning only once, and in sum for Reds fans, Brook Robinson was Carlton Fisk on steroids. During the World Series, he hit .429 with two home runs, and at third base, he turned impossible plays into routine ones while going to his left, to his right and by using his arm to silence Reds rallies.

The Big Red Machine also was the Little Red Wagon against Orioles pitching with a team batting average of .213. In contrast, the Orioles clobbered Reds pitching for a .292 team batting average with 10 homers and a slugging percentage of .509.

The Reds discovered what I did: Man cannot live by slugging alone, not if you want to win world championships. While thinking about it all, I couldn't eat mom's wonderful dinner afterward. I eventually figured I could handle something lighter such as an Arby's roast beef sandwich. After I bought it, my eyes said yes, but my stomach said no.

Blame my Killer B's . . .

Brooks and Burkhart.

Little did I know another B-word would cause me pain for the 1971 season.

Beer.

CHAPTER 5

The New Red Machine

It was the middle of November 1970, and I couldn't shake the thought of Baltimore Orioles third baseman Brooks Robinson and Major League umpire Ken Burkhart becoming The Great Satans for my Big Red Machine in the World Series. You had Robinson with his bat and his glove, constantly torturing the Reds during clutch situations, and you had Burkhart, who still hadn't a clue what happened at home plate in the sixth inning of Game 1.

Then it got worse. The local folks at George Wiedemann Brewery Company had a five-year contract with Jim McIntyre and Joe Nuxhall to broadcast Reds games on WLW radio, but the deal expired at the end of the 1970 season. The new sponsor was Stroh Brewery Company from Detroit, which meant several things, and none were good.

For better or worse, beer and baseball had been linked forever – from advertising on the outfield walls of ballparks since Genesis 1:1 to Anheuser-Busch purchasing the hometown Cardinals in the 1950s – and the Reds were no different than their peers. Courtesy of its heavy German citizenry, the area from southwestern Ohio through northern Kentucky had dozens of breweries in the early 1900s, and several became tied to the Reds. Hudepohl became the team's TV sponsor in 1956 for a run of 20 years. There also were the 23 seasons of pitching and broadcasting legend Waite Hoyt doing Reds radio on WLW for the Burger Beer Broadcasting Network. Since Hoyt flaunted his allegiance so much to Burger, baseball, and the Reds, he figured retirement was his best option after Burger's contract expired following the 1965 season.

That's when Jim and Joe took over for Wiedemann. They were comfort food over the airways, and the more I think about it, they were bigger than that.

They were family.

I hung on their every word from the Hot Stove League, which was the nickname for baseball news spanning from the end of the season to spring training.

With the coming of a new beer sponsor, the Reds and McIntyre decided on a mutual split, and I fumed. I even wrote WLW a letter of complaint, and I got a "thank you for your interest" response that referred to the change in sponsors. The Reds did keep Nuxhall, their former pitcher who ended broadcasts saying, "This is The Old Lefthander rounding third and heading for home," and that was the least the Reds could do, but I still fumed.

Then it got even worse. Jim McIntyre's replacement was somebody named Al Michaels, so we went from "Sparky who?" in Cincinnati to "Al who?" within a year. This Michaels guy had zero experience broadcasting Major League Baseball. His previous job was as the radio voice of the Hawaiian Islanders in the Pacific Coast League, and he was just 26 years old. I couldn't care less that he was the 1969 "Hawaii Sportscaster of the Year." He sounded weird over the airways. I listened to his first spring training broadcast for the Reds in March of 1971, and he had this nasally sound or something. He made you cringe after home runs of Reds players by saying, "She's gone," and he also wasn't Jim McIntyre.

Those were just the main issues, but you could tell Joe Nuxhall liked him, and by the end of spring training, I sort of did. Then somewhere around the All-Star Break, it was like, *OK, I'm getting into this WLW era of Al and Joe on the radio.*

What I couldn't embrace by the middle of the 1971 season were the Reds, because they were dreadful. Their slide from Big Red Machine excellence to whatever they were for most of that year, well, let's see. It began with Bobby Tolan's crash to the floor of a basketball court on Jan. 7 in Frankfort, Kentucky, where he ruptured the Achilles tendon in his right heel during a pickup game. He tore it again in May while running in the outfield, and just like that, the Reds' center fielder was out for the season, along with his 57 stolen bases in 1970 and offensive numbers of 16 homers and 80 RBIs. The left-handed hitter also showcased his ability during the previous season of swinging well against both lefties and righties on the pitching mound for a .316 batting average. Beyond Tolan's bad leg, there were the sore arms of starting pitchers Jim Merritt and Wayne Simpson. The team also had a collective slump at the plate, which began in October against the pitching aces of the Orioles during the World Series and lasted into 1971, where only Pete Rose and Lee May owned a consistent pulse at the plate.

Tolan's injury was the first clue of misery to come for the Reds, and the second was Opening Day on Monday, April 5, 1971.

It was freezing.

We discovered as much as a family, because we were there in winter gear for that Opening Day at Riverfront Stadium that had held its first Major League game in June of the previous year. This afternoon harkened us back to our days in northern Indiana, where snowflakes remained a tease from Easter through about Mother's Day. It also was chilly for the visiting Braves from the frequently toasty city of Atlanta. Even so, the Braves won 7-4 with my guy Pete Rose doing the unthinkable with no hits after five at bats, and the Reds proceeded to drop their next three games for an 0-4 start.

They never recovered. They flirted with reaching .500 for the season in late August, but they finished 79-83, 11 games behind a significantly inferior San Francisco Giants team in the National League West. Only three things kept my baseball sanity in 1971: (1) lots and lots of free ice cream from the Mount Healthy Dairy Bar courtesy of Coach Miller since our Aardvarks team rarely lost; (2) the diamond beyond our backyard constantly featuring pickup games thanks to the Moore boys; and (3) my Knothole League umpiring duties producing more than a few bucks for me to buy more baseball stuff.

I still followed the 1971 Reds closely enough to record nearly every pitch in my scorebook, but this time, I did so while infatuated with Al and Joe on the radio instead of Jim and Joe, and by autumn, it was almost *Jim who?*

What was I thinking in the beginning?

Al Michaels was great. The networks agreed. After a pitstop with the San Francisco Giants and UCLA basketball following three seasons with the Reds, he won multiple Emmys doing Super Bowls, World Series games, and other major sporting events. I ran into Michaels often. In fact, I had several chats with the affable man who said of Team USA's upset of the Russians during the 1980 Winter Olympics "Do you believe in miracles? Yes!"

We even discussed his radio broadcasting days with the Big Red Machine, but I never told him I didn't like him in the beginning.

Too embarrassed.

Going back to the disaster that was the 1971 Reds, it didn't stop me from seeing more games that season at Riverfront than I did the year before. My brother Dennis saw more than that since he went from food and drink vendor at Crosley Field to the same role at the new place. Surely awfulness was just a passing fad for a Reds team loaded with talent, and my guy Pete Rose led the way. So I knew I'd attend even more games in 1972 at Riverfront, and during the years and decades beyond that.

In the meantime, I looked forward that winter studying the Cincinnati Bengals, an entertaining NFL expansion team that made the playoffs just two years after its berth under the legendary Paul Brown as owner, general manager, and coach. Little did I know as a fan that I would eventually huddle with Brown when I became a journalist, and we eventually had the same alma mater of Miami University, just 35 miles to the north of town. Once, when I was a 23-year-old reporter working for *The Cincinnati Enquirer*, Brown called me into his office after a Bengals practice during their training camp in Wilmington, Ohio. He suggested I do something as a former star center field and middle linebacker for my Milwaukee high school.

"I read what you wrote today in the paper," Brown said, referring to a first-person story I did from Richmond, Indiana, where I participated in a Reds tryout camp. I performed well, and I was encouraged to advance to the next level, but I stuck to writing. "What you did with the Reds, why don't you do something similar with the Bengals?"

Was Brown serious?

I mean, I was.

No.

Speaking for the whole family, Cincinnati was our soulmate. It never bored us, and it was so scenic, and you had Bob Shreve showing movies all night on weekends on local TV, and The Cool Ghoul hosted scary TV movies. Dad had his golfing partners on weekends. Both parents had their bowling leagues during the week. Our friends were growing during the three years since we left a bunch in South Bend, and I just knew the Big Red Machine would roar down baseball's highway again.

Then Dad came home from work with some news.

We were moving.

What? No.

Where?

To Chicago.

When? Why? We've got this great baseball diamond behind our backyard, and I did well for the freshman baseball team at Mount Healthy High School after playing for the freshman football team. Oh, and Coach Miller needs us for the Aardvarks, and I really enjoy that money from umpiring. Can we take the Mount Healthy Dairy Bar with us? And I don't want to follow the Cubs again. I've got my Big Red Machine.

We were going anyway, my dad said, trying to sound as upbeat as possible, even though he knew we weren't buying it.

He said the move would happen by the end of August.

You mean THIS August?

Yes, and we had no choice, because that's what the AT&T bosses told my dad who went from becoming the company's first Black supervisor to sprinting toward becoming its first Black manager. I felt that familiar burst of sadness and excitement, but grief won this tug of war with several jabs to the heart. There were uppercuts to the jaw as we moved closer to our departure time. Just like my last days in South Bend,

Indiana, three years earlier at Benjamin Harrison Elementary School, there was sorrow among friends and teachers at Mount Healthy High School, but no tears surfaced from any of us. Only despair, and it mostly came from me, wondering a lot of things, but this was near the top of my list: How well can we get WLW around the suburb we're heading to on the southwest side of Chicago?

It turned out I could get the 50,000 Watts of WLW Radio in Woodridge, Illinois, where we moved into a condo since my dad was told he should be prepared for another transfer in about a year or less, but only to a more permanent spot.

The best thing about the Chicago move was that the relatives in South Bend and Notre Dame football were just an 1 ½-hour drive away. Other than that, this switch from southwestern Ohio to northern Illinois wasn't good, and neither were the reports coming from the 1971 Baseball Winter Meetings in November from Scottsdale, Arizona.

Reds officials panicked, or so it seemed to me. After the Big Red Machine imploded during the 1971 season, they traded the right side of the infield in first baseman Lee May and second baseman Tommy Helms for a bunch of obscure folks from the Houston Astros. Actually, there were eight players dealt from both teams, but Lee May? He was "The Big Bopper from Birmingham," and despite the quiet bats of most of his teammates in 1971, he slammed 39 homers, and he was named the Reds' Most Valuable Player.

As for Helms, he never could hit, but who cared? I didn't. The Reds had those sluggers, and nobody made the relay throw on double plays better than Helms, who spent that winter grabbing his second consecutive Gold Glove. I, along with the other most diehard of Big Red Machine fans, also knew the importance of Jimmy Stewart, among the top role players and pinch hitters in baseball, and the Reds just threw him into the deal.

That was crazy, but this was crazier: The Reds sent May, Helms, and Stewart to the Astros for the obscure likes of Cesar Geronimo, Denis Menke, Jack Billingham, Joe Morgan, and Ed Armbrister, a Minor Leaguer.

I hated the whole thing until I didn't, which was when those former Houston players showed by early summer 1972 why Reds general manager Bob Howsam was a baseball genius. In conjunction with some adjustments involving Reds holdovers, those former Houston players helped to form the New Red Machine. It was faster (much, much, much faster, as in the fastest team in baseball), and it was better defensively (as in the game's slickest fielding team). It also had better pitching with the consistently effective Billingham as one of the leaders in the starting rotation. Not only that, but it retained the ability to bash opponents into oblivion, just in different ways than the First Red Machine.

Something else was apparent to those of us who spent our existence kicking the tires and checking under the hood of the Machine every few hours. The new version had room for more parts to get stronger throughout 1972 and the rest of the decade.

That said, when it came to the Reds careers for each of those former Houston players, I didn't see anything close to the following coming.

Nobody did.

- Ed Armbrister: He became one of baseball's elite pinch hitters. He even batted .296 for the 1976 season when the Big Red Machine won the second of its consecutive world championships. He also contributed to the Reds' victory in Game 3 of the 1975 World Series with the most dissected sacrifice bunt in history.
- Denis Menke: While Tony Perez was a disaster at third base, Menke was adequate or slightly better. The Reds improved on defense in a flash since Reds manager Sparky Anderson plugged Perez into Lee May's old spot at first base, where Perez did less harm, and it kept his lethal bat in the lineup.
- Jack Billingham: He threw more than 200 innings per season in four of his six years with the Reds. In addition, his 0.36 ERA after pitching in the 1972, 1975, and 1976 World Series was the lowest in the history of the event until Madison Bumgarner of the San Francisco Giants came along 38 years later.

- Cesar Geronimo: He was the best defensive center fielder in baseball with four consecutive Gold Gloves, and he provided just enough offense and speed at the bottom of the lineup to make the New Red Machine even scarier. During my exclusive interview with Bob Howsam decades later, he had more to say about Geronimo's importance, and I was amazed, almost as much as by some of Geronimo's catches.
- Joe Morgan: Well, all he did was evolve into the game's best second baseman ever. That was enough, but when the Reds won their back-to-back world championships in 1975 and 1976, he was the National League MVP both years. He eventually added to his 10 trips to the All-Star Game, five Gold Gloves, and Silver Slugger award with entry into the Baseball Hall of Fame. In addition, he became a frequent person on the other end of my phone calls, and he had riveting thoughts on the Big Red Machine and baseball's treatment of African Americans in general.

Those were the future resumés for those guys. As for the present, which became 1972 faster than I expected due to the inertia from our Cincinnati move to Chicago, nothing changed regarding my baseball psyche.

It was early February, and spring training opened for the Reds in Tampa. Looking ahead, I wished I could see the Findlay Market Parade in April in all its glory, and I wished we could do what we had planned to do for the beginning of the 1972 season, and that is, attend Opening Day at Riverfront Stadium for a second consecutive year. I also wished I could spend the upcoming season flipping the TV dial to Paul Dixon, Bob Braun, or Nick Clooney to see if Sparky, Pete, and other Machine folks were about to make a cameo or three.

So much for wishing, but the Reds still were my guys. It was just going to become more challenging to follow them.

Then it happened *again*.

In mid-February of 1972, Dad came home from work with that familiar look as he gathered the whole family in the living room. He told us his AT&T bosses had given him plans for that more permanent move.

We were headed to Milwaukee, where he would be a manager in charge of multiple states. He said the move would occur by the end of March, and I began thinking, "At least I'll have enough time to find everything I need to watch or to hear the start of the season for the New Red Machine. And Wisconsin. Isn't that touching Canada, or even the North Pole? Uh-oh. I wonder if I can get WLW?"

The move to Wisconsin was flawless, and it was welcomed. We didn't like Woodridge, Illinois, or even Chicago, because we loved Cincinnati, and except for its German influence, Milwaukee wasn't Cincinnati, but it wasn't bad. That partly was because our parents found another house that catered to the needs of their sports-minded boys. Like our home in Cincinnati, this one had a huge field beyond its backyard. It was perfect for football, soccer, or even baseball games despite lacking a diamond. If nothing else, it was splendid for shagging flyballs, fielding grounders, or convincing younger brother Darrell to get between Dennis and me on the bases for a few sessions of "Rundown."

Compared to Cincinnati, we lacked the kids our age in the neighborhood, but we had the field, and we had us, and that was enough. I also discovered those who ran the local Little League program embraced youth umpires with my experience, and they paid about as much as what I got in Cincinnati.

There also was Milwaukee's James Madison High School, where I was the first African American on the baseball team, and as a senior, I was the only Black player on our 1973 undefeated football team. I played middle linebacker, and I led our defense in tackles. Between the sports activities, I became the news editor of the *Madison Messenger*, our high school newspaper that won national awards, and I joined the publication as a sophomore. To continue a theme, I was its first African American writer and then editor of any kind. I said to myself often back then, with Watergate, *The Washington Post* and Bob Woodward and Carl Bernstein always in the headlines, "I want to be a journalist," and my declaration became reality through four years at *The Miami Student*, the oldest college newspaper west of the Alleghenies at Miami (Ohio) University, 32 years writing for major newspapers and then a career as a national sports columnist for internet sites while doing significant TV work and authoring books.

So Milwaukee worked for us, especially for me since the high school journalism program of Mary Griesbach set my course for the future.

It was just cold.

No, it was freezing, and snow always lived somewhere on the radar. When we first drove from Chicago to our new place on Milwaukee's north side in late March of 1972, the sun eased through the gray sky after we stopped at a nearby restaurant. Those clouds thickened around the time we ordered our food. When we finished eating, we weren't greeted by snowflakes, but by a blizzard, and just like that, we knew we were even farther away from the more predictable climate of southwestern Ohio.

There were positives about Milwaukee, though. My dad got the family partial season tickets to see the Bucks of Kareem Abdul-Jabbar and Oscar Robertson at the Crosley Field of NBA facilities called the Milwaukee Arena, which later was known as The Mecca. We also had partial season tickets to see the other tenants of the building, which were the Marquette Warriors, the powerhouse college basketball team led by colorful coach Al McGuire.

There also was a Major League Baseball team in town, but only theoretically. The 1972 Brewers began their third season in Milwaukee after one year in Seattle as an expansion team called the Pilots. Nothing about the Brewers was appealing. Their softball-like uniforms were a boring blue for away games with mustard-colored sanitary hose. Their team logo was a baseball glove (Don't ask.) They were as woeful on the field as my Big Red Machine was wonderful, and they played in the American League, which was a yawner for us National League chauvinists. We went to Brewers games anyway, and lots of them, because baseball was our thing, at least one of our things, and it was a big thing.

It mostly helped our sanity that the Brewers played in Milwaukee County Stadium, and I said "mostly" since that often was the coldest spot of a cold town.

Hot chocolate always was available at Brewers games, along with whatever fans put into their thermos to keep warm. Their home ballpark also served the world's best brats with its "Secret Sauce" that graced the same meat served at Bucks and Warriors games. Even though I preferred just "Take me out to the ballgame" during the seventh-inning stretch, the Brewers took advantage of the city's German heritage by throwing in the "Beer Barrel Polka" as folks in the stadium sang and danced throughout the song.

That was different, even enjoyable. The ballpark's other charm was two-fold, especially for a sports historian like me: First, the Green Bay Packers always played two of their home NFL games at Milwaukee County Stadium, and even though they had won only four games the previous season, you still felt the ghost of Vince Lombardi whenever you left the turnstiles for the stands. Second, you couldn't shake Hank Aaron's shadow, even before he left the Braves after the 1974 season to play his last two Major League seasons with the Brewers.

About Hank Aaron: The Braves moved to Milwaukee from Boston for the 1953 season, and the next year, he made his Major League debut with the team. He helped the Braves make back-to-back World Series trips in 1957 and 1958 to face the New York Yankees, and the Braves captured the first one with much help from his overall game.

No way, I thought as a baseball fan during my youth, that I would do something such as become closer to Henry Louis Aaron than any reporter in history. It was a 40-year relationship, and like Joe Morgan, Hank told me with passion that he thought Major League Baseball was trying to faze African Americans out of the game. I was the Hank Aaron whisperer, so whenever he wished to discuss that topic (or any other), he called me, and he called me often.

After Hank died in his Atlanta home at 86 on January 22, 2021, his widow Billye asked me to do two things: help her with the funeral program for baseball's all-time greatest player, and serve as an honorary pallbearer.

Hank and Milwaukee never lost their love for each other, and it began in the 1950s, when he helped this little (by MLB standards) Wisconsin town do the unprecedented by drawing two million folks per season for four consecutive years. Still, by the early 1960s, the Braves' attendance began to decline, partly due to rumors that ownership flirted with bolting Wisconsin for what it viewed as a more lucrative setting in Georgia.

The Braves left Milwaukee for Atlanta following the 1965 season, and even though much of Wisconsin appreciated the return of Major League Baseball (sort of) with the Brewers, they missed the Braves. They also missed the National League, which the Brewers later joined in 1998. But in 1972, when the Sam Moore family came to town, it was only an American League city. So I couldn't see my Big Red Machine live unless I did what I occasionally did, which was to make that two-hour drive from our house to Wrigley Field for a Reds visit to Chicago.

Those trips didn't occur until later during our Milwaukee stay. In 1972, I was just trying to figure out how to follow my Big Red Machine with consistency.

The first players' strike in Major League Baseball history delayed the season, which I hated, but then I loved it. That gave me more time to develop strategy. This wasn't Chicago, where I picked up WLW on most days, especially for night games, and the Cubs still did the unusual back then by televising virtually all of their home and away games locally on WGN. That allowed me more chances to catch the Reds. The Big Red Machine also was among the favorites for the NBC Game of the Week, and in addition to those things, my interest in the media continued to grow, along with the stack in my room of newspapers and magazines. Many of those publications contained articles on the New Red Machine, the one with those former Houston players who eventually became family.

Then, out of nowhere, I had my baseball equivalent to Saul getting knocked from his horse to became Paul after a blinding light from heaven.

With Opening Day 1972 at hand on Saturday, April 15, the Reds faced the Los Angeles Dodgers at Riverfront Stadium in Cincinnati to begin the entire Major League Baseball season with an afternoon game. Local TV never was an option. I was deep inside Cheesehead country, where those among the Beer Barrel Polka crowd couldn't care less about the Reds, and they barely cared about the Brewers. The Reds game also wasn't on national TV, which left radio, and our desktop one wasn't getting anything at 700 on the AM dial except a few mumbled syllables in the middle of static. This was before cable television and the internet, so receiving updates somewhere during games was not an option.

What to do? WHAT TO DO?

I had my transistor radio, and I went outside to see if I could get a better signal (or any signal), but nothing was happening there. So I returned to the house, and my blinding light from Abner Doubleday (or maybe Mr. Thurman's science class back at Mount Healthy Junior High School) told me to head to our partially finished basement in search of a conductor for additional electrons (or was that protons?)

Whatever the case, I placed the antenna of the transistor radio against various metals throughout the lower level of our house until I found a water pipe in what we called The Little Room for trophies and for books. Suddenly, Al and Joe on the radio were fairly clear, and during that season and subsequent ones, their broadcasts usually were nearly perfect for night games when the WLW signal was at its zenith. I nailed the strategy. From Opening Day 1972 through the bulk of my Milwaukee summers that ran through 1976, The Water Pipe was the primary way I followed the Reds.

Relatives. Friends. Visitors. All those folks thought I was a bit goofy with The Water Pipe, the transistor radio, and the Big Red Machine addiction, but I had an itch to scratch.

I kept scratching.

What Al and Joe reported about the 1972 Reds wasn't the best from April through the middle of May, when the former Houston players struggled to find their way, but then came the rest of the regular season. The New Red Machine guys weren't those busts for the Reds of 1971 with a losing record all year, or the brutes for the Reds of 1970 with the ability to scare opponents by swinging from their heels on just about every pitch.

These 1972 Reds were different. They stressed defense overall instead of here and there. They pitched better, which meant they had multiple guys who actually could keep the other team from scoring, even beyond their usual collection of solid relievers. They supercharged their speed, with Morgan's swift feet matching those of a healthy Bobby Tolan.

These 1972 Reds also were grittier. After they topped .500 for the first time on May 16, they won the National League West by 10 ½ games with a 95-59 record. They had the second-most victories in baseball to the Pittsburgh Pirates, who played one more game than the Reds and won the National League East by 11 games. The Pirates were loaded, with future Baseball Hall of Famers Roberto Clemente and Willie Stargell leading the way, but the Reds also had a few Cooperstown guys in waiting.

So I knew what nearly everybody else who followed baseball knew, and that was, the NL Championship Series would be close.

But this close?

I was a wreck from beginning to end. The teams split the opening two games in Pittsburgh and the next two in Cincinnati. Since this was a five-game series, that meant the fifth and decisive game was slated for Riverfront Stadium on Wednesday, Oct. 11, 1972, during the afternoon, and that also meant I was screwed.

Yes, all MLB playoff games were on national television, and even if they weren't, I still had my transistor radio and The Water Pipe. So that wasn't the issue, but this was: It was a school day in Milwaukee, and I played on the James Madison High School football team, and we practiced soon after the end of classes. The Reds-Pirates game was scheduled to start around the time we took the field for a couple of hours of blocking and tackling. In other words, this wasn't October 1968, when I smuggled my transistor radio into my Benjamin Harrison Elementary School classes to hear the World Series between the Tigers and the Cardinals. Since I valued my arms and my legs, I knew it wouldn't be wise at football practice to hold an electronic device in my hands with Coach Quinn screaming during swamp drills.

I also knew about those other options, but I wasn't going to skip school by claiming my baseball fever was some other fever. We weren't raised that way, and skipping football practice wasn't happening, either. Remember: I was born in the same hospital in South Bend, Indiana, where Notre Dame legend George Gipp died – as in, "Let's win one for the Gipper," as opposed to "Let's skip one for the Gipper." That left me with two options: (1) Try not to mess up too much on the field while wondering if Pete, Joe, Tony, and Johnny were doing enough against Roberto, Willie, and the rest of the Pirates; (2) Run like crazy after practice during that 1-mile trip from James Madison High School to our house on 94th street.

I'd never removed shoulder pads faster, and my shower was quicker than quick. I also got dressed in a flash and began the dash of dashes, refusing to turn on my transistor radio for an update of the game and resisting the urge to imagine what was or wasn't happening during what had to be the seventh, eighth, or ninth inning.

The game could be over.
I hope the Reds didn't lose.
What if they did lose?
Was there another Brooks Robinson or Ken Burkhart?

As soon as a I opened our front door, I rushed to the right toward the living room, where my brothers Dennis and Darrell were sitting, just staring at their older brother gasping for breath and wondering why he was looking prepared to hear them say something like Martians had just landed behind our house.

"What's wrong with you?" Darrell said with wide eyes, but Dennis sensed the source of my disorientation, and he pointed at the TV screen. "It was a long rain delay in Cincinnati," Dennis said, appearing as calm as I was frantic, and he added, "So they just said the game isn't going to start until a few minutes from now."

Thank you, God.

Or so I thought.

That was before the Pirates took an early 2-0 lead, added another run after the Reds scored twice and were up 3-2 in the bottom of the ninth. Of the game that would decide who goes to the World Series.

This was too much, especially with Dave Guisti on the mound. He was *The Sporting News'* Reliever of the Year from the previous season, and Johnny Bench led off the inning. My expectations were zero. They were lower than that after the count reached 1-2, and it was irrelevant to me that Bench was likely to win the NL Most Valuable Player award for the second time in three years. I could sense what was coming, so I prepared to hurt. With that 1-2 count, I knew the right-handed-throwing Guisti would deliver an off-speed pitch, and he did toward the right side of the plate for the right-handed Bench.

I just knew Guisti knew my dirty little secret of the past three years on how to stifle the offense of the Big Red Machine. Just throw soft stuff to the heavy swingers like Tony Perez, Lee May, and Johnny Bench, and you'll humiliate them.

This time, before Johnny had left the on-deck circle to hit against Guisti, Katy Bench yelled her version of "Just win one for the Gipper" to her son. She rose from her box seat to tell Johnny to hit her a home run, but I didn't know that then. I prepared myself for sadness through the rest of the day, and then for weeks, months, and years. Reds playoff losses and Notre Dame losses in general left permanent scars inside me. I expected to see one of those awkward, lunging, one-handed swings by Bench at Guisti's backdoor changeup for a strikeout, and I knew it would worsen the already dreary days in both Cincinnati and Milwaukee.

Instead, Reds announcer Al Michaels previewed his "Call For The Ages" that happened eight years later, and I mentioned it earlier. In February 1980, he sat behind an ABC microphone in Lake Placid, New York, to describe Team USA in hockey shocking the Russians to move a victory shy of snatching Olympic gold.

"Do you believe in miracles? Yes!"

With Guisti hurling and Bench swinging eight years earlier, Michaels delivered his "Call For The Ages" for the Reds.

1 and 2.

Change, hit in the air to deep right field.
Back goes Clemente.
AT THE FENCE!
She's GONE!!!!
Johnny Bench, who hits almost every home run to left, hits one to right.
The game is tied.

To understand the poetry wrapped in fantasy of Bench's home run is to recall the omnipresence of Roberto Clemente during the 1971 World Series. Game after game, Clemente did to the Orioles back then what the Orioles did to the Reds in the 1970 World Series. Just like Brooks Robinson spooked the Reds for the Orioles at the plate and with his glove and his arm, Clemente was that same guy for the Pirates against the Orioles during the 1971 World Series as a right fielder who wouldn't stop proving immortals sometimes play baseball. This also was the Clemente of 12 Gold Gloves, which meant he specialized in breaking the hearts of opposing teams and fans by chasing and catching the impossible.

Clemente also climbed walls.

So near the end of Game 5 of the 1972 National League Championship Series, there was Bench, swinging for fame in the clutch, and with the ball rising deep and then deeper to right field (*back goes Clemente, at the fence!!!*), you saw the fame-killer drifting toward the warning track, teasing the universe that he just might catch the thing at the last second, but then he turned his back to home plate and looked toward the heavens.

Not even The Great Clemente could end this fame.

The thrills on Oct. 11, 1972, at Riverfront Stadium, weren't over, not if you were into the New Red Machine, my Big Red Machine. The ninth inning continued after Bench conquered The Great Clemente, and after a while, George Foster stood on third base for the Reds with two outs and with Bob Moose on the mound in relief of Guisti. I rushed for my cassette tape recorder, because I wanted to get the call from NBC announcer Curt Gowdy, which I did, but my description was better after Gowdy yelled, "In to the dirt!" to describe Moose's wild pitch as Foster raced home to send the Reds to the World Series.

And what were my words memorialized that day on a plastic film of polyester with a magnetic substance (you know, a cassette tape)?

Come on.

Go!!!!

The run!!!!

THE REDS WIN THE PENNANT!!!

No way the Big Red Machine would lose another World Series, especially as the New Red Machine, with defense, speed and (Thank you, God) pitching.

The Oakland A's boasted that their uniforms were Kelly Green, Fort Knox Gold and Wedding Gown White. Really? I mean, it was difficult to take them seriously, and they wore white spikes. Our clean-shaven lads preferred black spikes. It showed they were disciplined by hugging rules and regulations, and in contrast, they faced A's folks expressing their free spirits and rugged individualism through handlebar mustaches, ranging from manager Dick Williams to obscure players such as Gene Tenace and Joe Rudi.

Who were these guys?

The only A's player anybody knew beyond the San Francisco-Oakland Bay Bridge was Reggie Jackson, and he wouldn't play again until 1973 after he tore his hamstring stealing home during the American League Championship Series. Vida Blue had name recognition after capturing AL MVP honors and the AL Cy Young award the previous year. One of his pitching teammates was Catfish Hunter, and who could forget somebody named "Catfish?" But the Reds had Pete, Joe, Johnny, Tony, and Sparky, and everybody knew them.

Somehow, the A's wouldn't go away. Somehow, the combination of Tenace and Rudi (Who were these guys?) turned into Brooks Robinson 2.0 against the Reds. Somehow, after one-run decisions through Game 5 of the 1972 World Series, the A's were up three games to two in the best-of-seven matchup, but the Reds ripped them at Riverfront Stadium during an 8-1 slaughter to set up a decisive Game 7 in Cincinnati.

I was a mess. Again.

How did it come down to this?

Surely the Reds will win.
They have to win.
I think they'll win.

They didn't, and it was excruciating. One moment, the normally sure-handed Bobby Tolan was botching a couple of routine plays in center field. The next, Reds pitchers were failing to keep Gene Tenace from looking like Johnny Bench. Somehow, Tenace went 8-for-23 with four home runs and nine RBIs to become World Series most valuable player, and he was a lifetime .241 hitter. Then there was Joe Rudi. Somehow, with the brilliant sun threatening to burn a hole through his sunglasses in left field at Riverfront Stadium, he made a twisting, leaping, backhanded catch against the wall in the bottom of the ninth inning to strangle a potential game-winning rally for the Reds.

During those other games of the 1972 World Series, my stomach flipped and flopped while I watched from our Milwaukee living room, but that feeling intensified by a bunch in the bottom of the ninth of Game 7.

The visiting A's led 3-2 with two outs, Darrell Chaney stood on first base as the tying run, and my guy Pete Rose strolled to the plate as the winning run. He did nothing that World Series. He hit .214, which was 89 points below what would become his career batting average, but here was his chance to keep me from going sleepless through at least the rest of 1972. He faced Rollie Fingers, among the game's best relievers, and the switch-hitting Rose was batting from the left side of the plate against the right-handed-throwing Fingers. The first pitch was hittable, because it sailed right down the middle of the plate, and Rose swung.

The NBC center-field camera showed the ball rising high and somewhere in the direction of left-center field. I was too stunned to move, so I offered neither a yell nor a whisper with my brothers screaming nearby. I kept thinking, hoping, wishing within milliseconds, "Maybe it's gone. Maybe the Reds just won Game 7 of the World Series in the bottom of ninth. Maybe they did so courtesy of my guy, the hometown hero, the Reds player I watched that September night in 1969 making that diving catch below us with his face sliding across the mud.

Maybe Fountain Square is moments away in Cincinnati from becoming packed and loud."

Maybe not.

Well, definitely not.

Joe Rudi (who else?) raced over to that part of the warning track in left-center field for a two-handed catch, and he and his teammates challenged the Major League record for jumping up and down with glee. Since this was my train wreck, I was glued to the screen, and the sight was horrible, but not as much as something else that happened during the A's celebration. I couldn't get that particular sight out of my head. Since the sporting gods combined with the newspaper gods again, I had a chance to bear my soul regarding that particular sight 12 years later when I worked on a profile for *The Sporting News* and the *Atlanta Journal-Constitution* on Charles Finley, the former A's owner and baseball maverick. I spent much of a day with Finley on his 1,280-acre farm in LaPorte, Indiana, near Chicago.

We discussed everything. There was Finley's generation of feuds with the baseball establishment since he wanted walks after three balls, orange baseballs and designated runners, designated hitters and night World Series games long before several of those things happened. He called Bowie Kuhn "the village idiot," because the baseball commissioner wouldn't allow him to sell his A's players during the pre-free agency era as freely as he did the chicken and the pigs on his farm. He also was noted for exploding at people for reasons only known inside his soul, and this was typical: He tried to fire A's second baseman Mike Andrews in the middle of a World Series after he misplayed a ball.

Even so, within the two decades Finley owned the A's through 1980, they became a mini-dynasty. They won three consecutive world championships in 1972, 1973, and 1974, and it began with the 1972 World Series against the Reds.

Finley and I talked about all of that. Then, after he gave me one of the orange baseballs he urged Major League officials to use during the 1960s, we ended the interview near sunset, sitting on a swing in his front yard, and I told him about my love for the Big Red Machine. The more

I told him how sick I was after the Reds' Game 7 loss, the more he chuckled. I told him I really got miffed during the A's postgame celebration when it swung to a new high (or low, if you were the definitive Big Red Machine fan like me) after Finley climbed on top of the visitors' dugout at Riverfront Stadium with his wife, Shirley, and they threatened to grin the night away while doing a jig or something before the cameras.

It was like dancing on the grave of my Big Red Machine, and that was the sight I couldn't get out of my mind.

Finley laughed and laughed before he began to sniffle. With misty eyes, he thought about Shirley before he glanced into the distance and said, "We got a divorce about a year after that. I was so wrapped up in baseball that I even lost my happy home."

When I saw the pain on Finley's face, I almost wanted to forgive the poor guy for doing that jig or whatever it was on the visitors' dugout at Riverfront. But then came The Phone Calls two weeks later. After I sent Finley the stories I published in both *The Sporting News* and the *Atlanta Journal-Constitution*, he left a bunch of profanity-filled messages on my answering machine. He claimed he never got emotional talking about his former wife, and when I called him back, he said from his place in LaPorte, Indiana, "You (censored). I oughta come down there and kick your (censored)."

It was just Charlie being Charlie.

So in my heart, I forgave Mr. Finley for his answering machine messages and for his response to my call, but not for that jig or whatever it was.

CHAPTER 6

An Almost Dynasty

It took just shy of forever for me to get over the 1970 World Series, and the same went for this one in 1972, with Joe Rudi, white spikes, Gene Tenace, and owner Charles Finley and his wife dancing on top of the visitors' dugout at Riverfront Stadium. All winter long, the ugliness that was the 1972 World Series played as an endless loop in my head. There were little things surrounding that collapse of my Big Red Machine, but they became huge things, and not in a good way.

For one, I began watching *The Today Show* on NBC when the main folks were Frank McGee, Barbara Walters, and Joe Garagiola, the former baseball catcher turned sportscaster for the network. The morning after Game 7, I figured I would cleanse my damaged baseball soul by flipping to those folks to hear more on Henry Kissinger's trip to Saigon to discuss a proposed cease-fire in Vietnam. If not that, then maybe Barbara or Joe would deliver the inside scoop on something like Ringo Starr and singer Lulu making cameos on Monty Python's *Flying Circus*. I watched from the start, and during the latter part of 1972, *The Today Show* always began with video accompanied by the somber sound of The Lute Concerto in D major, RV 93 by Antonio Vivaldi playing in the background.

I couldn't take my eyes off another train wreck meant for me. On the screen was Pete Rose's flyball leaving the sky for the glove of Joe Rudi in left-center field, and then you saw Rudi and his A's teammates jumping and smiling and hugging each other as the music kept making the scene more poetic and majestic.

It was disgusting, but I kept watching.

Why? Why? Why?

Why wasn't that music playing for my guy Pete Rose? Why wasn't he running around the bases with camera shots alternating between that scene of the Reds hometown hero after belting a World Series-winning, two-run homer in the bottom of the ninth inning of Game 7 and the jubilant crowd at Riverfront Stadium? Why weren't we seeing Johnny, Joe, Tony, and the rest of his teammates pouring out of the dugout like maniacs?

I knew why. The Big Red Machine, well, my Big Red Machine, choked, and even though I didn't have to watch that A's celebration on *The Today Show*, I had to watch.

Then, after I suffered through more of my train wrecks elsewhere in national and local media over the next few weeks and months, I couldn't wait for the 1973 season. Since the 1972 Reds almost won it all during their first year as the New Reds Machine, the upcoming season couldn't become less than great. At least that was my thought – until Johnny Bench foreshadowed health issues to come for the 1973 Reds.

Doctors found a lesion on Bench's right lung after the previous season, and they performed surgery in December 1972 by cutting through his chest and under his arm to reach his neck before determining the legion was benign. He never hit 40 or more home runs again after surgeons also went through ribs, bones, and nerves. Reds officials were so concerned about their 25-year-old catcher with two National League MVP awards within the previous three years that they spent that same December trading for Bill Plummer, who backed up Bench. Hal King became the third-string catcher (and the potential No. 2 guy depending on Bench) after a trade with the Texas Rangers.

Hal King.

Remember that name.

The baseball gods did. Even though Bench mostly remained Bench during the 1973 season with his bat, glove, and arm, Hal King used one swing of his bat that summer to leave the shadows and claim legendary status with the franchise.

Years later, King contributed to the early success of my professional journalism career, and our first interaction was surrealistic, but all I cared about in 1973 as a teenager and definitive Big Red Machine fan was redemption. The Reds needed to work toward that after blowing the 1972 World Series to an A's team without its best player (Reggie Jackson), without a strong fan base (they eventually moved to Las Vegas), and without the normal decorum for a Major League franchise of the 20th century (bizarre mustaches, white spikes, and an owner who hadn't a problem dancing with his wife on top of somebody else's dugout).

I spent much of my 1972 Milwaukee winter watching the prosperous ways of the Bucks and Marquette basketball via our partial season tickets for both teams, but the bulk of my sports thoughts were elsewhere. I stayed obsessed with all things Reds. I followed them through publications and the Chicago sports talk radio shows I picked up clearly in Wisconsin. Their baseball discussions often included the Reds, and then Milwaukee's sports talk radio became strong about that time, and I was a regular caller.

My nickname was "The Cincinnati Reds fan."

Of course, it was. It couldn't be anything else since I likely was the only person in Wisconsin gathered around a water pipe in the basement of their home to catch the later innings of Opening Day from southwestern Ohio on Thursday, April 5, 1973. My junior year at James Madison High School got in the way of me hearing the earlier innings. The game featured Reds pitching ace Don Gullett against future Baseball Hall of Famer Juan Marichal of the San Francisco Giants, but to my chagrin, the Giants won with a late spurt of runs.

The Giants also took Game 2, but then the Reds grabbed nine of their next 10 games, and life was grand for my Big Red Machine.

The core of the old gang remained in Johnny Bench, Tony Perez, Joe Morgan, Bobby Tolan, and my guy Pete Rose, but Sparky Anderson began pushing the Reds closer toward their glory years with several huge moves. He finally made Dave Concepcion the full-time starter at shortstop with his gifted glove, solid bat, and swift legs. He moved Cesar Geronimo to his natural position in center field after he mostly played right in 1972, and Tolan went from center to right. In early June, Sparky added rookie Dan Driessen and his quick bat to the lineup by benching weak-hitting Denis Menke at third base, and Ken Griffey Sr. moved closer to his Major League debut in late August.

But back in early May, Johnny Bench dominated the Reds headlines after he showed with three swings that his lung surgery was yesterday's news. The same Steve Carlton that he slammed three homers against during a game in 1970 when the Baseball Hall of Fame pitcher was with the St. Louis Cardinals was the same Carlton that Bench belted for three homers during a game on May 9, 1973, when the left-hander played for the Philadelphia Phillies.

The Reds kept their Bench-inspired momentum through the rest of the month, and even though they were a half-game from the National League West lead on May 25, I figured they were streaking to a double-digit advantage in the division by the Fourth of July. They were so good, and this was evolving into the greatest baseball year of my life.

The combination of Al Michaels and Joe Nuxhall never sounded better on WLW, which was crystal clear in Wisconsin for night games and good enough during the day from The Water Pipe. At the same time, my James Madison High School baseball team ranked among the best in Milwaukee, and I sparked the Green Knights with my line drives in the gaps as a leadoff hitter and stolen bases while playing a Cesar Geronimo-type center field.

My 1973 glowed in more ways. Since I joined my dad as a history and political science junkie, the Senate Watergate Hearings with Sam Irvin and Howard Baker were must-see TV every day that spring and summer. The U.S. Congress was investigating the President Richard Nixon administration for its role in the break-in the year before into the Democratic National Headquarters in Washington, D. C. When our parents asked us where we wanted to go that June for our family vacation, it was a no-brainer. I shouted "Washington, D.C.," and my dad agreed, and since he counted the most in those kinds of decisions, we were off to the nation's capital to see everything. We were even in the hallway of the Russell Senate Office building when Alexander Butterfield rocked the universe by revealing the existence of a taping system in the White House. That week-long trip did something I previously thought was impossible: It interrupted my moment-by-moment focus on the Reds.

Neither ESPN SportsCenter nor cellphones existed in 1973, so it wasn't until I returned to Milwaukee to read my publications and to huddle around The Water Pipe for Al and Joe on the radio that I realized the Reds were in trouble.

They were in serious trouble.

In fact, they were in free fall, sliding from that half-game deficit behind the Houston Astros and the San Francisco Giants atop the National League West on May 25 to 10 games behind the Los Angeles Dodgers on June 29.

What?

How?

I'm never going on vacation again.

Then it got worse. The Dodgers came to Cincinnati on Saturday, June 30, seeking to finish off the 1973 Reds for good during a four-game series. I wasn't going to miss a single pitch from The Water Pipe or elsewhere, and I mostly didn't. The opener was torture. During a slugfest, the Dodgers scored six runs in the top of the eighth inning to wipe out a four-run lead for the Reds, but then the Reds scrapped together two runs in the bottom of the ninth to send the game into extra innings. The Dodgers eventually won 8-7 in 13 innings. It pushed their lead over the Reds to 11 games, and I was sick.

I was Brooks Robinson and Ken Burkhart sick.

I was Joe Rudi and Gene Tenace sick.

I was sicker the next day during the first game of a doubleheader. As I listened by The Water Pipe on the afternoon of Sunday, July 1, 1973, the Dodgers were just an out away at Riverfront Stadium from leading the division by 12 games over the Reds with two outs and a 3-1 lead in the bottom of the ninth. It didn't matter the Reds had two runners on base. Up next for the Reds wasn't the magnificent Joe Morgan or Tony Perez, owner of a famously clutch bat, or Johnny Bench who lifted that home run over the head of Roberto Clemente the previous year to help the Reds win a pennant, or my guy Pete Rose. It was Hal King, the obscure catcher the Reds acquired from the Texas Rangers during the offseason when they worried about Bench going under the knife of a surgeon.

King had done nothing with the Reds. He owned just one hit after 10 at bats since joining the team, but Reds manager Sparky Anderson had this hunch, and he had the knowledge of King playing for the Atlanta Braves years before and smacking a grand slam after seeing a screwball from the Dodgers' Don Sutton.

Who was the Dodgers pitcher this time?

Don Sutton.

Since Anderson rested Bench for that first game of the doubleheader, backup Bill Plummer started, and Plummer was the next batter scheduled at that point, but Sparky went with King as a pinch hitter. Moments later, I wasn't sick anymore, not after Sutton either forgot about his personal history with King or didn't care by hurling (yep) a screwball toward the bench player with the count two balls and two strikes.

Before I unleashed one of my loudest shouts ever for the Reds, I heard the following from The Water Pipe with my transistor radio, and it came from Al Michaels leading the way with Joe Nuxhall screaming in the background.

"The Reds down to their last strike. Two balls, two strikes, two outs and two on, and it's 3-1 Dodgers in the bottom of the ninth inning.

"Sutton on the rubber. Has the sign. Don at the belt. A glance at (Tony) Perez (on base), and the 2-2 pitch to King is swung on and hit to deep right field, back goes (Willie) Crawford, all the way back, GOOOONE!!!"

Nuxhall yelled through his mic, *"All right!!!" after* he kept delivering his familiar line of *"Get outta here!!!"* as King's shot kept going, going and then over the fence. Michaels turned sage after that. In the calmest of tones, he said, *"Boy, I'll tell ya. If anything can turn the season around, it is that play right there."*

Boy, Al told us correctly.

The Reds survived another thriller during the second game of the doubleheader on Perez's game-winning single in the 10th inning. Then they won again the next day before they eventually took eight of nine games. Soon enough, it was Labor Day, and the Reds and the Dodgers were tied for the NL West lead. The Reds went ahead that next day of Tuesday, Sept. 3, and they rolled all the way to capturing the division by 3 ½ games with the best record in baseball at 99-63. They did all of that by overcoming everything, and I'm not just talking about that monster of a double-digit deficit they had to slay.

If the 1973 Reds had a first-half MVP, it was Dave Concepcion, but they lost their shortstop and his brilliant season in progress (.287 batting average, eight home runs, 22 stolen bases and Gold Glove-caliber fielding) to a broken leg in late July after he slide into third base. That was a season-ending injury, and so was the sore arm for starting pitcher Gary Nolan.

Then there was the ongoing drama of Bobby Tolan, and not only because his batting average barely topped .200 late in the season. I cringed reading endless media reports about his battles with Reds officials who already fumed over two things: his offseason basketball injury that cost him the 1971 season, and his miscues in center field during Game 7 of the 1972 World Series. I couldn't understand why he defied team rules by growing facial hair. Then in August, with the Reds trying to keep the pressure on the Dodgers, he went AWOL from the team, and then he was suspended, never to be part of the franchise again.

So sad. When we played our pickup baseball game in Cincinnati on the diamond in the park behind our backyard, left-handed hitters often imitated Tolan's hitting stance. He stood nearly erect in the batter's box, and he held the bat straight toward the sky as he raised it above his head before dropping it into position before the pitch. He was African American, too, which meant we pulled for him even more, but something happened to Bobby Tolan as a rising superstar with the Reds, and maybe it was simple. Maybe it was his inability to recover fully physically and mentally from his Achilles tear in January 1971 on that basketball court in Frankfort, Kentucky.

Growing up, Sam Moore's family was a close-knit unit.

Terry, Dennis, and Darrell were together often as youth.

We rushed to Dad Moore as kids as soon as he returned home after his janitorial duties at Indiana Bell in South Bend, Ind.

Samuel Moore was nearly always the only African American in the room along his way toward becoming the first Black supervisor in the history of AT&T and one of its first Black managers, if not THE first.

Here's a certificate for one of the three holes in one Samuel Moore made in his life.

Annie Moore won her share of bowling trophies.

Annie Moore was often the first and only African American at her workplaces.

During Terence's senior year at Milwaukee's James Madison High School, he led the 1973 undefeated football team in tackles as an inside linebacker.

In addition to football, Terence was a standout baseball player throughout high school.

Foreshadowing things to come, Terence was the news editor of his high school newspaper in Milwaukee.

Terence made his first TV appearance on a Milwaukee station showcasing top local high school journalists.

Except for sports journalism and teaching, Terence's favorite job was umpiring, and he kept the clicker from his teenage gigs.

In Terence's own scorebook, he marked the happenings of nearly every Reds games during the 1970 season.

The Sam Moore family during our Milwaukee days.

Terence joined the Miami (Ohio) University student newspaper during his first day on campus in September 1974.

*After Terence's freshman year at Miami (Ohio) University,
he played in a Milwaukee summer baseball league.*

One of Terence's biggest thrills as a fan was attending Game 3 of the 1975 World Series.

*This is Terence during his senior year in the Miami (Ohio)
University yearbook as sports editor of The Student newspaper.*

*In July 1978, Terence wrote the first story ever about Ken Griffey Jr.,
when the future Baseball Hall of Famer was 8 years old.*

*Terence interviews a Cincinnati Reds player in June of 1978
in the home clubhouse at Riverfront Stadium.*

An Almost Dynasty

Terence frequently chatted with baseball legend Reggie Jackson through the years.

Terence huddles with Pete Rose in the visitors' dugout at Candlestick Park in San Francisco.

Terence and Hank had a nearly 40-year friendship.

My Big Red Machine

Kobe Bryant answers a question from Terence when he was an Atlanta Journal-Constitution columnist.

When Lou Holtz was named University of Notre Dame football coach in 1986, Terence did the first interview.

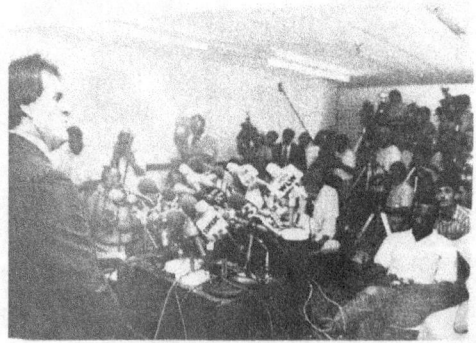

In August of 1989, when Pete Rose held a press conference in Cincinnati after

116

An Almost Dynasty

he was banned from baseball, Terence was in the front row (bottom right). Photo Credit: The book "Pete Rose: My story."

Here's another photo of Terence at Riverfront Stadium in August of 1989 when Pete Rose (left) said during his press conference that he did not bet on baseball.

Terence with Atlanta Falcons star quarterback Michael Vick.

Terence gave Hank Aaron's widow, Billye, one of the first copies of his book on her late husband.

Dusty Baker and Terence talked often through the decades.

Terence visited the Baseball Hall of Fame for the first time in June of 2024.

An Almost Dynasty

While in Cooperstown, Terence saw one of the cans from Pete Rose's soft drink that led to his first interview with his all-time favorite baseball player.

Not surprisingly, Terence discovered the Baseball Hall of Fame has items and photos everywhere regarding Carlton Fisk's walk-off homer in Game 6 of the 1975 World Series.

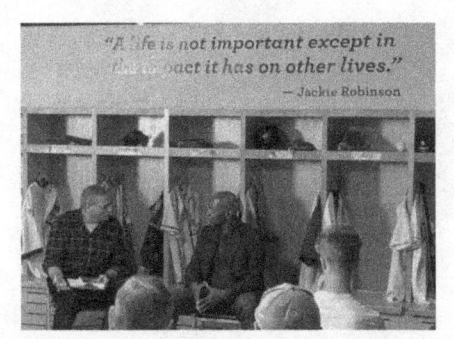

Terence talked about his Hank Aaron book before a packed room at the Baseball Hall of Fame.

My Big Red Machine

On the west side of Cincinnati, Terence saw this sign on the wall near the spot of Crosley Field's home plate.

During the early summer of 2025, Terence visited the spot in Cincinnati that featured the home plate of Crosley Field.

At one of the Cincinnati office buildings near the spot of old Crosley Field, there was this photo of Pete Rose.

Terence at work in a press box as a professional sports journalist of nearly 50 years.

By late summer 1973, Tolan was the only prominent member of the First Red Machine to slip into oblivion. Even Lee May and Tommy Helms stayed prominent with the Houston Astros after they were dealt away after the 1971 season in the Joe Morgan Trade of the Century.

As for 1973, thanks to the wisdom of Bob Howsam in the front office and of Sparky Anderson in the dugout, the Reds kept rolling beyond Nolan, Concepcion, and Tolan. To compensate for Nolan's loss, they acquired Fred Norman from the San Diego Padres in mid-June, and he went from 1-7 with his former cellar dwellers to 12-6 the rest of the season with the Reds. I embraced the move from the start, mostly because Reds hitters wouldn't have to face him anymore. This all went back to my dirty little secret on how to gum up the gears of the Big Red Machine. The left-handed Norman of 5-foot-8 was another one of those soft-throwing pitchers who gave Reds sluggers fits. *So, welcome, Freddie*, I thought, while forming the widest of smiles. And at shortstop, the Reds replaced Concepcion with previous starter Darrel Chaney, owner of a steady glove and a weak bat, but who cared about the latter? We had the rest of the Big Red Machine hitting ahead of Chaney. Finally, with Tolan gone, rookie Ken Griffey Sr. and 24-year-old George Foster flashed signs the rest of the season of All-Star Games to come as at least decent outfielders with consistently slick bats.

If you combined those changes with the usual exploits of Pete, Johnny, Joe, and Tony, you could see why the 1973 Reds were playoff bound, but none of that would have occurred without Sunday, July 1, 1973, and Hal King's leap from the shadows against the Dodgers.

Four years after that, I worked as an intern for *The Cincinnati Enquirer* on July 3, 1977. It was the summer between my junior and senior years at Miami (Ohio) University, and I sought to fulfill my editor's wishes for an off-day story involving those Reds. At the time, they were 8 1/2 games behind (who else?) the Dodgers and fading fast, so I had this thought: *What does Hal King think about this, and where is he?*

Nobody knew. Not these 1977 Reds, not other reporters, not baseball executives and scouts, but along the way, with the internet and cell phones still not things, somebody led me to the Mexican League. I needed more than that. After exploding the charges on the Enquirer's old WATS line, which was the Wide Area Telephone Service from AT&T for businesses to make long-distance calls with a flat rate, I dialed Monclova, Mexico. I contacted officials of the Coahuila team, and they gave me a number to reach the 33-year-old King who was on a road trip. When I reached him, he was stunned. He also was thankful for a reporter's call from the city of his last and final Major League season in 1974.

"Hey, it's a funny thing," King told me over the phone. "I just got up from bed a few minutes ago, and I was just dreaming about Joe Morgan and George Foster. We were riding in an elevator. I don't know where we were going."

In 1973, the Reds were going from purgatory to paradise after King's home run, and he told me during our 1977 conversation that he swung so hard at Sutton's screwball that he ripped his cleats. He said he preferred to stay in the present ("I don't like to think back to the past. I mean, I just hit a home run yesterday.") But then he agreed to help me on deadline with more thoughts on Sunday, July 1, 1973, you know, just this time.

"I'd say that was my biggest thrill," said King, who played parts of seven Major League seasons, and who had only the Mexican League wanting his services after his 1974 season in Cincinnati produced just three hits after 17 bats. The year before that, when he became baseball royalty overnight for the Reds against the Dodgers, he finished 1973 with a .186 batting average after eight hits in 43 at bats, but three of those hits were pinch-hit homers, including a grand slammer in the clutch. Still, there was that one hit for King, and he said of the memory, "That's something that gave me a name all around the country. *That* country."

I thanked King for his time, and when I told Jim Montgomery what I had, the normally mellow sports editor of the *Enquirer* threatened to scream "Stop the presses" in the middle of the newsroom. He did his version of that by saying between puffs on his cigarette, "Oh, that's front-page stuff," and the praise I received the next day for the piece was overwhelming. It ranged from the top bosses at the *Enquirer* to those receiving the paper at their doorstep. Montgomery also sent me a note saying, "Terry: Good job on Hal King, good perseverance." It was among several stories I wrote during the summer of 1977 on the Big Red Machine that got me hired fulltime at the *Enquirer* the next year.

But back in October 1973, I was an overjoyed Reds fan, knowing the upcoming National League Championship Series was only a formality before my guy Pete Rose and his teammates finally snatched the franchise's first world championship since 1940. Rose, by the way, won the third batting title of his career in 1973 after hitting .338, and that was fueled by his NL-high 230 hits. He was named the National League's Most Valuable Player, and given the two such honors for Bench within the previous three years, that meant a Reds player grabbed the award during three of the previous four seasons. That also meant the Big Red Machine was edging closer to reaching its full potential.

I'd never been more confident about anything.

After the Reds sweep the Mets and then whoever they face in the 1973 World Series, should they hold the victory celebration around Fountain Square the next day or wait until the weekend, especially since they officially became a tri-state favorite of Ohio, Indiana, and Kentucky by drawing more than two million folks at home for the first time ever?

Then after this world championship, will the Reds win two, three, or how many more before the end of the decade?

Oh, wait. First, the Reds must beat the Mets during the best-of-five National League Championship Series. The Mets were in last place for most of the year in the NL East and only showed a pulse in September. They finished 82-79 for the worst record ever to win a division or a pennant in baseball history.

That team? Against my Big Red Machine?

Puhleeze.

Uh-oh.

The Reds won the opener of the 1973 NLCS (barely) at home, but the Mets manhandled them during the next two games with victories of 5-0 in Cincinnati and 9-2 in New York, and then there was that brawl in Game 3. With victory mostly assured for the Mets at old Shea Stadium, Rose remained Rose by sliding hard into Mets second baseman Bud Harrelson in a failed attempt to break up a double play. The tiny yet scrappy Harrelson blurted things at the significantly burlier Rose, and the next thing you knew, Rose shoved Harrelson to the ground before second base became a pile of Reds and Mets players, pushing and grabbing each other as the packed house of nearly 54,000 jeered in the background.

When that part was over during Game 3, New York fans pounded Rose in left field at the bottom of the inning with cans, batteries, and even a whiskey bottle, which prompted Sparky Anderson to take his team off the field. I missed it all. It was a day game, and I had school followed by football practice, but between tackling drills, I anticipated the worst for my Big Red Machine with its wheels going flat and swerving toward a ditch. Somehow, the Mets, with fewer no-name guys than the Oakland A's during the 1972 World Series, were a Game 4 victory away in New York from giving the Reds their most humiliating loss since they officially became the Big Red Machine in 1970.

The Reds got a reprieve.

Due to extra innings, I was able to see it.

I was at football practice, and when I discovered Game 4 was still going, I ran faster than the wind to catch the top of the 12th at Shea Stadium, where Rose waited for my arrival, at least that's what the baseball gods told me through the sight to come. With the score tied at 1-1, he blasted a pitch over the right-field wall for the eventual game-winner, and then he sprinted around the bases with fist raised as the crowd continued its afternoon-long booing of the guy who gave Harrelson a bruise above his eye.

For one moment, courtesy of my guy Pete Rose, the previous horrors for the Reds during the 1973 NLCS didn't matter, and mercifully, I missed all of Game 5, which was another day game happening during football practice.

The Reds weren't even competitive during a 7-2 loss that put the Mets in the World Series, where they were exposed as frauds. The A's won their second consecutive world championship, and the rest of us were trying to figure out how the Big Red Machine broke down again in the postseason. Despite all that firepower, the Reds hit .186 for the NLCS while the Mets weren't much better at .220. But contrary to what sports historians like to say, it wasn't as simple as the Mets having Baseball Hall of Fame pitcher Tom Seaver, and the Reds having much less than that on the mound.

This was simpler: The Big Red Machine choked. *My* Big Red Machine choked, and I was a mixture of upset, angry, and mystified, because this happened for the second consecutive year. I sort of excused the Reds for vanishing in 1971 due to the Bobby Tolan fiasco and the fluke that was nearly the entire roster forgetting how to hit. In 1970, well, OK. The Orioles did have a bunch of future Baseball Hall of Famers, including Brooks Robinson who became the main character from several horror flicks, and they all manifested themselves into one in the flesh against the Reds at third base. But losing to those A's? No way. Then dropping the NLCS to those Mets? Their motto was "You gotta believe," but for those Reds, it was "You gotta be kidding me," and the bad news kept coming for my Big Red Machine.

Or so it seemed.

Al Michaels revealed during the offseason he was leaving, and for the first time in decades, this change of Reds announcers on WLW had nothing to do with the beer sponsor. Michaels left to become the play-by-play guy for the San Francisco Giants, and he sought to expand his resumé as a national announcer by doing, not only baseball, but football, Olympics, and just about everything else. So here we were again regarding the Reds' broadcasting situation, and we got lucky the last time. After Jim McIntyre was forced out after the 1970 season, the Reds hired Michaels, a guy who would go on to collect multiple sportscaster of the year awards, become a staple for prime-time NFL broadcasts, and get his star on the Hollywood Walk of Fame.

Despite the Michaels shocker and the Mets fiasco, sunlight burst through the dark sports clouds around me. The rays had nothing to do with baseball. Our James Madison High School football team went undefeated to win the Milwaukee City Conference Championship, and from my inside linebacker spot, I led the Green Knights in tackles. Then the other sports team of my heart continued as the antithesis of the Reds.

That's because the No. 3-ranked Notre Dame football team from the hometown of South Bend, Indiana, spent New Year's Eve in the Sugar Bowl, where the Fighting Irish slid by No. 1 Alabama in a thriller for their first national championship in seven years.

A few weeks later, there was more brightness in my sports hemisphere, and it involved the Reds after they thought outside the box again for their play-by-play radio guy. They were rewarded again, and so were Reds fans. With Michaels, they ignored his young age for a Major League announcer of 26 years old to hire him anyway, and in late January 1974, they went with Marty Brennaman, owner of more college basketball and football games on his resumé than those involving baseball of any kind. Nevertheless, I was impressed with his style from Day One. He was a no-nonsense guy from Portsmouth, Virginia, with a captivating voice and with strong ties to the University of North Carolina in Chapel Hill and other parts of that state, but he joined the Reds after calling football and basketball games for Virginia Tech.

How did that turn out? Well, Brennaman spent 46 years as a Baseball Hall of Fame announcer in Cincinnati through 2019, and to the delight of me and other listeners, he had wonderful insight, he spoke his mind, and after every victory, he would declare "and this one belongs to the Reds."

Marty Brennaman was part of our family, just like his partner Joe Nuxhall. Even so, after the Reds hired Brennaman, team executive Dick Wagner contemplated replacing Nuxhall as the color man. Fortunately for Wagner and his health, he avoided a mutiny in Reds country by keeping the Old Lefthander rounding third on the air.

So, with Marty and Joe on the radio set for my hours at The Water Pipe, I still had this nagging issue during the spring of 1974.

Why wasn't my Big Red Machine a dynasty?

It was almost *something*, but what?

I also had other concerns beyond finishing my senior year strong on our loaded James Madison High School baseball team. *Where to go for college?* I knew I wanted a newspaper career since sports editor Bill Dwyre of the *Milwaukee Journal* came to my high school journalism class in the spring of 1972 to discuss his job. I had a great start working for the *Madison Messenger*, which earned the national distinction among high school newspapers of First Class from the Columbia Journalism Review during my time as news editor. I also wrote sports stories. One of my college choices was the University of Notre Dame, which was perfect for everything, but I had too many relatives in South Bend who might wish to stop by, and that wouldn't be conducive for studying. Marquette had an impressive journalism department, and it was right there in Milwaukee with the parents and the brothers. As an added bonus, the Warriors (as they were called back then before becoming the Golden Eagles) had that nationally renowned basketball program whose games we often attended.

Then again, maybe it was time to leave home, and I kept remembering a trip we took as a family in the late 1960s during our Cincinnati days to see a high school basketball tournament 35 miles to the north in Oxford, Ohio. The setting was breathtaking, and the town evolved around Miami University, known as the Cradle of Coaches, with members ranging from Paul Brown and Woody Hayes to Bo Schembechler and Ara Parseghian, who was the sports god disguised as the football coach at Notre Dame. While glancing at a brochure I got in the mail from the school, I saw it was also home to the oldest college newspaper west of the Alleghenies. Not only that, but when I called from Milwaukee to Oxford that spring of 1974 to speak with somebody on the newspaper, the editor-in-chief answered and said that unlike other colleges, the section editors allowed gifted freshmen to write from the start.

Here was the other thing, and it was among the biggest things: If I went to Miami (Ohio) University, as it preferred to be called then, I would be close again to the Findlay Market Parade, Paul Dixon/Bob Braun/Nick Clooney, Skyline Chili, Fountain Square, my Big Red Machine in general, and my guy Pete Rose in particular.

I was off to Miami that fall.

In the meantime, I had the 1974 season to follow that spring and that summer for the Reds, and the Dodgers were getting on my nerves. They wouldn't lose, and it didn't help the Reds got off to a mediocre start.

On Opening Day, with all eyes on Cincinnati beyond just its baseball heritage of 105 years, Hank Aaron walked to the plate in the first inning for his Atlanta Braves and tied Babe Ruth in career home runs at 714 with his first swing of the season. I didn't see it. I was in school, but the whole family was around the TV a few days later on the night of Monday, April 8, when Aaron blasted his record 715th homer over the left-field fence at Atlanta-Fulton County Stadium. For African Americans, the moment resembled April 15, 1947, when our ancestors gathered before the radio for the debut of Jackie Robinson of the Brooklyn Dodgers. Otherwise, April of 1974 was as forgettable for me as it was for the Reds. They finished the month 10-9, and they already were five games behind the Dodgers.

The Dodgers just weren't likeable, or maybe it was because they wouldn't lose. They had a bunch of guys who tried their best to yank the sparkplugs out of my Big Red Machine, and sometimes, they were successful. I'm talking about Steve Garvey at first base, Davey Lopes at second base, Bill Russell at shortstop, and Ron Cey at third base. That infield was the Dodgers' core for much of the decade, but in 1974, they were joined by others such as the effective catching duel of Steve Yeager and Joe Ferguson. They also had this ridiculous depth in starting pitching with Andy Messersmith, Don Sutton, Doug Rau, and Tommy John.

They had something else. If you were a Reds fan, they had two guys who were possessed by the same evil spirits as Brooks Robinson, Joe Rudi, Gene Tenace, and whatever got inside the Mets during the 1973 National League Championship Series.

They had Jimmy Wynn and Mike Marshall.

Every game in 1974, it seemed like Wynn was slamming a home run or rocketing a shot off the wall, and they usually were the game-winners in dramatic situations. Not only that, but every game in 1974, it seemed like Marshall was getting the save by making hitters look silly with his screwball after minutes or maybe seconds on the mound.

This was for sure: With Wynn and Marshall leading the way, the Reds couldn't beat those Dodgers. The Reds dropped nine of their first 10 games to them, which helped seal the Big Red Machine's fate for the year as the continuation as an almost dynasty. The scenario never changed during that 1974 season. Whenever the Reds played in Los Angeles for night games starting at 11 p.m. Eastern Time, I went to bed with my transistor radio next to my pillow. If I began to dose, I always knew when Wynn was at the plate or Marshall was on the mound. That's because all I heard was the crowd roaring in the background, drowning out Marty and Joe on the radio, trying to describe what I really didn't want to hear.

Just like in 1973, the 1974 Dodgers steamrolled their way into Cincinnati around the Fourth of July for a four-game series, but unlike the year before, there was no Hal King moment for the Reds to slow the charging Dodgers.

On July 1, 1973, the Reds used King's pinch-hit, game-winning homer in the bottom of the ninth inning during that series opener as inspiration to win three of the four games. That cut the Reds' deficit to the Dodgers in the division from double digits. This time, during early July of 1974, the Dodgers grabbed three of four games from the Reds to leave town with a 9 ½-game lead. It was up to a season-high 10 ½ games within that week. Still, I kept thinking Hal King, Hal King, Hal King. Such a moment didn't come in July, but surely it was destined to appear in August or September. The Reds weren't going out like this, not with their most talented roster since the birth of the Big Red Machine.

The Reds had their Famous Four doing wondrous things. In addition to Johnny Bench resembling his NL MVP self of 1970 and 1972, Tony Perez slammed his way toward 28 home runs and 101 RBIs. Joe Morgan was Joe Morgan, finishing 1974 with 58 stolen bases and an on-base percentage of .427 to lead the National League. Then there was my guy Pete Rose, whose batting average dipped below .300 for the first time in 10 years, but he still led the Major Leagues in games played, plate appearances, runs scored, and doubles.

Those Reds were complemented by Dave Concepcion returning from his broken leg, and he joined center fielder Cesar Geronimo, Morgan, and Bench in acquiring Gold Gloves after his masterful play at shortstop. On offense, Concepcion reached base enough with his .281 batting average to manage 41 steals.

Outfielders Ken Griffey Sr. and George Foster combined with third baseman Dan Driessen as young guys who kept suggesting with their bats that they would become significant for the Reds sooner rather than later. The 1974 Reds could pitch, too, with solid starters in Don Gullett, Clay Kirby, Jack Billingham, and Fred Norman, and the Big Red Machine always had a stellar bullpen for Sparky Anderson, a la Captain Hook. Pedro Borbon and Clay Carroll still led the Reds' stifling group of relievers.

And those Reds kept winning.

It's just that the Dodgers wouldn't lose.

Then the Dodgers did begin to lose, but only a little, and at the same time, the Reds stormed through the middle of September with nine victories in 12 games. They spent the end of that stretch shaking off their Dodger blues of earlier in the year to take the opening two games of a three-game series at Dodger Stadium, and out of nowhere, the Reds trailed in the NL West by 1 ½ games on Sept. 14.

Such perfect timing. With the Reds charging, I listened to Marty and Joe at The Water Pipe in Milwaukee between making final decisions on what to pack into our black and gold 1970 Chrysler New Yorker. My parents and I had a 6 ½-hour drive to Oxford, Ohio, and my freshman year at Miami University was slated to start within a week. I couldn't wait. Yeah, I was excited as a good student about the great academics ahead around a public college known for its Ivy League education. Yeah, I wanted to see the place again that poet Robert Frost said had "the most beautiful campus that ever there was." Yeah, there was that Cradle of Coaches thing, and the award-winning food, and the Beta Bells, a bell tower near the center of campus that would chime every 15 minutes, but all of that ranked behind this: I soon would be just 35 miles to the north of Ground Zero for another one of the greatest comeback stories in Major League Baseball history.

Instead, we arrived in Oxford with the Reds reeling after five losses in six games, partly due to a collapse in pitching, and that was the bad news. Here was the good: I didn't need The Water Pipe anymore. Before, during, and after classes, I heard Marty and Joe loud and clear on WLW

Radio through the earpiece on my transistor radio, but it was agony. The Reds were right there, ready to complete the miracle with me nearby, but now they were 4 ½ games behind the Dodgers with eight games left in the season.

Oh well. At least they've stopped tugging at my emotions. So now I can place my whole focus on making this transition from high school to college.

Then the Reds began to streak again.

This was too much.

The Big Red Machine won one, two, three, *six straight games.* Just like that, with freshman English taking a slight hit for a while, the Reds were 2 ½ games out of first place. They would capture the division if they won their last two games in Atlanta, and if the suddenly wobbly Dodgers got swept during a three-game series at Houston.

Neither happened. The Braves beat the Reds both games in Atlanta, the Dodgers won their opener against the Astros, and that was it. The only team in baseball with more than the Reds' 98 victories were the Dodgers with 102.

A few days later, I was in Millett Hall, where Miami played home basketball games and kept its athletics hall of fame in the lobby. There were all of those famous members of its Cradle of Coaches – Earl "Red" Blaik, Paul Brown, Weeb Ewbank, Woody Hayes, Bo Schembechler, Ara Parseghian, right on down the line, and then there was Walter Alston, a Miami graduate who lived 5 miles away from Oxford in his hometown of Darrtown when he wasn't at his job.

What was his job? Well, according to Alston's plaque on the wall in Millett Hall, he was a Miami guy like me, and he won four World Series titles and seven pennants as a Baseball Hall of Fame manager for the Dodgers.

I still didn't like them.

But guess what? The baseball gods and the newspaper gods combined with The Big Dodger In The Sky to make me at least like Walter Alston. It happened when that fan at Miami University became a journalist for *The Cincinnati Enquirer*, and Alston invited the journalist (OK, me) to spend an evening with him at his Darrtown residence.

Yeah. Crazy. Especially since I went from liking Walter Alston to loving him, along with the doughnuts from his wife.

CHAPTER 7

The Real Dynasty

Since I didn't have to worry about the Reds in the 1974 World Series, I had time to do something like study the rest of my freshman academic year at Miami University in Oxford, Ohio. We were on the quarter system back then. After each of the three, I found a note in my Dennison Hall mailbox saying I made the Dean's Merit Roll. One of the notes came with a letter inviting me to the "Miami Freshman Scholarship Banquet" in April, adding, "Only 727 students out of approximately 3,550 freshmen achieved at least a 3.00 during this stretch. You have made an excellent beginning in your college career. We hope this will inspire you to maintain such an excellent academic average each succeeding quarter."

Yeah, well.
It depends on how the Reds are doing.
That's what I thought to myself.

This was the first time since before October of 1968 – when I smuggled that transistor radio into classes at Benjamin Harrison Elementary School in South Bend, Indiana, to hear the St. Louis Cardinals versus the Detroit Tigers – that I didn't care about the World Series. For me, the matchup couldn't be worse.

You had the Oakland A's, and get this: They were basically the same group that used somebody named Joe Rudi and somebody else named Gene Tenace to slip past the superior Reds during the 1972 World Series. Afterward, A's owner Charlie Finley and his wife did their little jig, waltz, or whatever that was on top of the visitors dugout at Riverfront Stadium, and I still couldn't get that sight out of my head. The A's took the World

Series again the next year against a New York Mets team that shouldn't have been there. It should have been the Reds, but the Reds choked during the 1973 National League Championship Series.

Now the A's were back again, and they faced the Dodgers, and I couldn't stand the Dodgers. That's because the Reds couldn't beat them. Not with Jimmy Wynn swinging and Mike Marshall hurling, and they did so at extraordinary levels.

I didn't watch a single pitch of the 1974 World Series. I discovered afterward the A's handled the Dodgers in five games for Oakland's third consecutive world championship, and then the emotions began. Instead of the A's, that should have been my Big Red Machine holding the Commissioner's Trophy after the 1972, 1973, and 1974 seasons.

With Pete Rose, Joe Morgan, Johnny Bench, and Tony Perez leading the way, nobody in baseball during those years matched the quality of the Reds' roster, and they looked mightier for 1975. They just needed to get past the Dodgers, and I hated the Dodgers, so the following scene was perplexing for me in December 1974. I was at a Miami home basketball game at Millett Hall on Miami's campus, and somebody pointed to an older man sitting by himself in the distance. He looked familiar with his tall frame and stoic look, but I couldn't make the connection.

Who is that?

Somebody told me it was Walter Alston, the same Walter Alston who managed the Dodgers (did I mention I hated the Dodgers?)

Oh, wow!

Um, OK.

I didn't know how to react.

Yes, Alston was a future Baseball Hall of Famer whose former players included Jackie Robinson, a hero of mine. I also discovered within days after I arrived on campus that Alston was a Miami graduate and a member of its Cradle of Coaches. From his home in Darrtown, he regularly made the eight-minute ride on his motorcycle to Oxford since he lived just a right turn and then a left away from campus. I later saw Alston at a Miami home football game. Within keeping of his low-key nature that led to his nickname of "The Quiet Man" – as well as "Smokey," which he acquired as a young pitcher courtesy of his sizzling fastball around that part of Butler County – he vanished within seconds of those football and the basketball games.

During the summer of 1978, when I worked for *The Cincinnati Enquirer*, I spent that evening with him in Darrtown, where we watched Monday Night Baseball together from his living room, and he was a pleasant soul. His wife brought me freshly baked doughnuts to enjoy as Alston and I chatted mostly between innings.

This was the strangest thing: From the time Alston greeted me on the porch while smoking one of his Tareyton cigarettes through the guided tour he gave me of a modest home for somebody with four World Series rings, and then through my surrealistic time watching baseball with this legend of the sport in front of his TV set, I couldn't dislike him. It was partly because of our Miami University connection, and partly because he was such a nice man, but mostly because I tried so hard not to remember how much I hated the Dodgers.

Think about the Honda motorcycles in Alston's garage that he likes to ride.

Concentrate on his splendid carpentry work you just saw from the massive toolshed he built with his own hands.

Enjoy the doughnuts.

All I knew as a Big Red Machine disciple in the late fall of 1974 was that Alston managed the Dodgers, and that made me cringe.

Then came the spring of 1975 in Oxford.

There was joy throughout my baseball world. Between studying for classes when I wasn't working for the college newspaper, I experienced the atmosphere of my first Opening Day in southwestern Ohio since AT&T abruptly moved our family in August 1971 from Cincinnati to Chicago and then to Milwaukee six months later.

Everything was the same: the Findlay Market Parade; the constant Reds talk on those local live TV variety shows; the first pitch of the entire Major League Baseball season unfolding along the Ohio River. Everything was just grander this time, because the Big Red Machine was supposedly in its prime, and the opening three games of the season were at Riverfront Stadium against those same Dodgers of Miami's Walter Alston, and the Dodgers squeezed past the Reds near the end of the 1974 season to reach the playoffs and eventually the World Series.

I wanted to attend the opener badly, but I couldn't get a ticket for a game that always sold out months in advance, and this time, those Dodgers were in town. The Reds were scheduled to see them early and often in April, and during the last "Anderson from Florida" show on WLW radio from Tampa on the final day of spring training, I listened from my dorm room when Reds manager Sparky Anderson told Marty Brennaman, "I have never looked forward to something as much as I look forward to seeing the Dodgers seven times in the first 10 days."

Anderson delivered his words with conviction. Which meant, if nothing else, I had to get the best ticket I could find for Game 2, and somebody I knew always was driving from Oxford to Cincinnati. That was splendid for me since I didn't have a car until the end of my senior year at Miami. What also was splendid was the Reds winning the opener over the Dodgers that Monday afternoon in April 1975, and then two days later, I was in the Blue seats – the box seats, the premier ones, right along the third-base side – to see the Reds take a thriller. They were down by one to the Dodgers in the bottom of the ninth, but then they scored twice, with Dave Concepcion ignoring the groin injury that kept him from starting and heading to the plate as a pinch hitter to rip a game-winning single.

As a nice bonus, the tying and winning runs for the Reds came against Mike Marshall, the reliever who rarely was less than great the year before.

I was ecstatic, and the next day, I listened with more glee from Oxford as the Reds completed the three-game sweep of the team they previously couldn't beat. But those victories appeared to be flukes for the Reds since slightly more than a week later, Marshall helped the Dodgers bring back 1974 all over again with a four-game sweep of the Reds in Los Angeles. I also traveled to Cincinnati from Oxford to witness other shaky Reds losses through the end of April, but then manager Sparky Anderson made one of the most brilliant moves in baseball history. Since the Reds were mediocre and listless despite all those elite players, he decided they needed another elite player in the lineup.

Did I say Sparky was brilliant?

This sounded nuts at the time.

On Saturday, May 3, with the Reds in fourth place in the National League West at 12-12 and four games behind the Dodgers, I listened to Anderson's pregame show when he said he was switching Pete Rose in the starting lineup from left field to third base. Since I was *the* Pete Rose guy, I knew he hadn't played the infield on a regular basis since 1966 when he started at second base for the Reds, and Anderson said he wasn't without that knowledge. He said this was bigger than that. He said he wanted George Foster's bat in the lineup, period. He said the best way to do that, while keeping everything else as potent as it was elsewhere in the Reds' batting order, was to swap Rose at third base in place of the anemic-hitting combination of John Vukovich, Doug Flynn, and Darrel Chaney.

After The Swap, the Reds went 41-9 in the next 50 games and 96-42 overall for the rest of the season.

Rose often attacked grounders at third base with the finesse of a Sumo wrestler on a balancing beam, but he didn't embarrass himself with just 13 errors in 349 chances, and he was flawless during the postseason. Foster also evolved into one of the game's most feared sluggers, and the Reds already had a few of those. Better yet, they went from their Fabulous Four of Rose, Bench, Perez, and Morgan to their Great Eight of those players and Foster, Ken Griffey, Dave Concepcion, and Cesar Geronimo. They formed the best set of regulars ever to grace an MLB starting lineup.

Among my favorite parts of going to Reds games in 1975 was just before the first pitch. That's when Paul Sommerkamp spent the 23rd of his 36 seasons as the Reds public address announcer preparing his baritone voice to deliver the following before every home game as each member of the Big Red Machine left the dugout one by one to take his spot at Riverfront Stadium after hearing his name.

Your attention, please.

Presenting the Cincinnati Reds.
The catcher . . . Johnny Bench.
The first baseman . . . Tony Perez.
The second baseman . . . Joe Morgan.
The shortstop . . . Dave Concepcion.
The third baseman . . . Pete Rose.
The left fielder . . . George Foster.
The center fielder . . . Cesar Geronimo.
The right fielder . . . Ken Griffey.

And the pitcher . . . you know, whoever the Reds had on the mound, but for my Big Red Machine, it was mostly about whoever was at the plate.

During late May of 1975, I attended my last Reds home game before heading back to Milwaukee from Oxford for the summer. They smashed the Montreal Expos 6-0 for a 28-21 record, and they still trailed the Dodgers in the division, but it was only by 1 ½ games. You just knew my Big Red Machine was on the verge of shifting to higher and then higher gears during the next few days and weeks, and it happened. In mid-June, with the Great Eight nearly fully meshed, the Reds were up in the division by 3 ½ games when I got in the family car in Milwaukee with my two brothers and drove the two hours to Wrigley Field.

We were rewarded for coming.

These weren't those other generations of Cubs, so the Reds could beat these guys. More precisely, the Reds could massacre them.

Don Kessinger remained the Cubs' shortstop, but instead of Ernie Banks at first base, they had Andre Thornton. They had Manny Trillo at second base instead of Glenn Beckert, and they had Bill Madlock at third base instead of Ron Santo, and they had Pete LaCock in left field instead of Billy Williams, and they had George Mitterwald at catcher instead of Randy Hundley. In the Cubs' pitching department, there wasn't anything close to Ferguson Jenkins among the starters or the relievers, and the manager was the forgettable Jim Marshall instead of Leo Durocher who joined Banks, Williams, Santos, and Jenkins in the Baseball Hall of Fame.

With my brothers and me cheering from the left-field bleachers, the Reds won 11-3 that Saturday afternoon after smashing the Cubs 18-11 the previous day. For us, it was another game on Chicago's northside back to the future of Crosley Field, the Reds' jewel of an old ballpark from 1912 through its finale, which was four games after June 20, 1970, which was when my brother Dennis and I attended the last Saturday game there.

Like Crosley, Wrigley was quirky, but only with ivy on the outside of its brick outfield walls instead of Crosley's little hill of a warning track against the left-field fence and massive scoreboard that formed the back side of center field. Like Crosley, Wrigley was built to fit inside a neighborhood, so, thankfully, both ballparks lacked the sameness of the flying saucer stadiums of the 1960s and the 1970s or of several of the 21st century structures that tried but failed to become the Crosley and Wrigley of their generation. Like Crosley, Wrigley usually helped the Reds fatten their already gawdy offensive numbers, and since that other generation of Cubs wasn't around anymore, the 1975 Big Red Machine watched its batting average soar while also accumulating victories more often than not in the Windy City.

Other than that Chicago trip, the bulk of my Reds knowledge in Milwaukee during the summer of 1975 came from my growing pile of sports periodicals, my transistor radio with an assist from The Water Pipe, and my time in front of the TV screen, where the Reds were becoming regulars on national broadcasts.

I also had the local sports talk radio shows that labeled me "The Cincinnati Reds fan," and I called the most popular one in Milwaukee during late June when Baseball Commissioner Bowie Kuhn was the guest.

The host: Good evening, you're on Sports Line.

Me: "Yes, commissioner. I used to live in Cincinnati, and I still go to college down in southern Ohio, and a thing that has gotten a lot of people upset in southern Ohio is the fact that Cesar Geronimo was left off the All-Star Game ballot this year. Here's a man who won the Gold

Glove last year and batted around .300 for virtually the entire season, and I think he ended up around .285, but why was he left off the ballot?

Kuhn: "I can only answer it this way. As I told you, we have this large nominating group of 140 experts, and they do their best job, and as you get down to, you nominate 18 outfielders, and when you get down to the 18th, 19th and 20th outfielder, it's awfully tough. As I recall, Geronimo was about 19th. I'm not sure about that, but I think he was about 19th. Which means he would have been the next fellow nominated if he had been one slot higher. So there are a lot of good outfielders, and always, when you cut off something, the guy just below the cutoff is apt to feel that he got the short end, but you have to have a system, and that's how the system works."

Me: "Well, I'll see you in Cincinnati in October for the World Series."

Kuhn: "(Laughter) Well, they're doing pretty well."

Yes, the Reds were, and so was I as a baseball player that summer, even though I didn't make the Miami team after a tryout during the fall of 1974. The Miami roster was loaded. It included future Major League players such as second baseman Bill Doran, who eventually was elected to the Houston Astros Hall of Fame, and Charlie Leibrandt, a starting pitcher for the 1985 Kansas City Royals who won the World Series and later for the Atlanta Braves during the early 1990s when they began their MLB-record run of 14 consecutive division titles. Miami coach Bud Middaugh praised my defense in center field, but he said I couldn't hit with enough power against the quality pitching on the team's schedule.

I accepted Coach Middaugh's critique, especially since he was headed to Miami's Hall of Fame, but then came the summer of 1975, soon after my brothers and I returned from that Wrigley Field trip. We participated in one of our favorite pastimes, which was visiting the batting cages near our Milwaukee house. We often drew a crowd. So, as I lined shots around the cages with relative ease, I mostly shrugged over the complimentary remarks I kept getting from somebody watching a few feet away, and then I looked in his direction.

George Scott.

Wait. George Scott?

Yep, it was George Scott, the All-Star first baseman for the Milwaukee Brewers. During that 1975 season, he was headed for another one of his eight Gold Gloves, and he eventually led the American League in home runs with 36 and in RBIs with 109. He waved me out of the batting cage, and he said, "Man, you're good. What team do you play for?"

I told Scott I didn't make my college team.

"Shoot, let me write a letter to that coach," Scott said, laughing, making my day, and it would have been the highlight of my baseball summer, but my Big Red Machine kept resembling the invincible force I initially envisioned back in 1970 during the early stages of the First Red Machine. Unlike that version, this one had pitching and overwhelming speed and tremendous defense and no Tommy Helms or Woody Woodward in the batting order to give opposing pitchers time to catch their breath for a split second.

My only frustration with the 1975 Reds came down the stretch, and it involved manager Sparky Anderson's tendency to take his foot off the gas pedal of his high-powered baseball vehicle. He needed to floor that thing, right through Labor Day and the last pitch of the World Series. I kept thinking "116." That was how many games the 1906 Cubs won during the regular season to set an all-time record. I wanted that record, but I also kept thinking, saying, and fuming, "Why doesn't Sparky feel the same way?" My questioning of the otherwise dandy manager involved his use of Johnny Bench, the generational catcher, whom Sparky played 16 times in left field, nine times at first base and three times in right field.

No, no, no, Sparky. That man should remain behind the plate.

This isn't like the aging Cubs stars of 1969.

Among the theories for their collapse was that manager Leo Durocher kept putting his old geezers in the lineup every day, and they were exhausted by September from playing nothing but day games at Wrigley Field back then. But members of the Reds' Great Eight are in their prime, dude, and Riverfront Stadium regularly flips on its lights, and don't you even care about "116" and the 1906 Cubs?

I still loved Sparky, so the Bench thing was minor.

It was irritating, but minor.

As for the major part of this story, I knew game by game, inning by inning, and second by second something like a "once in a lifetime" season was happening with my Big Red Machine, and my guy Pete Rose was among those leading the way.

I couldn't wait to get back to Oxford, Ohio, that fall for the start of my sophomore year at Miami. When I returned to campus, I saw the Reds rip the Braves 12-5 at home in late September for their 106th victory, and they were in the middle of finishing the season with a five-game winning streak and taking 10 of their last 11 games. They fell short of "116" overall with 108 victories, but I wasn't complaining. The Reds extended their momentum into the postseason after they manhandled the Pirates during the National League Championship Series with the smoothest of three-game sweeps.

That series showed the diversity of the Big Red Machine's might since the Reds outscored the Pirates 19-7 overall with only two home runs.

So, with the World Series ahead, I still hadn't learned my lesson as an NL chauvinist, because I still refused to believe some AL team really could be dangerous (see the 1970 Orioles and the 1972 A's). I had close to no fears about the Reds facing the Boston Red Sox, and most of my overwhelming confidence had to do with the Reds. If you included the NLCS, they owned an eight-game winning streak, and they had taken 13 of their last 14 games, and they were going to play road games during the 1975 World Series at Boston's version of Wrigley Field and Crosley Field, which meant players on my Big Red Machine were about to make the Green Monster at Fenway Park their best friend during these October days.

The Red Sox have Carl Yastrzemski.

Yeah, well. OK.

And this rookie Fred Lynn is doing MVP things as the Red Sox's center fielder, but it isn't as if he is Cesar Geronimo.

I've seen Red Sox pitching guru Luis Tiant through the years on the NBC Baseball Game of the Week, and his windup makes him resemble a Cuban Flying Wallenda. That's entertaining. He also has guts on the mound, but I'm guessing neither Johnny Bench nor Joe Morgan is shaking in his cleats over thoughts of facing El Tiante or any of those other Red Sox guys in their starting rotation or bullpen.

Uh oh.

As I watched in shock from my Miami dorm room, the Red Sox clobbered the Reds 6-0 in Game 1 at Fenway Park. Not only did they score all of their runs in the seventh inning against flame-thrower Don Gullett and the Reds' vaunted bullpen, but for nine innings, Tiant twisted and hurled his way toward holding the Big Red Machine – a team that scored more runs in the Major Leagues during the regular season than anybody – to zero runs and five hits.

After Tiant willed himself to a complete game, with much help from the Reds' feeble swings at the plate, I thought I was experiencing one of those auras from a migraine attack. Instead, I was just seeing visions of Brooks Robinson, Gene Tenace, and Joe Rudi torturing my memory. That was until Game 2 returned order to the planet. It was close, though. Too close. It took ninth-inning magic from Dave Concepcion and Ken Griffey to knot the World Series at 1-1 after they delivered the tying hit and the game-winning hit, respectively, at Fenway Park to help the suddenly offensively challenged Reds overcome a 2-1 deficit.

That set up one of the sports thrills of my life.

I thought it was a joke.

The day before Game 3 of the 1975 World Series, which was switching to Riverfront Stadium that Tuesday night after Game 2 in Boston on Sunday afternoon, Chip Grobmyer walked into our Miami dorm room with some news. He had joined me as a Big Red Machine disciple, and that was how we met. During the previous fall, I rushed toward my freshman dorm of Dennison Hall on maybe my third or fourth day in college. I forgot my transistor radio before heading to classes, so I had thoughts of flipping on WLW as quickly as possible to see what the surging 1974 Reds were doing that afternoon in pursuit of Jimmy Wynn, Mike Marshall, and those Dodgers.

After I flew up the stairs to the third floor, I heard Marty and Joe loud and clear through an open door. The radio belonged to Chip, and he gave me game details. We shared our Big Red Machine passion over the next few months, and the next thing we knew, we were roommates in 203 Hepburn Hall from our sophomore through senior years.

On this October day of our sophomore year, Chip said his brother, Jack, was going to Game 3 of the World Series with his wife, Barb, but then Chip added his brother and his sister-in-law had two extra seats to sell. He said he was going to purchase one of them, and he asked me if I wanted to buy the other one.

Are you kidding me?

Not that it matters, but how much?

$10.

Just like that, I challenged the world's record for yanking cash out of a pocket, and $10 was the face value of that 1975 World Series ticket, which featured a white background with red and blue lettering saying the following: Game 3, loge reserved, $10, admit one, Riverfront Stadium, Cincinnati. Then there was the 1975 World Series logo above the classic Reds logo with Mr. Red running inside the wishbone C carrying "Cincinnati" on its top half and "Reds" on the bottom.

So, during a strikingly clear night in the low 70s on Oct. 14, 1975, I spent the last of my three baseball games sprinkled with pixie dust as a fan in Aisle 335, Row 1, and Seat 104. That placed me right behind Cesar Geronimo (or Fred Lynn when the Reds were batting) in the row nearest to the wall at Riverfront Stadium in straightaway center field. This was nirvana for several reasons. For one, historians later placed that Game 3 of the 1975 World Series among the greatest World Series games ever. For another, the Reds won. For another, the game-winning hit came straight in the direction of my center-field seat.

About the game . . . Wow.

I lost my voice by the seventh inning.

Players slammed six home runs, three by each team. The Red Sox led, and then the Reds went ahead by four. After chipping away here and there, Boston trailed by two in the top of the ninth before Dwight Evans smashed one of those homers for the Red Sox with a teammate on base for a 5-5 tie and extra innings.

Then the real drama began. In the bottom of the 10th, Cesar Geronimo led off with a single, and Sparky Anderson signaled for pinch-hitter Ed Armbrister to sacrifice Geronimo to second base. Ambrister's bunt bounced toward the sky around home plate in the direction of first base. As That Man (OK, Red Sox catcher Carlton Fisk) moved over to grab the ball, Armbrister hesitated before running, bumped into Fisk and watched Fisk rush a throw to second base in an attempt to nail Geronimo. The ball sailed over the head of Red Sox shortstop Rick Burleson, and with nobody out, the Reds had Geronimo at third, Armbrister at second, and me joining 55,000 other folks in the ballpark screaming for reasons opposite of the screaming by Red Sox manager Darrell Johnson and Fisk around home plate.

Our screaming contained glee. Not so much for Johnson and Fisk, whose screaming mixed with cursing. They wanted the umpires to call Armbrister out for interference, but everything looked perfectly fine to me. Then again, I was in center field, and I also was a Reds fan.

The call stood. So, with nobody out, the Red Sox walked Pete Rose to load the bases for a potential force out at any base, and after Merv Rettenmund struck out, Joe Morgan climbed into the left side of the batter's box. As the crowd went from loud to louder, the man nicknamed Little Joe became Big Joe after he swung every part of his frame of 5-foot-7 and maybe 160 pounds to drill a shot over the head of Fred Lynn in center field and straight toward every part of me yelling in Aisle 335, Row 1, and Seat 104.

The Reds won 6-5 in 10 innings.

As I contributed to the nonstop yelling, stretching from the yellow and then red seats above us to our green seats and then to the blue ones across the way, the ball from Morgan's Game 3-clinching hit kept rolling, rolling, and rolling some more in my direction on the artificial surface beyond the center-field wall. Looking back, it was a sign from the baseball gods to ignore whatever scariness would transpire the rest of the way during a World Series that already had produced needless tension for Reds fans. *Be calm, be steady, be strong.* That was what the baseball gods were telling me as Morgan's ball kept tumbling closer and then closer to me.

With apologies to the baseball gods, they weren't the ones with the belly in turmoil, trying to stay Big Red Machine faithful during the most excruciating string of one-run decisions ever played. The Red Sox took Game 4, and then the Reds survived Game 5, and then came Game 6 at Fenway Park, where those highlights mixed with horrors wouldn't stop for the Reds.

There was the three-run lead in the bottom of the eighth inning with six outs left before their first world championship in 35 years. There was the three-run homer later in the eighth by former Reds player Bernie Carbo to tie things with two outs. There was George Foster delivering the throw of his life from left field in the bottom of the ninth to send the game into extra innings after nailing the Red Sox's potential game-winner at the plate. There was Joe Morgan's game-winning homer in the top of the 10th, but before it beame official, it landed in the glove of Dwight Evans, sprinting, leaping, and then crashing into the right-field fence. Then came the bottom of the 12th, and That Guy kept leaping, waving, and clapping after hitting the foul pole in left field at Fenway Park at 12:33 a.m. on Wednesday, October 22, 1975, and there was me, rising from my pile of Econ notes at my dorm room at Miami and heading to The Water Tower for hours in the middle of Oxford, Ohio.

I was numb for Game 7. As I watched from my dorm room, I slid into a trance, partly from little sleep due to That Guy at 12:33 a.m. earlier in the day and partly because I hadn't a clue how badly I did on that Econ test later in the afternoon.

Good thing I was numb, because with constant noise around Fenway Park, the Red Sox led 3-0 through six innings as the Big Red Machine became the Little Red Wagon, but what else was new? The Reds were World Series cursed, and I prepared myself to accept their fate as the most gifted "almost" champions in baseball history. Then I began feeling a little something in the top of the sixth when Tony Perez rocketed a blooper pitch from the Red Sox's Bill Lee over the Green Monster. It was a two-run homer to pull the Reds to within one. Then I was back to normal (or so I thought) in the eighth when my guy Pete Rose tied the game on a single, and then the Reds went ahead in the top of the ninth after Joe Morgan's bloop single in shallow center field scored Ken Griffey from third base for a 4-3 lead.

There was one out in the bottom of the ninth, then two. Then Carl Yastrzemski pushed a lazy flyball toward Cesar Geronimo in center field to make the 1975 world championship official for my Big Red Machine, and I was, well, I was – I didn't know.

I guess I was relieved.

As for anything else, That Guy from Game 6 zapped away the ultimate joy I should have experienced after Game 7, but I had a dose of giddiness around Fountain Square in Cincinnati for the victory parade, especially after seeing my guy Pete Rose in the distance.

On the 45-minute drive back to Oxford, I thought about how dominant my Big Red Machine would be in 1976 with its key members returning after discovering neither the Dodgers nor the American League teams during the World Series were invincible. I also thought about how the Reds finally winning it all gave me a chance to direct more brain power toward my classes, but also to *The Miami Student* newspaper, which I joined as soon as I walked on campus. Even though I was an Econ major, I still wanted to fulfill my high school dream of becoming a sports journalist, and with encouragement from my Jackie Robinson parents, I always searched for ways to make my visions reality.

Few things topped this. During November of 1975, my past, present, and future sat in the stands of Millett Hall during a Miami home basketball game. There was a Reds connection, and it was a huge one. It was Joe Nuxhall, with the voice that had become part of my soul since we first moved to Cincinnati in the fall of 1968. The voice was there during my days next to The Water Pipe in Milwaukee, and the voice continued through my Big Red Machine capturing its Great White Whale a few weeks earlier. I discovered later that Nuxhall grew up 10 miles away from campus in Hamilton, Ohio, and even though he never attended Miami (remember: He started pitching in the Major Leagues during

World War II at the Major League-record age of 15), he viewed this college with its gorgeous setting as his college.

I couldn't believe what I was seeing. *Joe Nuxhall.* I had to talk to Joe, but I didn't want to just *talk* to Joe. I figured I needed a reason. Since *The Student* sports editor was covering the basketball game, I ran over to him to ask if anybody had ever done a story on Joe Nuxhall and his apparent love for Miami, and if not, could I do the first one.

The sports editor said, "Go for it."

That was the easy part. Now I had to approach one of the cogs of my Big Red Machine that I adored, and the Joe Nuxhall cog was as significant to its operation as any of the others. He was so approachable, greeting me with a smile, and it grew when I told him the truth: I loved his work, and I loved the Reds, and I loved the idea of working in sports media someday, and I loved this opportunity to ask him for an interview. He paused, which made me nervous, and then he said something that made me even more nervous, but only until I thought about his words for a few seconds. He said, "If you can, why don't you wait to interview me when the season starts," and then there was more. He said, "You can interview me in the press box at Riverfront Stadium, and I can give you the information on who to contact."

Suddenly, I got it. Even though I was just an aspiring journalist as a sophomore working for a college newspaper, this man I knew only through radio already was trying to help my career, and he didn't have to do it. As fate would have it – and fate did that often throughout my life – I got to know Nuxhall well after my professional journalism career began. We conversed often for decades, and that was before and after Reds games, right through his retirement in 2004 before his lengthy battle with cancer ended with his death in November 2007. I never asked him if he delayed my interview with him on purpose during that night at Miami in the fall of 1975.

I never asked, because I knew the answer.

Here's the bottom line: Joseph Henry Nuxhall contributed to one of the most important days of my life, which was Friday, May 14, 1976, because it was my first time in the clubhouse or the locker room of a professional sports team. It wasn't just any clubhouse, either. It belonged to the Big Red Machine, my Big Red Machine, and it all went back to Nuxhall.

First, there was everything before and after that moment of moments for me, starting with the rest of the 1976 season for the Reds. With spring training approaching, I lacked my yearly Big Red Machine anxiety, but my yearly Big Red Machine excitement was in full throttle. Neither I nor anybody else who knew a resin bag from a batting tee wondered if the Reds would win the National League West. The only question was, "Will they do so just after the All-Star Break, or what about near Memorial Day since they might never lose again?" The National League Championship Series and the World Series were just formalities for the 1976 Reds, or so were the thoughts of baseball wisemen who kept saying such things, and this was long before this edition of the Big Red Machine fulfilled just about all of those predictions. So it made sense that I never heard Reds manager Sparky Anderson sound so confident – even cocky – during his radio interviews with Marty and Joe during spring training in Tampa.

One day I tuned into WLW on my transistor radio from Oxford, and I heard Sparky say, "Nobody can stop us, Marty, not when we don't want to be stopped."

All righty then, and this wasn't just talk.

Along came Opening Day 1976 on Thursday, April 8, with Major League Baseball's traditional opener in Cincinnati at a heightened level of color, fanfare, and anticipation throughout southwestern Ohio. The game went as advertised for those who paid attention to Sparky, those baseball wisemen, and common sense. The Reds pounded the Houston Astros 11-5 before a stuffed house of 52,949 at Riverfront Stadium, and then they ripped the Astros 13-7 the following day before kicking them out of town to end the three-game series with a 9-3 victory. The Big Red Machine continued its steamrolling ways on the road in Atlanta, where the Reds won 6-1 to outscore their opponents 39-16 for a 4-0 start.

Nobody was surprised, and this also was worthy of a yawn: The 1976 Reds eventually led the National League in runs scored, batting average, slugging percentage, on-base percentage, doubles, triples, home runs, RBIs, and stolen bases. They also led Major League Baseball in fielding percentage.

Strangely, the Reds dropped five of their next seven games after that opening surge, but I could speak for those who joined me at Riverfront for a 14-7 loss in April against the San Francisco Giants during the middle of that slide. Nobody flinched, and the same was true regarding another dip for the Reds in early May. You just knew the hitting would never slump, and they were peerless as a team on the bases and in the field.

With the Great Eight in its first full season together – since George Foster started in left field from Opening Day with Pete Rose now settled at third base – all the Reds needed was decent pitching, which was shaky pitching during those early stretches of rockiness. Then, with the Reds' bullpen still solid as ever, starters Gary Nolan, Jack Billingham, Pat Zachry, Don Gullett, and the rest began moving in late spring toward finishing with a team ERA of 3.51, which was right at the overall average for the Major Leagues, and the rest of the season contained zero drama for the Big Red Machine, with Sparky mostly driving in cruise control.

Even so, I kept watching closely, just to make sure the Reds didn't swerve across the center line toward danger of a needless crash. I still visited The Water Pipe in Milwaukee during that summer, but as far as driving to Wrigley Field, the Reds took the first of their two yearly trips to Chicago early in 1976 when I was still in college. The other one occurred later when I was back on campus. In general, as the leaves began to fall, along with any doubts by anybody that this was baseball's best team, I had no Big Red Machine complaints, not even about Sparky's use of Johnny Bench.

In 1976, Bench caught for the Reds, and that was about it. He played only five games in left field and one at first base. Otherwise, when Sparky wasn't resting the greatest catcher ever, he was behind the plate and sprinting toward one of his 10 Gold Gloves. Not coincidentally, he led the National League in putouts for the first time in his career with 651, and his .997 fielding percentage led the Major Leagues.

There was this nagging thing hovering over the 1976 Reds, though, and it foreshadowed unpleasantness to come for the Big Red Machine Nation. Whenever folks in the national media mentioned the 1975 World Series, which was often due to its many twists and turns over seven games, they usually led with That Guy and his home run in their highlights, focusing on his leaping, jumping, and clapping in that 12th inning. Game 6 of that World Series lived more than Game 7, and the only thing the Reds possibly could do to change that (with an emphasis on the word "possibly") was to do what they did during the 1976 playoffs.

They blew everybody away. *Everybody*, and it began during the NL Championship Series against the Philadelphia Phillies who won just one less game than the 102 of the Reds. Just like the 1975 Reds, the 1976 Reds could have (should have) had a flashier record, but with Sparky seeking more than ever before to rest guys prior to the playoffs, they split their last 10 games of the 1976 regular season. During a September game in Los Angeles, Sparky started the forgettable Don Werner at catcher, the equally forgettable Bob Bailey in left field, and George Foster in center, which was a huge leap for somebody who barely could handle his less-demanding position of left field. But none of that mattered in mid-October.

The Reds swept the Phillies in three NL Championship Series games, and during the 1976 World Series, they met the New York Yankees of fiery manager Billy Martin. The Reds doused Billy's inferno and his Bronx Bombers by outscoring them 22-8 in another four-game sweep, and my Big Red Machine became the first team ever to win all of its postseason games since baseball went to division play in 1969.

Oh, and in the '76 Series, Sparky didn't make a single offensive or defensive substitution (except for pitching changes) in the four games.

It was complete domination.

During this World Series, I watched comfortably from my same Miami dorm room where I squirmed the year before against the Red Sox, and I focused on next season. I wondered if the 1977 Reds could become the first National League team ever to three-peat as world champions.

With much help from the 1972 Reds, the A's did so in the American League from 1972 to 1974, and you had the five-peat of the Yankees through 1953 after their four-peat through 1939, so maybe the Reds could top even those marks.

After all, the Great Eight of Bench, Perez, Morgan, Concepion, Rose, Foster, Geronimo, and Griffey started in 80 combined regular season and postseason games in 1975 and '76. The Reds' record in those 80 games? 64-16. That's an .800 winning percentage, which in a full season would translate to a 130-32 record.

So it was simple, right?

Keep the Great Eight together.

That's not what happened.

I gasped when I heard during Christmas break in Milwaukee on Dec. 16, 1976, that the Reds traded Tony Perez and pitcher Will McEnaney to the Montreal Expos for, let's see, who again? Woodie Fryman and Dale Murray? Never heard of them, and most folks hadn't, because they were ho-hum pitchers.

The Reds looked clueless.

Tony Perez was the Pennzoil that kept the Big Red Machine running smoothly. All of its pistons were different, and they sometimes worked against each other, which is what I saw when I began dealing with most of those same Reds for *The Cincinnati Enquirer* as a professional journalist, and which is why my Big Red Machine needed nothing less than Perez to handle its squeaks to keep it operating as one.

Even as a Reds fan next to a water pipe, I could have told management about Perez's value to the clubhouse, especially after Friday, May 14, 1976.

CHAPTER 8

The Transition

Oh, about Friday, May 14, 1976 . . .

Thanks, again, Mr. Nuxhall.

I mean, Joe.

Several months earlier in Oxford, Ohio, Nuxhall wanted to postpone doing an interview with me as a sophomore reporter for the Miami University student newspaper, and he suggested I reschedule for this moment. With a nudge from Nuxhall, Reds public relations director Jim Ferguson gave me a press credential for the game that night at Riverfront Stadium against the New York Mets. Before I knew it, I was there at the headquarters of my Big Red Machine to interview the Reds radio announcer who had Miami University in his blood and who was much more than that during the history of my 20 years on earth.

I was so nervous.

A friend from college drove me the 45 minutes from Oxford to Cincinnati, and as we had planned, I met Nuxhall at Riverfront. It was the first time I was in a Major League Baseball press box. Moments before, it was my first time going through a media gate of a professional team, and then it was my first time going up a media elevator. During all of these "firsts," I encountered so many Reds employees and stadium security folks who were extraordinarily kind. I saw many of them again and again through the years, and they often said with emotion while smiling, "I remember you when you first started." I thanked them (again) for their eternal kindness.

When I arrived at the press box, I was overwhelmed. It began with the massive view of the field from an angle I never knew existed. This remained the heyday of newspapers, so by the first pitch, the place was packed with veteran writers, all White, all mostly older than my dad in his mid-40s and all wondering who was this Black kid looking slightly terrified?

The clanging of typewriter keys filled the air. That sound became more dominant since this was an enclosed press box with a plexiglass view to the field and to the stands.

I saw Bob Hertzel, the Reds beat reporter for *The Cincinnati Enquirer*, and he invented the phrase "Big Red Machine" during a story he wrote on July 4, 1969. I saw Hal McCoy, the future Baseball Hall of Fame writer for the *Dayton Daily News*. They both would become highly influential to my career. There were several icons of New York sports media such as Dick Young and Jack Lang. Then there was Nuxhall, the Old Lefthander who took me into the WLW radio booth to meet Marty Brenneman, the future Hall of Fame announcer, and that almost was too much.

I stood there with Marty and Joe, the guys I followed often by The Water Pipe in Milwaukee, and they were shockingly normal. Then Joe and I returned to the press box for the interview. Since it was a couple of hours before the first pitch, most of the writers were elsewhere. We sat side by side in the front row, and after I glanced to my right at the spectacular view beyond the plexiglass, where the grounds crew was pulling the batting cage into place, I somehow got out my first question without stumbling much.

It involved Nuxhall's Miami University connection.

When did it start?

I was stunned by his answer.

"Well, of course, this was back in 1963, but we had a service station in Hamilton, my brothers and myself, and the radio station, WMOH, which did Miami football and basketball for many years, came to sell us advertising, and we weren't sure whether we wanted to buy any or not, so we told them to come back," said Nuxhall, and thank goodness I had my cassette tape recording at the time. Even though I brought my notebook, I barely could write down his words since I was so amazed to hear his voice without the need of my transistor radio. He continued with his Miami story, saying, "They came back about a week later, and they said, 'Would you be interested in doing Miami basketball?' I said, 'What are you talking about?' He said, 'Doing the play-by-play of Miami basketball.' I said, 'I don't know anything about that. I know basketball, but as far as doing play-by-play, that's different.' He said, 'I'm not asking that. Will you do it?' I told him that I would try anything once, and this is how it all began, with me going to Miami's basketball coach Dick Shrider who also was the assistant athletics director, and he said, 'Sure. That would be real nice,' and this is how my broadcasting career started. I did basketball at Miami for about four years."

How cool. Joe Nuxhall, my Joe Nuxhall, got his broadcasting start at my college, and he's right here in front of me with that voice.

We talked some more, including how Nuxhall got the call in 1966 to become the color analyst for Reds games on WLW after his Miami basketball stint gave him experience behind a microphone, and he eventually remained the emotional voice of the Reds for nearly four decades. We talked about other Miami things, and about his broadcast partners through the years, and about the early 1976 struggles for the Big Red Machine. Then I stood up and thanked "Mr. Nuxhall" ("You can call me Joe") for his kindness, not wanting to overstay my welcome, and as he shook my hand, he asked me a question.

I was stunned again.

"Have you been to the clubhouse?"

The clubhouse?

"Yeah, that credential will get you into the clubhouse."

I had no idea. Despite those words from Mr. Nuxhall – OK, Joe, I still had no thoughts of heading to the sacred domain of my Big Red Machine, even though "Joe" told me I was allowed to do so. He added, "Just take the elevator down to the bottom, turn to your right, and as you keep walking, you'll see it to your left. You can't miss it."

Thanks, Joe.

For the sake of my desire to work in that Riverfront Stadium press box someday, along with others throughout professional and collegiate sports, I knew I had to ignore my slightly wobbly legs to follow Joe's instructions. I did, and when I got to the front door, I felt like Dorothy stepping from the poppy field to the Land of Oz. A security guard glanced at the credential on my belt, nodded without saying a word and opened the door to the Land of the Great Eight, and everywhere I looked, it was red, perfect or both. The door. The carpet. The lockers. The furniture. The lighting. The atmosphere. The coaches. The players.

Then I turned to my right after walking down the short hallway, and there was Johnny Bench, sitting at his locker, and I resisted the urge to slap the side of my face to see if I would awaken from a pillow. Cesar Geronimo stood straight ahead, and Dave Concepcion sat nearby. On the far side to the right, there was Joe Morgan, sounding like Joe Morgan, speaking to a clubhouse attendant about cleats, or about post-game dinner choices, or about the latest episode of *Jeopardy*. I noticed Joe Morgan kept talking, and the clubhouse attendant kept nodding and listening. (I discovered later as a professional sports journalist that Joe Morgan often kept talking and talking, usually to the delight of the listener).

While some writers interviewed players at their lockers, others huddled near the loaded food table in the middle of the room. They weren't waiting to eat. Soon after I became a professional journalist, I discovered writers in those situations wanted a central spot to see when guys they wished to interview were available. It also was a way for the writers to study the overall mood of the team before dashing to meet deadline.

No more than five minutes after I first entered my Big Red Machine fantasy land, somebody headed toward the far corner of the clubhouse to my right with a huge cake full of candles, and everybody – players, batboys, clubhouse attendants, announcers, coaches, reporters – moved in that direction. Many folks sang happy birthday to the guy standing with his face toward the back of his locker as he held his jersey in his hand.

I joined the crowd, and the guy turned around.
Wow. Tony Perez.

He looked awesome.

To celebrate his 34th birthday, he lit a cigar, and I guess it was Cuban since he was from that island. The universal love for him was striking, along with his charisma, and prior to this, I had only experienced Atanasio Perez Rigal standing on a baseball field while I watched from a ballpark seat. Ken Griffey Sr. greeted Perez with a handshake, and George Foster stood at a locker to Perez's right.

It doesn't get better than this, I thought to myself.

Then it did. Sparky Anderson emerged out of the multitude with that snowy white hair. He said a few words to Perez, then to Bench, then to others before he slipped around the corner and down the hallway to his office I would later visit often. But not on this day. Even though it wasn't the case, I thought my credential was different than those of the veteran writers throughout the clubhouse, and I switched fairy tales in my head. I went from thinking this was the Wizard of Oz to Cinderella, glancing at my watch, fearing the clock was about to strike the Big Red Machine version of midnight, but only for me.

Surely one of the clubhouse attendants was minutes or even seconds away from tapping me on the shoulder and saying, "Son, it's time for you to head back to wherever you came from out of nowhere."

I wanted to stay, but I felt I had to go.

The problem was that I didn't see the main guy I wanted to see, and as I took a few steps toward the hallway leading to the clubhouse door, I looked behind me. That main guy was walking in my direction, or perhaps it appeared as much. No way Pete Rose was coming toward a sophomore writer for the student newspaper at Miami University.

"Hi, I'm Pete Rose. What's your name?"

Uh, T-T-T Terry Moore.

"You write for *The Cincinnati Enquirer*?"

No, I'm a writer for The Miami Student newspaper at Miami University in Oxford.

"Well, you'll work for the *Enquirer* someday. You can do an interview with me."

Rose nodded, retreated to his locker near that of Morgan on the far wall to the right, and I wanted to faint. I couldn't believe what just happened. The Rose thing, the Perez thing, the whole clubhouse thing, the Nuxhall thing. Then I left my baseball Land of Oz to experience everything involved with the reporters thing.

It began with batting practice. From the clubhouse, I was told to make a couple of right turns, and then move straight ahead to depart through the tunnel behind home plate, which I did, and before long, I was in the suburbs of the Land of Oz. I was mesmerized by two sets of sights around the floor of Riverfront Stadium. First, there were the Reds players trickling out of the home dugout on the first base side. They either went to the batting cage, where the usual suspects prepared to rocket shots toward the farthest parts of the red and yellow seats in the sky, or to the field, where players trotted to various parts of the artificial surface for groundballs and fungoes to remain baseball's best defensive team.

Then there were the writers. With my future always in mind, I cared as much about the journalism unfolding around me as I did about my Big Red Machine *right there.*

I didn't talk. I just watched and listened.

Some reporters stood around the cage, asking questions to players and coaches between swings. Others did interviews inside or outside the dugout, and most of them had notebooks, flipping pages while using their pens to jot down a little, a lot, or nothing at all.

During the game, I sat at the top of the multi-tiered press box to study everything below and around me. I noticed how the writers kept track of every pitch in a scorebook, just as I had done for years with the help from The Water Pipe. The writers scribbled into their notebooks between delivering thoughts on those typewriters, which were making their last stand with huge portable computers becoming the rage. What intrigued me more were the conversations amongst the writers. They involved the players, managerial decisions, folks in the stands, other writers, the weather, politics, or whatever else was on somebody's mind, and the conversations were nonstop, ranging from informative to humorous to cynical to vicious.

Among the best things about the press box was the dining room down the hall. It was for media folks and Reds officials. In addition to a pregame meal, a kindly elderly gentleman stayed ready behind a counter until the last pitch. He made whatever type of sandwich you desired, and if you were thirsty for something soft or stronger than that, no problem. The same went for snacks and desserts, and it was all free.

My dominant thoughts involved the working press box more than the food or even the game, which was a disaster for the Reds. The closer the game moved to the ninth inning, the more the conversations among the writers slowed and the typing increased. As soon as the Mets made the last out for a 5-1 victory, the wild dash began for the top of the press box with yells of, "Hold the elevator" from those lagging behind. I wanted so badly to follow them back to my Land of Oz in the Reds clubhouse, just to see how the writers conducted postgame interviews, especially after a loss, and I knew my credential would take me there. But my ride back to Oxford was waiting for me at a designated place.

Before I left the press box, I stood there, looking toward the field as the groundskeepers did their thing and fans eased their way toward the exits, and then I glanced around, with several writers still pounding their keyboards on deadline.

I like this. I can see myself doing this.
Man, I want to do this.

As a spiritual person, I knew there was no such thing as coincidence, so I realized the events of Friday, May 14, 1976, were leading to something grand for me in journalism. But first things first. I had to finish my junior and senior years at Miami, and despite heading for a business degree in Economics, my thoughts on the road back to Oxford from Cincinnati that night were on *The Miami Student* and beyond as a sportswriter. I also thought about the state of the Reds, but despite their loss to the Mets, no worries. I knew my Big Red Machine would do what it eventually did, which was, it joined the greatest teams in baseball history after bullying its way to the easiest of world championships for back-to-back titles.

My college also knew about dominance. Miami had its Cradle of Coaches, and throughout my years on campus, many of the sports teams were the best in the Mid-American Conference, and they frequently joined the nation's elite. That dominance began and ended with the football team that went 33-1-1 through the fall of my sophomore year in 1975. During that stretch, Miami even reached the pages of *Sports Illustrated* for operating as a mid-major program from southwestern Ohio that nevertheless defeated the big boys of Florida, Georgia, and South Carolina in consecutive years while finishing 12th, 10th, and 15th in those seasons, respectively, in the Associated Press poll.

Then came the college football mystery of 1976 during the fall of my junior year, when Miami began 0-6 and didn't win its first game that season until two days after the Reds swept the Yankees in the World Series on Oct. 21.

With Miami headed for its first losing football season in 34 years, I went into professional sports journalist mode for *The Miami Student*. I had this idea. I stayed all day on the phone during late October to call as many of the living football members of the Cradle of Coaches I could find, and I got most of them: Paul Brown, Woody Hayes, Bo Schembechler, Ara Parseghian, Weeb Ewbank, Bill Mallory, Carmon Cozza, and Paul Dietzel. They were all stunned by Miami's football collapse, and they were all tremendous with their responses. It was a huge story for *The Miami Student*. In fact, veteran newspaper writer Bill Ford, who covered Miami football and basketball for *The Cincinnati Enquirer*, told me on campus while waving the paper containing my article high in the air for a few seconds, "Now *that* was a helluva piece," which was some compliment, but only if you understood it came from *Bill Ford*.

At the time, Ford was a 60ish White man who didn't mind having his face turn the reddest of reds after a few belts of his favorite libation, which was any libation. He was the epitome of an old-school journalist, with his crusty look, colorful language, and unique brand of cynicism that bordered on brilliance. He hated everything, but he had the softest heart, and he was a splendid reporter and a terrific writer. I discovered those things when I saw him at Miami University sporting events, and I sought his knowledge, primarily through observation. I discovered even more Bill Ford things when I became one of his colleagues at *The Cincinnati Enquirer*, but back in October 1976, I was just a junior at Miami, always looking ahead, and I thought about something after Ford praised my Cradle of Coaches piece.

Do you think The Cincinnati Enquirer would print it?

"I'll give you the number to the sports editor," said Ford, pulling out his reporter's notebook to jot down the information for Jim Montgomery. I called within the hour, and I discovered Montgomery was a Texan of few words. He would become my first boss as a professional sports journalist. He was fabulous for young writers of ambition like me, but in late October 1976, he hadn't a clue I existed before our conversation that lasted less than a minute. After I mentioned what I wrote on the Cradle of Coaches and that Bill Ford liked it (which was huge), Montgomery told me to telecopy the story to the *Enquirer*. "I'll take a look-see," he said, hanging up the phone, and I'm not sure he said goodbye.

It didn't matter. The *Enquirer* ran my Cradle of Coaches story the next day, and it was at the top of the front page of the sports section.

Soon after that, I did a satirical column for *The Miami Student* on the collapse of Miami's football season, and I played off the themes of a new book back then by my journalistic idols Bob Woodward and Carl Bernstein. Their book was called "The Final Days," detailing the end of the Richard Nixon presidency. The Miami football coach was Dick Crum, so my column was called, "Dick Crum and The Final Daze." While the Woodward and Bernstein book mentioned Nixon wandering the White House in the middle of the night after a few drinks and talking to the portraits of former presidents, my column featured Crum wandering the lobby of Millett Hall and guzzling Gatorade while talking to the photos on the walls featuring Miami's Cradle of Coaches members.

The *Enquirer* ran excerpts of my "Final Daze" column, along with the nearby *Dayton Daily News*, the *Columbus Dispatch* in Ohio's capital city, the *Cleveland Plain Dealer* and other newspapers around the state. I was feeling this journalism thing, and I was obsessed with making as many connections as possible. Then again, that approach wasn't revolutionary for me. Given the national brand of Miami sports during the 1970s, and even before that in spurts, especially in football, local and national journalists kept finding their way to Oxford, Ohio. I spent my freshman and sophomore years trying to huddle with as many of those journalists as possible, and it just expanded my junior year.

I also remained in contact with Bill Dwyre, the *Milwaukee Journal* sports editor who inspired me as a sophomore at James Madison High School during the spring of 1972 when he spoke to our journalism class. He preached the separation of fan from reporter when covering teams, and he warned against journalists getting too close to players and coaches. "Your job is not to cheer for teams, but to report about them," Dwyre would say, even to the point of removing his *Milwaukee Journal* writers from one beat to another if he felt they were becoming pals with the folks they were covering. Dwyre also became one of the first sports editors to ban his reporters from the long-time practice of traveling on the same planes with teams. In addition, his reporters weren't allowed to eat the free food offered by teams at games.

Except for the free food part, I turned Dwyre's words into action during the spring of 1977 when I was named the sports editor-elect of *The Miami Student*. The university switched from the quarter system to semesters at the start of my junior year, which meant my official sports editor duties were slated for the fall semester of 1977 during the start of my senior academic year. Instead, *The Miami Student* sports editor for the second semester of my junior year decided to leave his post early, and to my delight, I was the sports editor. I operated my department as if I were Bill Dwyre, which was easy. We ran the entire *Miami Student* like a regular newspaper, and we had the talent to do so, with editors and reporters who frequently broke stories. We kept school administrators as well as coaches in the athletics department on edge in a way that would make Bill Dwyre proud, and that was among my objectives.

There was something else: Before I received my sports editor's gig that spring of 1977 from *The Student* – going from the first African American writer ever for the oldest college newspaper west of the Alleghenies to becoming its first African American editor of any kind – I got a Christmas present from *Enquirer* sports editor Jim Montgomery. Once again, his call was short when he asked me in December if I wished to spend the summer of 1977 as an intern at the paper.

Um, yes!

I began to reminisce.

After my freshman year at Miami, I spent that summer of 1975 working as a stock boy at the same record distributorship in Milwaukee that hired me the previous year when I graduated from high school. Following my sophomore year at Miami, I hung tailpipes at an automative store during that summer of 1976 when I wasn't putting oil cans on the shelves. Between those real jobs, I still umpired youth baseball, but those real jobs helped me pay for college while I wondered every day why the clock wasn't moving faster toward 5 p.m.

At that automative store, I had a 45-minute lunch break (and they meant 45 minutes) between acquiring more scratches on my face and arms from those tailpipes. I ate at a nearby park with the food I brought from home, and before and after prayers beyond saying grace for lunch, I fantasized about doing something that didn't require clocking in and out.

Something to take advantage of my imagination.

Something I enjoyed.

Something I could do forever with a smile.

Something like what I heard from Jim Montgomery, and as he explained over the phone in December 1976, this wasn't just any internship. He said he and his lieutenants in the sports department treated their interns like full-time reporters, and he also said the interns got paid like it, with a salary resembling that of first-year reporters due to the rules and regulations of the newspaper union. My eyes grew wider, so this was easy: I had the choice of beginning my *Enquirer* internship early or later, and I chose to do so as quickly as somebody could take me from Oxford to Cincinnati, which was a week after the second semester ended during my junior year in May of 1977.

I needed a place to stay for the summer, and my spiritual theme of "there is no such thing as a coincidence" continued when *The Miami Student* editor-in-chief Sue McDonald told me she had friends who were living in Cincinnati for the summer in a house. She said they had an extra room I could use at a minimum cost. I snatched it in a hurry. I still didn't have a car, which would be the case until my last semester at Miami, but that wasn't a problem. For assignments other than those at Riverfront Stadium, which was in walking distance from the *Enquirer*, the editors gave me the same free taxi privileges enjoyed by their full-time employees.

At the top of the hill from the house, there was a bus stop, and that route of 15 to 20 minutes took me about a block or two from the *Enquirer* building at 617 Vine Street. The house was down the hill from The Christ Hospital. Whenever I walked in that direction to catch the bus, I thought about Johnny Bench. In December 1972, the Reds catcher had a benign tumor removed from his right lung, and courtesy of the surgeons at that hospital, he continued to play at a future Hall of Fame level.

Before The Christ Hospital, The House, The Bus Stop, and The Internship, I had The Schoolwork staring me in the face between daydreaming. I was only a couple of months from finishing my junior year at Miami, but I couldn't wait. I was sprinting during the spring of 1977 toward making the transition from fan to journalist. I knew it, because the signs were there. Near the end of spring training in Tampa for the Reds, hoping for a rarity in professional sports with a third consecutive world championship by taking the 1977 World Series, I still listened to Marty and Joe on the radio. I still wanted to know about Reds players on the rise after the exhibition season and those needing a baseball revival before the official first pitch. I still got that Cincinnati style of baseball fever with Opening Day up next, starting at the Findlay Street Market, where all of the traditions were ready and waiting as usual.

But this was the strangest thing.

I wasn't as pumped as usual.

The loss of Tony Perez didn't help. *Are you kidding me?* I still couldn't believe Reds officials traded away their clutch hitter during games and their glue player in the clubhouse to the Montreal Expos for virtually nothing. Now the Reds had promising yet unproven Dan Driessen at first base, and unlike Perez, Driessen would swing more as a gap hitter in one of the power spots in the batting order.

That said, the main thing for me was the transition: Bill Dwyre's words were becoming more powerful within my psyche ("You're not a fan, you're a journalist"), and I also saw how professional sports journalism worked in real time on Friday, May 14, 1976, when I spent much of the day in the Reds clubhouse and the press box at Riverfront Stadium. If those things weren't enough, I was just weeks away from operating as a real sports journalist for the *Enquirer*, with the likes of Bill Ford and other long-time reporters who growled while typing, and I was sure they would study my every move. There was only one Bill Ford at the *Enquirer* or in the history of the world, for that matter, but many of the others on the sports staff filled with veterans were in the vicinity of Ford as in by-the-book journalists.

That was great for me, and so was this: During my first day of orientation as an *Enquirer* intern in mid-May 1977, the paper gave me a Reds season credential for all games at Riverfront, with access to the media gate, the media elevator, the press box, both clubhouses, the field for batting practices, and both dugouts. I wasted little time testing out that new Reds season credential. Following the nods along the way from the suddenly familiar security folks at the media gate and on the press elevator, I was down at the tunnel level, preparing with slightly more confidence now to make that entry again into the Reds clubhouse. I got another nod from a security guard, and I noticed something different along the way up to that point. In contrast to Friday, May 14, 1976, all of these security guards added polite conversation after their nods. Was it me as a suddenly familiar face – especially since I was one of the few Black journalists ever to sit in the press box at Riverfront Stadium or visit the clubhouse when I did so the year before – or was it the power of the Reds season credential?

Maybe both.

Then came the surrealistic. It happened after I walked into the Reds clubhouse, and without doing so intentionally, I stood nearly where I was the previous year, but only before departing that time.

Once again, Pete Rose approached from afar.

No, no, you're kidding me. This can't be Pete Rose coming this way from that same area as he did on Friday, May 14, 1976, but it is.

Where's the Twilight Zone music?

"How's it going, Terry? Are you working for the *Enquirer* yet?"

I was flabbergasted, but I answered, saying, "Well, sort of, but I'm still going to Miami, and I'm just working for the Enquirer this summer as an intern."

"You'll be there full-time," said Rose, with those sparkling eyes, and then he left, but I couldn't move while thinking about what just happened. There was so much to digest. Seconds earlier, I had my all-time favorite baseball player greet me out of nowhere again, and that was enough, but he did so nearly a year apart at almost the same spot.

More impressively, he remembered my name.

Peter Edward Rose remembered my name. How did he do that, and what does it mean, and isn't this wonderfully crazy?

Speaking of crazy, early into my *Enquirer* internship that summer of 1977, I noticed a bunch of sights and sounds around the clubhouse, dugout, and batting cage at Riverfront that I missed during my first visit on Friday, May 14, 1976. I wanted to rub my eyes, just to make sure I was seeing what I was seeing, but I would have exposed myself even more as a 21-year-old intern dropped into the middle of the big time. I also resisted gasping, especially when I saw more than a few key members from my Big Red Machine guzzling beer at their locker. Several downed can after can with the greatest of ease, and there was an endless supply of whatever brand they preferred across the room in a container.

There also was the smoking. Yes, there was smoking. *Smoking by members of my Big Red Machine? Surely we are in the final days.* Until that summer, I didn't know about the tunnel for the Reds leading from the clubhouse to the home dugout. I discovered in a hurry that players and coaches (oh, and Sparky, definitely Sparky, who smoked like an old Buick with white hair) used parts of that area to puff on their cigarettes. They did so before batting and fielding practice, between innings or whenever they just felt like it.

Then there was the cursing, and it was everywhere, mostly just for cursing. I discovered in the world of Major League Baseball teams, cursing was as common as breathing. *You mean, some of my Big Red Machine guys wouldn't perform well as Sunday School teachers for fear of letting something slip that isn't found in Matthew, Mark, Luke, or John?*

My summer internship consisted of stories assigned by *Enquirer* sports editor Jim Montgomery and his assistants, and while several of them involved the Reds, the bulk of them were about something else (a local diver competing in Israel during an international meet, a high school wrestling coach, a Cincinnati golfer with a low handicap despite missing his right hand). Then there were the extra stories.

Well, that was my thought.

During the summer of 1977, I functioned as if *Enquirer* sports interns had the ability to write about whatever they wanted, just as long as they did the other stuff. In other words, I already was employing the old sportswriter's rule that I would learn later from Bill Ford or from one of those other jewels of journalistic wisdom on the paper: Keep going until somebody tells you to stop, and I discovered Jim Montgomery never said no to a good idea, especially if you offered to do it during your day off or after hours. Since I always had resumé-building on my mind, and since it was summertime, and since my Big Red Machine and Riverfront Stadium were so accessible with that Reds season credential, most of my extra stories involved the Reds in particular or baseball in general, and many of those extra stories were significant.

I wrote a story on baseball mud. While walking around the tunnel at Riverfront Stadium before a Reds game, I looked through the open door of the umpires' room. I saw each of them with a bucket between their legs, and they were rubbing something out of the bucket onto dozens of baseballs. It was mud. It was a special kind of mud, but the umpires had no idea where it came from. All they knew was that the mud helped pitchers get a better grip, and that the mud wiped the shine off balls without damaging them.

After I talked to others around the ballpark before making a bunch of phone calls, I discovered Major League Baseball officials began purchasing this mud in the early 1950s from a family owning a lake in Willingboro, New Jersey. My story went nationwide through the Associated Press. I even found the following note in my office mailbox from Mel Woody, the *Enquirer's* cantankerous assistant sports editor: "Real good piece! Woody."

While working on the baseball mud story, I also had one of my most striking "Toto, we're not in Kansas anymore" moments in the transition from fan to journalist. This part of the transition actually began a month earlier than the baseball mud story when I was in the press box at Riverfront on Wednesday, June 15, 1977. Word surfaced during that game against the Philadelphia Phillies that the Reds had made a significant trade. They were seven games behind (who else?) the Dodgers, and they wanted a spark, but this guy? At least that was the reaction of reporters everywhere, heating the air with sizzling words after slamming their fists on the table in front of them over the new member of the Reds.

Who?

Tom Seaver, somebody said.

Huh?

I was confused.

Seaver already was on the fast track as a Baseball Hall of Fame pitcher with the New York Mets, and according to East Coast media reports, he would go straight from retirement someday into sainthood after spending a lifetime doing stuff like savings puppies from towering infernos. His nickname was "Tom Terrific" with that smiling face and engaging voice, and he led the Miracle Mets of '69 before taking the "You Gotta Believe" Mets past the significantly more powerful Big Red Machine and into the 1973 World Series. But to hear these reporters tell it, Seaver's image was more fantasy than reality. Even though I heard them while trying to stay out of the way of objects tossed around the press box over the trade, I refused to believe what they were saying, but then came my interviews for that baseball mud story. I had fun with it. I asked everybody from players to fans to umpires about where they thought the mud came from, and I wanted their reactions when I told them the details.

Everybody was great.

Until I got to Seaver.

The owner of three Cy Young Awards sat at his locker in the Reds clubhouse, writing something on the newspaper sitting on his lap. I waited five minutes or so to make sure I wouldn't interrupt his concentration, just in case he actually was plotting strategy on how to attack hitters for his next-scheduled start in a couple of days.

Hi, Mr. Seaver.

I'm Terence Moore of The Cincinnati Enquirer.

Is this a good time to get you?

Without acknowledging my presence, Seaver continued to stare at his newspaper before jotting down a few more things, and after 30 or 40 seconds or so, he finally lifted his head toward me with a disgusted look, saying, "Can't you see I'm doing my crossword puzzle?" Then he lowered his head again to the paper.

I had not a clue what to do. Veteran writer Earl Lawson of the *Cincinnati Post* witnessed the whole thing, and he waved me over after uttering an expletive, and then he said I had to realize some of these guys are, well, like I just witnessed. Then Lawson said, "Wait him out." Even though I wanted to leave, I went back to Seaver's locker and stood there, as he did his crossword puzzle for another five minutes.

Then Seaver folded up his paper, swung around on the seat of his chair and asked me with that same disgusted look, "What did you say again?"

Welcome to the big leagues, young man.

Even though that was the first time something like that happened to me as a professional sports journalist, it wouldn't be the last. I appreciated Tom Terrific preparing me for my future, which included dealing on a regular basis with noted media tough guys such as Indiana University head coach Bobby Knight, New York Yankees manager Billy Martin, and Oakland/Los Angeles/Oakland Raiders owner Al Davis. Fortunately for me and my overall sanity, none of the players from my Big Red Machine were Seaver-like in attitude, but some of them had their ways, which I would discover over time. As an intern, I was just trying to learn about everything as quickly as possible and adjust when necessary.

In addition to the baseball mud story, there was my Hal King exclusive about the Reds obscure third-string catcher who literally jumped out of his shoes in July 1973 to slam a pinch-hit, walk-off homer to spur the Reds from sitting 11 games behind the Los Angeles Dodgers to winning the National League West by 3 ½ games. King vanished for three years, but I tracked him down playing deep in the hills of the Mexican League.

That also went nationwide through Associated Press.

I did other "extra" stories as an *Enquirer* intern. I did a profile of Dan Driessen, the young player with the unenviable task of replacing Reds favorite Tony Perez at first base, and the story was well-received by the *Enquirer* bosses and the paper's readership. Driessen and I had this connection, and it went back to Riverfront Stadium's media gate, which also was the players gate. Long before and after games, that gate was packed with fans clamoring for autographs or just a handshake. With apologies to Bill Dwyre ("Keep that separation between players and reporters"), Driessen and I used to spend time joking about how many of those fans thought I was Driessen. Most of them refused to believe otherwise, so when I wasn't rushed, I would shake their hands or sign whatever they wanted, but I did so with my name, of course, as they responded with puzzled looks.

I also did a feature on the Reds blowing up their starting pitching by mid-summer since they were resembling the early days of the Big Red Machine. They could pound you to death, but you could do the same against their hurlers. So another one of my extra stories involved the Reds going with youthful pitching replacements – 21-year-olds Manny

Sarmiento and Mario Soto, 24-year-old Paul Moskau and 25-year old Doug Capilla – and they gave me insight on the pressure they felt trying to help an otherwise loaded Reds team three-peat.

The story was striped across the top of the front page of a Sunday sports section, which was the premier section of major newspapers during those days.

By the end of the summer, *Enquirer* sports editor Jim Montgomery felt so comfortable with my work that he sent me to cover the U.S. Women's Amateur Golf Tournament in town, and I did a profile on 20-year-old golfer Beth Daniel, who eventually won the event and later putted, chipped, and drove her way into the World Golf Hall of Fame.

As for the future Baseball Hall of Famers on the Big Red Machine and several of their teammates, they continued to spend the summer bashing the daylights out of folks, led by George Foster with Major League highs in home runs (52) and RBIs (149) while batting .320. He was named NL Most Valuable Player, which meant the award went to a Reds star for the sixth time in eight years. But opponents still were clobbering Reds pitching, especially before those youngsters arrived. I was there at Riverfront that June night when San Francisco Giants first baseman Willie McCovey set a Major League record with two home runs in the same inning. His second blast was a grand slam, and he used his 39-year-old wrists to rip it against the 40-year-old arm of Joe Hoerner.

I was behind Hoerner after what became a 13-8 loss for the Reds when he attempted to leave the media/players gate. The booing was so loud, combined with arms and legs swinging in his direction, the security guards pulled Hoerner back inside the tunnel, almost knocking me over, to save the reliever from the howling masses.

Hoerner retired a month later.

Too bad he didn't take other Reds pitchers with him.

In mid-July, with the historically rugged bullpen for the Reds showing no signs of stopping its implosion, the Big Red Machine spent an afternoon in Chicago dropping a 16-15 slugfest at Wrigley Field in 13 innings. I was in the sports department when one of the copy editors typed one of my all-time favorite newspaper headlines: "The wind blew, the balls flew, the Reds lose, so what else is new?" Courtesy of mostly their pitching woes, the Reds finished July with 16 losses in their last 21 games of the month, and they were 51-51 and 14 games behind the division-leading Dodgers in the NL West. My transition from fan to journalist was nearly complete at that point, because even though the bulk of the Reds players remained on my Big Red Machine, their losses weren't my losses anymore.

I was too focused on having the time of my life during the summer of 1977, and it helped that the Enquirer's newsroom was never boring, especially the sports department.

One day, I entered the *Enquirer* building to find a heavyset White man standing in the lobby. He wore dirty overalls and work boots. He had a toothpick in his mouth, or it might have been a piece of straw. He wanted to know how to get to the sports department.

I took him, and he told all of us gathered around him that he was good friends with Reds pitcher Woody Fryman, and then the man in overalls said, "Woody done left the team." It was true, and it wasn't necessarily a bad thing. Fryman came to the Reds before the season as part of the Tony Perez deal with the Montreal Expos, and even though Fryman was three years younger than Joe Hoerner, Fryman was another old and ineffective pitcher for the Reds, flirting with giving up an average of a touchdown per game when taking the mound.

Woody Fryman also wasn't chummy with Reds manager Sparky Anderson, at least according to the man in overalls, and then he said, "Woody retired. Headed back to his tobacco farm back in Ewing, Kentucky. Just wanted to tell y'all."

Only at the *Enquirer*.

I loved that place. Sometimes, when you walked into the sports area of the newsroom, old-timer Dick Forbes would stop typing a story on his regular beats of golf and Xavier basketball, and then he would yell out your name from the far corner of the room. After that, he would sling a genuine NFL football in your direction that he got from Paul Brown, his best friend who invented everything from the Cincinnati Bengals and the Cleveland Browns to the facemask and the playbook.

Forbes was fabulous, but nobody in the history of newspapers topped Bill Ford for entertainment.

Either before, during, or after writing a story in the newsroom, Ford would grab his suit coat from behind his chair, and he would declare in his raspy voice, "I'm going to my outer office," which was the neighborhood bar on the corner near the *Enquirer* building. I encountered Ford often through the years at Miami University, where he covered the frequently stellar football and basketball teams on campus. So I knew about his quirkiness, but he also was a stickler for journalist ethics, you know, as he saw them.

I was writing a story in the *Enquirer* newsroom on Tuesday, August 16, 1977, when the teletype machines for the wire services began going crazy behind me. One, two, soon there were 10 or more bells ringing loudly, which signaled during those days that The Mother Of All Stories was coming through. A copy woman dashed to the machine, ripped off the incoming sheet, and began running and screaming, "Elvis is dead! Elvis is dead! Elvis is dead!" She was referring to singing idol Elvis Presley, whose passing dominated the entire paper the next day to the chagrin of Bill Ford. I was in the newsroom when he started at the far end, ranting and raving with a red face, which had nothing to do with his outer office in this case. He finally waved the paper in the air while pointing to the front page, screaming, "For Christ's sake, we didn't even put a black border around the edge of the paper when JFK got shot."

No way I wished to leave the *Enquirer* that summer, but I had to. My senior year was calling 35 miles to the north at Miami.

CHAPTER 9

Goodbye, Machine

I had three highlights during my senior year at Miami University in Oxford, Ohio. Here was the first, and I couldn't stop rubbing my eyes: In March of 1978, the basketball team opened the NCAA Tournament in Indianapolis against No. 2-ranked Marquette, the defending national champion with four returning starters. It didn't matter. Supposedly overmatched Miami from something called the Mid-American Conference shocked Marquette, the sports universe, and me with an overtime victory.

No way, I just saw that.

I watched from courtside from Market Square Arena as sports editor for *The Miami Student* newspaper. Even though Kentucky destroyed Miami in the next round, those powerful Wildcats eventually stormed their way to the national championship, and Miami's ugly loss after a pretty win became more acceptable.

Two months later, I had another one of those thrills. With my parents grinning, shouting, and clapping in the background, along with my brothers, Aunt Flossie, Aunt Inez, and Uncle Ralph, I marched across the Millett Hall stage at Miami to receive my diploma in economics as a backup in case my journalism dream became a nightmare.

The dream lived, and it was in living color, which tied into the biggest thrill of the three during my senior year at Miami. I got a call a few weeks before that Marquette upset from Jim Schottelkotte, the managing editor of *The Cincinnati Enquirer*. He made what he told me back then official with job details on the paper's letterhead, and he sent the letter to my mailbox at 203 Hepburn Hall on Tuesday, April 25, 1978. In part, Schottelkotte wrote, *"Dear Terry. With all the processing completed, I can now formally welcome you to the Enquirer family. We have you down to start May 14 (or at least that week) as a first-year reporter in the sports section . . . We were quite pleased with the work you did during your internship last summer, so I don't think you should have any problem getting through the six-month probationary period we have for all employees. Again, we're happy to have you with us."*

Not as happy as I was to join them.

Eight days after I graduated from Miami on Sunday, May 7, 1978, I began the first of my nearly 50 years as a professional sports journalist. I also made history. I was the Jackie Robinson in the sports department of a newspaper founded in 1841, but that only made sense. The year before, I was the first African American intern ever for any section of the paper. I found the perfect apartment near the University of Cincinnati, just up the hill from downtown, and to the chagrin of Cincinnati Metro, I finally had a car. Right before my last semester at Miami, I bought a brand-new Datsun F 88 hatchback that was lime green with a manual gearbox, and I drove it to the *Enquirer* building to get my company identification card and something just as valuable for me: my 1978 season credential for the Reds, who were hoping to recover from their mediocrity of the previous year.

Just like my internship, Jim Montgomery and his assistants offered me story ideas, and just like my internship, I had more than a few of my own.

I wasted zero time delivering my thoughts to Montgomery on a piece to begin my career as a full-time sports journalist, and it involved my guy Pete Rose. Days before, his marketing folks announced his latest endeavor after serving as a pitchman for Wheaties, Nestle Crunch, Kool-Aid, Chevrolet, Aqua Velva, Geritol, Swanson's Hungry Man Dinners, Skechers, Pony, Jockey, and others. This time, Rose wanted to hawk his own soft drink.

The tan-covered can with brown lettering featured a photo of Rose diving headfirst with helmet flying, and below the word "Pete," there was the following: Chocolate flavored beverage, 9 ½ fluid ounces. Shake well!

The beverage was awful.

Even if you shook the can until your arm yanked from its socket, the taste didn't improve, but this was a perfect way for me to have my first extended conversation with Rose and my first piece as a full-time sports journalist.

Montgomery gave his blessing, and I rushed out the door toward my destiny. I couldn't stop smiling after I got to Riverfront Stadium. When you combined Friday, May 14, 1976, with my *Enquirer* internship from the summer of 1977, and with the fact I still was the only Black face people saw that didn't belong to somebody who played, swept or cleaned around the ballpark, everybody knew me. The security guards. The clubhouse folks. The elevator person. The kindly elderly gentleman making sandwiches in the dining room near the press box. I felt confident, but only until I walked into the Reds clubhouse and saw Rose on the far side of the room, sitting at his locker and cleaning one of his bats.

Be strong, Terry. Be professional.
Try not to faint.

As soon as I reached Rose, I said, "Hey, Pete. I finally graduated from Miami, so now I'm working full-time at *The Cincinnati Enquirer*."

"I know. I know," said Rose, which messed me up. *How does he know?* Anyway, I was getting ready to deliver my prepared lines that I had rehearsed while walking the 20 minutes or so from the *Enquirer* building to Riverfront Stadium, but I didn't need them. Rose looked up from cleaning his bat, and he said with his sparkling eyes, "Terry, you're here to talk about my soft drink?" I was so surprised by his words that I probably would have responded with gibberish, but Rose stood up and said, "Let's go talk in the dugout."

Rose led the way, through the tunnel, up the stairs, and then he sat in a folding chair on the edge of the dugout as I opened my notebook for my questions and his answers. He was tremendous, just as he would be during the numerous talks we would have in future years, but during this first one, I tried to keep my mind from drifting.

I couldn't help it.

I remembered when we first came to Cincinnati as a family during the fall of 1968, and kids scrambled from all around Cincinnati Gardens during a Royals NBA game when Rose was rumored to be in the box seats. I remembered Tuesday, Sept. 2, 1969, when we sat in the upper deck along the right-field line at Crosley Field for our first Reds game ever, and I became infatuated with Rose after he made that diving catch face-first while sliding across the damp grass in right field, and someone called him a "hotdog." Soon after that, I remembered seeing a commercial featuring Rose's former wife, Karoyln, standing in their kitchen, holding a jar and saying while smiling into a camera, "Hi, I'm Pete Rose's wife. In our household, we use Gulden's Spicy Brown Mustard," and that was all I needed to hear. From that point through the unforeseeable future, that was the only mustard I planned to use, and it happened that way.

I also remembered something else. During the spring of 1970, my dad's boss at AT&T had a cookout at his Cincinnati home for his supervisors and their families. We walked into the living room, and the first thing I noticed was a book on the coffee table with a photo of a left-handed-hitting Rose from the waist up wearing a Reds cap and jersey. The book was titled "The Pete Rose Story: Autobiography." While everybody else prepared to leave for the backyard and the burgers, brats, and ribs, I asked my dad's boss if I could stay in the living room to sift through the Rose book, and he said, "Help yourself."

I didn't stop reading until I got through the last page. The book was riveting, and it made my Rose poster come to life even more.

About the poster: It was a huge one of Rose wearing a mid-1960s Reds pinstriped home uniform, and he was running to first base at Crosley Field. I bought it when I was 12 years old before I officially was a Rose fan. I just liked the look. At the same time, I purchased another poster made by the same company, and that one was of Hank Aaron, my all-time favorite player who wasn't with the Reds. Both posters hung in my apartment in Cincinnati when Rose sat across the way from me in the home dugout at Riverfront Stadium, and he answered questions as if I weren't a 22-year-old reporter straight from college doing his first interview as a full-time sports reporter for a major metropolitan paper.

Rose was exactly the way I thought he would be.

Others? Not so much.

I had that bizarre encounter in the Reds clubhouse as an *Enquirer* intern during the previous summer with Tom Seaver ("Can't you see I'm doing my crossword puzzle?"), but he was more of a Met than a Red. Well, that was what I told myself back then as I eventually moved away from his locker in disgust. *There's no way I'll experience anything like that from any of the guys I followed regularly as a youth next to The Water Pipe in Milwaukee and during endless trips to Crosley Field and Riverfront Stadium*, which was also what I told myself, and I didn't.

That said, several of the primary players of my Big Red Machine were the antithesis of Pete Rose in that they were either slightly or greatly different than what I previously imagined.

- Johnny Bench: cooperative, but aloof. (BTW: I never asked him about the promise he didn't keep. It involved that time I was 14, pleading from the railing of a Crosley Field box seat for him to sign my scorecard after a game. While running, he said he would return after heading to the Reds clubhouse. He didn't.).
- Joe Morgan: the most talkative human being in the history of Major League Baseball or maybe of Planet Earth.
- George Foster: surprisingly soft-spoken for such a loud bat.
- Dave Concepcion: lively, not afraid of delivering an opinion.
- Ken Griffey: confident, almost cocky, but guarded.
- Cesar Geronimo: quiet. OK, no personality.
- Tony Perez: well, he was gone from the Reds during my *Enquirer* internship summer of 1977 and later when I joined the paper full-time.

Unofficially, Perez was still there, and I already knew his personality. I experienced Friday, May 14, 1976, featuring his birthday celebration inside the Reds clubhouse, and that showed me Tony Perez was another Pete Rose, which meant he was exactly what I expected. I also encountered Perez many times over the years as a non-Reds player and beyond. He never had a bad day as a jovial soul who made everybody feel good around him.

Then there was Sparky Anderson, the Reds manager who projected charm from afar, and even more so up close. He had that whitest of white hair. His folksy talk held your attention for long stretches. With regularity as Captain Hook, he also held the whole stadium hostage along his journey to one of his numerous pitching changes.

Will he or won't he?

No, Sparky never violated one of his biggest baseball superstitions, which was, even though he waited until the last microsecond every time, he always avoided stepping on the first-base chalk line heading to the mound.

I discovered *that* Sparky wasn't as dynamic as the real Sparky who could have been a charter member of the Charismatic Hall of Fame. His group interviews with reporters in his office were insightful and entertaining, but his one-on-one sessions were gold. I had several of them in his office before Reds home games at Riverfront. While puffing on his pipe, he would sit behind his desk in his undershirt and his shower shoes. He also would have on everything else involved with his Reds uniform minus his No. 10 jersey and his cap. Home games started at 8 p.m. back then, and there were several times at 7:35 p.m. or beyond that I thought I should wrap up the conversation, but Sparky often kept going. Which meant he kept talking, right up to reaching for his spikes and tying each bow and having me follow him to the tunnel as he buttoned up his jersey after he grabbed it from the closet.

The man had more to say. He wasn't Joe Morgan, owner of a constantly moving tongue, but George "Sparky" Anderson was close.

To put Sparky into perspective, I later determined something. Over the decades, I had frequent interactions with at least two dozen Major League Baseball managers, and they included the colorful likes of Billy Martin, who managed the A's and Yankees during my career; Frank Robinson, who managed the San Francisco Giants, Baltimore Orioles, Montreal Expos/Washington Nationals while I was working; and Bobby Cox, who managed the Atlanta Braves and Toronto Blue Jays.

None of them surpassed Sparky regarding everything.

Later, when Sparky became as beloved as the manager of the Detroit Tigers as he was with the Reds, we would have long sessions in his office at Tiger Stadium or at the team's spring training home in Lakeland, Florida. But my favorite conversation with Sparky occurred during the early 1980s when I worked for the *San Francisco Examiner*. We spoke around the pool of his hotel in Oakland, California, where his Tigers were in town on an off day before facing the A's. We reminisced about his Big Red Machine, which was my Big Red Machine, and from beginning to end, he was brutally honest.

"Nobody will ever know what it took each day for me to keep everything together with that team, the greatest team I've ever seen, the greatest of all-time," said Sparky, closing one eye while puffing away on his pipe. Then he told me something that the fan in me (yes, the fan was still there) didn't want to hear. "That team was done. Right after we won the 1976 World Series, they took us as far as we could go with that run."

Say it ain't so, Sparky.

After that, Sparky went deeper with several other things he told me in the past, and this was the biggest one: It wasn't always a lovefest happening in the Reds clubhouse despite the public thinking the opposite. "That's why the presence of Doggie was so important for us," said Sparky, referring to Tony Perez's nickname among his teammates. "Nobody didn't like Doggie, I'll tell you that, and he could smooth out the rough edges between guys," said Sparky, before getting more to the point. "There was no love lost between a lot of them guys, so my toughest job as the Reds' manager was trying to do my best to keep the guys who hated each other away from each other as much as possible."

Like Pete Rose and Johnny Bench.

I mostly saw the tension between the two when interviewing Bench, because his eyes shifted on occasion to wherever he thought Rose was in the room. Not coincidentally, their lockers were on opposite sides of the home clubhouse at Riverfront, and after Rose's gambling habits surfaced during the late 1980s – leading to his lifetime ban from baseball that remained until his death in September 2024 – his biggest critic for decades regarding his possible entry into the Baseball Hall of Fame was You Know Who.

During a simulcast appearance on the Dan Patrick Radio Show in July 2018, Bench thought about Patrick's question about Rose and Cooperstown, and then Bench responded with an incredulous look, "The thing that I tell people is, people who say, 'Yes, he should be (in the Baseball Hall of Fame),' then I say, 'Do you have kids?' Then they say, 'Yeah,' and then I say, 'Go home and tell your kids there are no more rules,' and it kind of makes you think about what it is." The summer after that, Rose appeared on Fox News to declare on the Brian Kilmeade Show about Bench's anti-Rose crusade, "It don't bother me, but you know Johnny Bench is one guy who should thank God I was born. Because he never would have made the Hall of Fame if I wasn't born. Because I'm the guy he knocked in a thousand times."

Sparky had to tightrope across that daily Rose-Bench friction for nine seasons, and there also was his juggling of other egos in the Reds clubhouse of those not named Pete Rose, Johnny Bench, Joe Morgan, or Tony Perez.

"Davey and them other guys would complain that I treated them differently than I did Rose, Bench, Morgan, Perez, and them guys," said Sparky, with his Cincinnati memories as brilliant as the California sun above us during our poolside chat. When he said "Davey," he meant Reds shortstop Dave Concepcion, and "them other guys" were George Foster, Ken Griffey, and Cesar Geronimo who joined "Davey" to complete the rest of The Great Eight starting lineup of the Big Red Machine. Sparky added, "I used to tell Davey and them guys, 'Yeah, I do. I do treat Joe, Pete, and them differently, because they deserve it.' I told Davey and them other guys, 'As soon as you get to that level, I'll treat you the same.'"

In contrast, Sparky was an equal opportunity manager when it came to the boys always running around the Reds clubhouse.

They actually were boys.

They belonged to Big Red Machine members, and most of those boys barely reached my shoulder, sometimes my belly button. Before they threatened to terrorize the place as kids being kids, Sparky used to bribe them. He kept a little refrigerator in his office filled with popsicles and ice cream bars, and he would offer a choice to the nice kids, but he would tell the naughty ones they needed to shape up or leave the treats to others. Those boys were 12 years old and under, and three of them I later saw regularly as adults.

There was Pedro Borbon Jr., whose father, Pedro Borbon Sr., was among the ace relievers for the Big Red Machine. Throughout much of the 1990s, Pedro Jr. became a key reliever for the Braves during a stretch of their Major League-record streak of 14 consecutive division titles. I was a columnist at the time for *The Atlanta Journal-Constitution*, and, yes, Pedro Jr. and I often discussed those old popsicle and ice cream days.

Ken Griffey Jr. was another one of those boys in the clubhouse, in the dugout, and around the batting cage. A member of the Reds grounds crew told me one day in 1978 during my first year as a full-time reporter for the *Enquirer* that I needed to do a story on Ken Griffey, and I told him with a baffled look, "I've done several stories on Ken Griffey."

The member of the grounds crew said, "No, not the father, the son. Ken Jr. is a great player in the Knothole League, but nobody's talking about it."

I did better than talking about it. I wrote about it.

On Sunday, July 30, 1978, *The Cincinnati Enquirer* printed the first story ever about Ken Griffey Jr., and it was by Terence Moore.

Ken Jr. was 8 years old.

Years later, one of Ken Jr.'s best friends told me Ken Jr's parents still had my story framed from the summer of 1978, and he said it was hanging from one of the walls in their home. This was the same Ken Jr. who eventually spent most of his career with the Seattle Mariners and parts with the Reds. He joined Barry Bonds as the greatest players of the 1990s, and then Ken Jr. sprinted into Cooperstown.

Finally, there was Eduardo Perez, the son of Tony Perez. He had playing stints with seven Major League teams, including the Reds from 1996-98. He then became one of the top baseball announcers for ESPN. Occasionally, when he traveled to Atlanta during my days as a national sports columnist for Forbes.com, we engaged in Big Red Machine talk, including the popsicles and the ice cream bars in Sparky's refrigerator. Then came the summer of 2024, when Eduardo was in town for a national ESPN broadcast involving the Braves. He waved me over to the edge of the batting cage at Truist Park. He handed me his cellphone, and I was at The Water Pipe again in Milwaukee, or at least it was Friday, May 14, 1976, in the Reds clubhouse in Cincinnati at Riverfront Stadium.

Tony Perez was on the other end of the Facetime connection from Puerto Rico, where he moved with his wife after his baseball days. He said, "What are you doing still working? I thought you would have been retired a long time by now."

Tony Perez? And he was remembering me through a Wi-Fi connection as, not only a journalist, but as a seasoned journalist – but certainly not as a fan.

Where has the time gone?

I saw nothing close to that Tony Perez Facetime conversation as my future when my dad climbed to the top of our house in South Bend, Indiana, during the mid-1960s to twist the antenna toward Chicago for Cubs games. Neither did I see the coming of that Tony Perez Facetime conversation nor any of the other lasting connections I would have with Big Red Machine folks, beginning with the summer of 1978, when Rose and I stayed attached at the hip.

In mid-June, Rose began a 44-game hitting streak to set a modern National League record and to finish second only to Joe DiMaggio's 56-game mark. I was part of the *Enquirer's* coverage of the streak. One day in July, I was flooded with messages from friends and relatives across the country. The Associated Press shot a photo that went nationwide of Rose swinging in the batting cage at Riverfront Stadium during the streak, and there I was, wearing a polo shirt and bell-bottom pants while leaning against the side of the cage watching the world's most famous hitter.

Later that summer, I surveyed dozens of Major Leaguers from both leagues to determine their choice for the game's most competitive player. Pete Rose was the winner, of course. It gave me another opportunity (and I always was looking for those opportunities) to huddle with my guy, and we spoke at length about the results.

Soon after that, one of the *Enquirer* photographers dropped a manilla envelope on my desk at the office and said, "You might like this," before he walked away with a smile. I didn't see what was inside until I got back to my apartment. My mouth dropped. Without me knowing, the photographer watched from the distance in mid-May when I interviewed Rose from the home dugout at Riverfront Stadium, and he snapped the shot (see the front cover of this book). It was a black-and-white beauty, showing Rose in his Reds uniform and me standing nearby with an Afro, sunglasses, striped pullover shirt, and a notebook in my hand.

Once again, the baseball gods combined with the newspaper gods. Fewer than a few sportswriters can say they have a photo of them doing their first interview as a professional journalist. Way fewer than that can say they have a such photo of them interviewing their all-time favorite player of a given sport.

I had yet another Pete Rose story of significance on the way in 1978, and that one challenged his 44-game hitting streak for local and national impact.

Before then, I wrote other things for the *Enquirer* when summer turned to autumn. I did high school football involving Moeller, the nation's best program, and I was there when its winning streak ended after more than three years on a field goal in the last seconds. Moeller's coach was Gerry Faust, who later went straight from Moeller – yes, a high school program, which tells you what a big deal Moeller was – to my hometown team of Notre Dame in South Bend, Indiana. I also covered big home games for Indiana University in Bloomington, where the football coach was Lee Corso, later of ESPN fame with his mascot heads, and where the basketball coach was Bobby Knight, noted for his explosive tantrums. My Reds coverage remained in spurts down the stretch of a season that went from decent to lousy and then to unbelievable. Just like that, they jumped from their grave to close the year winning seven straight games and nine of their last 10. After trailing (who else?) the Dodgers by 9 ½ games in mid-September, they finished two games from the National League West lead at 92-69.

I didn't know those were the last days of the Big Red Machine.

Nobody knew.

The long goodbye turned into a flash. First, the Reds had shipped away Perez during the winter of 1976 after their second consecutive world championship. Then, two years later, the most unlikeliest of the next cogs to leave the Big Red Machine flirted with doing so during the offseason, and that cog was Pete Rose. *Pete Rose? My guy? Not happening. He was born and raised in Cincinnati within a few pop flies of Crosley Field, and he grew up as a diehard Reds fan long before I knew the franchise existed.*

Nevertheless, despite playing all 16 of his previous Major League seasons in southwestern Ohio, there was the following paragraph near the top of an article stripped across the top of *The Cincinnati Enquirer* sports section on Thursday, Oct. 19, 1978: "Pete Rose officially dropped his baseball cap into the free-agent ring Wednesday with a formal letter to the Major League Players Association. The Cincinnati Reds' third baseman, who also sent a copy of the letter to Dick Wagner, the Reds' president and general manager, can negotiate with teams other than the Reds in 15 days."

I wrote that, but I didn't believe that.

For one, if Pete Rose really was leaving the Reds, I didn't believe the newspaper gods would be so cruel. They were. They forced me to go from that 13-year-old fan -- who saw Charlie Hustle make that diving catch at Crosley Field in September 1969 and who read hundreds of *Enquirer* articles on Rose and the Reds – to full-time reporter nine years later writing stories for that same *Enquirer* about his favorite baseball player threatening to bolt Cincinnati and the greatest team of all time.

Here's the other thing I didn't believe. Even though Rose signed his name to a bunch of papers, grabbed a couple of stamps, and slipped that envelope into a mailbox, he wasn't going anywhere outside the "513" area code. Well, that was what I thought, along with anybody else who didn't see money was becoming a persuasive thing in sports. Then, for the second time – yes, the second time – during an eight-day stretch after

Thanksgiving, somebody took a sledgehammer to the engine and the transmission of the Big Red Machine.

Pete Rose?

My Pete Rose swung this sledgehammer?

On Dec. 5, after Rose narrowed his choice to the four highest bidders, he signed what was the biggest contract in Major League Baseball history when he joined the Philadelphia Phillies with a four-year deal for $3.24 million. Again, that was the second sledgehammer. The first one was just as deadly, and it was banged like crazy against the roof, the fender, and every other part of the Big Red Machine just after Thanksgiving. It happened on Nov. 28, and I was in the *Enquirer* sports department. I couldn't believe what I was hearing, and I wasn't alone. One of the assistant sports editors hung up the phone after taking a call from one of our reporters, and he said, "Sparky's gone."

Gone?

Gone where?

To the Bahamas? Skyline Chili?

Gone as in dead? He's only 44.

Certainly not "gone" as in "fired" since he's already among the greatest managers in the history of Major League Baseball.

Sparky was fired. Reds president Dick Wagner wielded the sledgehammer on that one, and after he did his dastardly deed, Wagner justified it. OK, he tried. With a straight face, he claimed the guy who would win another World Series after taking over the Detroit Tigers to become the only manager to capture world championships in both leagues, and the guy who would finish with the sixth-most victories in the Major League history of his profession, and the guy who would make the Baseball Hall of Fame with ease – Dick Wagner claimed that guy was nothing more than a push-button manager.

When you added the Sparky Anderson firing to the Pete Rose departure, which both came after the Tony Perez giveaway two years before that, not only wasn't this the Big Red Machine anymore, but it wasn't my Big Red Machine.

Then again, the further I went into the 1978 season as a full-time journalist for *The Cincinnati Enquirer*, the less it became my Big Red Machine anyway. I was deep into my transition from fan to journalist, but I discovered an ongoing truth: You never complete that transition since you can't erase your rah-rah past from your soul. That isn't a bad thing. For journalists, memories of your rah-rah past help you produce captivating stories for those in your audience who are also doing their version of enjoying The Water Pipe or suffering under The Water Tower.

There was another ongoing truth I discovered: Courtesy of that rah-rah past in your soul, objective sports reporting never existed.

Your writing, your speaking, and your thinking as a journalist is eternally influenced by your upbringing. As a Big Red Machine disciple, I always had my emotions from Johnny Bench ripping a clutch homer beyond the reach of The Great Clemente, those Crosley Field things, and That Guy sending me to The Water Tower after Game 6 of the 1975 World Series. And goodness knows, I always bled Blue and Gold since Notre Dame football became a part of my psyche at birth near Touchdown Jesus in South Bend, Indiana.

As the years became decades for me as a sports journalist, I also had those I covered I really, really liked, and others I really, really didn't.

It happens.

Which brought me to the biggest ongoing truth of all, and I realized this one soon into my first full-time year at *The Enquirer* -- or maybe as an intern at the paper, or perhaps during my time as sports editor at Miami University. Given everything I just mentioned, the objective for journalists of any kind is to become the least subjective as possible. It starts by acknowledging your rah-rah past and your biases, along with your likes or dislikes for whomever for whatever reason, and working around those things.

So I was mentally prepared for the challenge I was offered by new *Enquirer* sports editor Frank Hinchey before the 1979 Reds season. He asked me to serve as the backup writer on the Reds beat when Ray Buck wanted days off.

Of course! And wow!

Can I really do this? Fewer than 10 years ago, I was dangling a program over a railing at Crosley Field trying to get Johnny Bench's autograph!

I can do this.

At 23, I was among the youngest journalists in the country serving as a primary or backup writer of a Major League Baseball team for a major newspaper. Maybe I was *the* youngest, but this was for sure: I was the only African American covering Major League Baseball in any capacity for a major newspaper outside Larry Whiteside of the Boston Globe. This was pressure for those reasons and for others to come. Not only that, but when the Reds opened the 1979 season at Riverfront Stadium against the San Francisco Giants, my rah-rah past still rattled around my soul, my subconscious, and my present since more than a few significant players remained from the vintage Big Red Machine.

Here was the batting order:
Ken Griffey, right field.
Dave Concepcion, shortstop.
Joe Morgan, second base.
George Foster, left field.
Johnny Bench, catcher.
Dan Driessen, first base.
Rich Auerbach, third base.
Cesar Geronimo, center field.
Tom Seaver, pitcher.

No Pete Rose, no Tony Perez, no Sparky Anderson, no way this team could remain as mythical as its forefathers of the 1970s.

As for Anderson, he was two months away from becoming the Tigers manager in Detroit, where he would win two American League Manager of the Year Awards during his 17 seasons with them. The new guy for the Reds was John McNamara, and he was no Sparky Anderson, not just because he was hired by General Manager Dick Wagner despite an underwhelming two years with the Oakland A's and four more with the San Diego Padres.

Whereas Sparky smiled and joked and entertained you in his office during one-on-one sessions, McNamara rarely removed the blank look on his face, and if he had a sense of humor, I never saw it. Given his overall vibes that usually said, "Stay away from me," his personal times with reporters were limited, at least when compared to those under Sparky, and definitely when it came to me. Once, I walked into McNamara's office at Riverfront Stadium to ask him about a relatively minor roster move by the Reds, and managers routinely commented to reporters about such things without drama. Instead, McNamara glared at me and replied in a monotone voice, "You need to ask Mr. Wagner about that." As I, along with other reporters, often did, I tried to ask the question in another way, and he got louder as he rose out of his chair, "You need to ask Mr. Wagner about that," and then he walked away without elaboration.

Oh, how I miss Sparky.

And Pete.

On Wednesday, April 4, 1979, Buck covered the Reds opener for the *Enquirer* at Riverfront, where the Giants belted the Reds 11-5, and I sat by his side in the press box studying his every move. He was a gifted reporter, writer, and teacher. He told me that, in addition to the Reds off-day, which was that next day, he was going to rest even more after a long stay in spring training by skipping Game 2 of the season that Friday night. He said he needed me to cover that game against the Giants, and I was prepared after studying Buck as well as Bob Hertzel, the previous *Enquirer* Reds beat writer who was masterful on deadline.

I knew about the notebook of odds and ends I had to send to the *Enquirer* copy desk before the 8 p.m. first pitch. I knew about "the running," which was the story I had to keep writing throughout the game since it needed filing by the 10 p.m. early deadline. I knew about "the topper," which essentially was the opening two or three paragraphs I had to write within minutes after the final out for the postgame deadline. I knew about "the re-write," which was the whole new story I needed to do after going to the clubhouses of both teams for interviews and then returning to the press box and then meeting that final of all deadlines. I knew about "the sidebar" I might need to write either before or after the game if something else happened such as injuries, trades, or other news.

I also knew everybody would be watching.

Boy were they, and not necessarily in a good way on that night of Friday, April 6, 1979. That was the first time I went solo as the person in charge of Reds coverage for *The Cincinnati Enquirer*, which was the paper of record for a team that had won more games during the decade than anybody. I was a combination of nervous, excited, and confident. Even though I always got to the ballpark early, I got there earlier than that this time. I collected enough material for a notebook of odds and ends and a pre-game sidebar, and I returned to the press box, where I wrote each piece as if they couldn't be anything less than great. I sent everything back to the *Enquirer* using one of the portable TV-sized computers of those times, and I did so way ahead of deadline since it was 20 minutes before the first pitch.

Then, suddenly, the always noisy press box went mostly silent, and I heard the voice of somebody standing behind me.

"Where's Ray Buck?" the person said to nobody in particular, but a writer at the end of my front row responded, "Oh, he's off today." The person behind me took a few steps away toward another writer, and I was stunned. The person behind me was a veteran columnist for one of the major southwestern Ohio newspapers involved with Reds coverage back then. That veteran columnist said, without looking at me, "So who's covering for the *Enquirer* today?" and somebody near the top of the press box responded, "Terry Moore."

Then the veteran columnist frowned before saying loudly enough for everybody in the press box and beyond to hear him, "Oh, this ought to be fucking interesting."

Chuckles rang out everywhere.

I didn't flinch. I just kept typing between glancing at the Reds preparing to take the field for the first pitch, but I felt helpless. I was a young Black journalist in a room packed with older White men, giggling all around me, and I knew if I said or did anything, it would not be good. So I tried to show zero emotion as I sought to stay professional while everybody else was the opposite.

Everybody except Paul Meyer, the Reds beat writer for the *Dayton Journal-Herald*. He rose from his seat to my right on the front row, put his arm around my shoulders and said, "Forget these bastards. If you ever need anything, let me know."

I appreciated the offer from Meyer, but I realized this was mostly a singular battle, just like the ones my dad experienced when he became the first Black supervisor in the history of AT&T during the 1960s and later one of its first Black managers. In fact, as those chuckles increased throughout the press box, I remembered what Dad told us about Nov. 22, 1963, and his story took place maybe 2 miles away from Riverfront Stadium at the Kroger Building, which was AT&T's downtown headquarters. Back then, that heavyweight of telephone operations flew Dad with regularly to Cincinnati from South Bend for training during his rise from janitor to electronical engineer to supervisor. Here's what Dad often told my two brothers and me what happened that afternoon: Somebody came through the door with breaking news for the packed room of all White men and Samuel Moore. The guy said President John F. Kennedy had just been shot and killed in Dallas. After a slight pause, everybody in the room stood up and cheered, and as they celebrated, they kept glancing at Samuel Moore.

"They wanted to see how the Black guy would react since President Kennedy was considered to be pro-Civil Rights, and Cincinnati was basically a Southern town," said Dad, adding that he gave them no reaction. He wanted to make sure his three sons understood that point, which is why he often said it again. "They were trying to get inside my head."

Dad kept doing his job. Mom did the same.

After Dad was transferred during the fall of 1968 from South Bend to Cincinnati, Mom had to deal with daily mind games as the first and only African American in the regional office of Associates Savings and Loans. She often talked about Martha, a middle-aged White woman who resented that her 30-something coworker was named the lead cashier and had a bigger desk. Once, Mom said Martha dangled a set of keys in her face before saying with a fake smile, "I can get into your drawer anytime I want."

Mom reported Martha to the main boss, who said meekly, "I'll take care of it," but Martha remained Martha. Mom countered with the ultimate mind game of showing no reaction, just like Dad during the cheering by his AT&T co-workers after JFK's death.

I didn't burden my parents with the mind games building around me in Cincinnati surrounding my first full-time job. I was equally mum to them along those lines during my 25 years at the *Atlanta Journal-Constitution*, where I became the first African American sports columnist in the history of the Deep South and where I was attacked racially on a consistent basis, both inside and outside the paper.

Why share those hateful things with my parents? Not only did they tell me what to do, but they showed me how to do it.

So, as Samuel Moore's words about Nov. 22, 1963 rang over and over again in my mind, I kept doing my job for the *Enquirer*, right through the weekend of Friday, June 1. That was when Pete Rose returned to Cincinnati, but this time as a member of the Philadelphia Phillies. I was heavily involved in the coverage as the No. 2 guy on the Reds, and besides that, my guy was back in town. His new team was struggling, and there were reports his non-Big Red Machine teammates were upset by media reports that they weren't following the all-out efforts of Charlie Hustle every second of every game.

When I asked Phillies shortstop Larry Bowa about those media reports, his eyes flashed, and he said, "We've always hustled." After a slightly long pause, Bowa added, while trying but failing to keep the disgust from his voice, "The main thing he brings to this club is valuable experience. He's been in the World Series, All-Star Games, the playoffs. So I think leadership is Pete Rose's main role on this team."

Got it.

Just don't harm the messenger.

As for the 1979 Reds, they weren't the Big Red Machine anymore, partly because Rose's leadership was in Philadelphia, and Sparky was gone, and Tony Perez was long gone, but they were good enough to hold off the Houston Astros through September to capture the National League West by 1 ½ games. They faced the "We are family" Pittsburgh Pirates of Willie Stargell and Dave Parker during what was a best-of-five National League Championship Series back then, and I wrote stories with Ray Buck for the opening two games at Riverfront, where the Pirates won both games in extra innings. Then after an off-day, the series switched to Pittsburgh for Game 3, and only Ray Buck and our columnist were scheduled to make the trip. When I arrived in the office that afternoon, sports editor Frank Hinchey said the paper blew it. "You should be there, too," he said. "So if the Reds win the game tonight and force a Game 4, I need you to get on a plane tomorrow morning and head to Pittsburgh."

No problem. Just like that, I was a diehard Reds fan again, but I was pulling for the old gang for personal reasons. I'd never been to Pittsburgh, and what young sports reporter wouldn't want to cover as many playoff games as possible for his resumé?

Instead, the Reds were listless during Game 3 at Three Rivers Stadium, and they lost 7-1 to end their season. The *Enquirer's* Ray Buck and other reporters mentioned how long Joe Morgan lingered in the visiting clubhouse to speak with anybody who wished to come his way. That wasn't unusual. Morgan loved to talk (and talk). The unusual part was he continued to wear every piece of his Reds uniform. He wanted to keep it on as long as possible, because he knew when he removed it, it would be for the last time.

Little did I know, the 1979 season would be far from the last time Morgan and I would cross paths, and we would do so in mighty ways.

Chapter 10

Pete and Joe

Just before the Big Red Machine became more ancient than awesome after the 1979 season, my journey back to the future with Pete Rose and Joe Morgan began through college football. Yes, college football, and of all teams, that journey involved Indiana University, which hadn't had a winning season since 1968.

Then came the newspaper gods and the sporting gods.

Again!

The 1979 Cincinnati Reds had lost the National League Championship Series, but soon afterward, I won a trip to southern California, and the impetus was Indiana University. After a season as the No. 2 writer on Reds coverage for *The Cincinnati Enquirer*, I returned to the Hoosiers in football and basketball as a beat before switching to Xavier basketball. Indiana football was the highlight of my sports year since Lee Corso and his players constructed one of the greatest seasons in school history with an 8-4 record while finishing 19th in the Associated Press poll. They accepted an invitation to the Holiday Bowl, which took place a few days before Christmas in San Diego, and after I asked *Enquirer* sports editor Frank Hinchey if I could go, he said within seconds, "Sure. Great job this year. Make the arrangements."

It was my farthest trip west past Madison, Wisconsin. The night before the Hoosiers won a 38-37 thriller over Brigham Young at old San Diego Stadium, I stood on a pier overlooking the Pacific Ocean under a brilliant moon, and I said aloud before closing my eyes, "I could see myself working on the West Coast someday."

Oh well.

At least I came this far once in my life.

A week after I returned to Cincinnati, I got a call from Charles Cooper, the sports editor of the *San Francisco Examiner*, and he said he enjoyed my pieces in *Baseball Digest*, which often re-printed my *Enquirer* stories on the Reds and other baseball subjects. Cooper also said the San Francisco Giants beat was open at his paper, and he wanted to see more of my clips. I sent them immediately, and within days, he flew me to the Bay Area for an interview.

I got the job before heading back to Cincinnati, and I was miserable. Just like Tony Bennett, I left my heart in San Francisco. It happened as soon as the Delta flight sprinted east away from the Golden Gate Bridge, but then there was this: I loved *The Cincinnati Enquirer*, along with southwestern Ohio and Miami University just up the road. In addition, with my parents and brothers in Milwaukee and the bulk of my relatives in South Bend, Indiana, they all were a relatively easy drive away as opposed to time zones away.

Worse, regarding my conflicting emotions, there was *The Cincinnati Enquirer* managing editor Jim Schottelkotte who ultimately hired me as the paper's first African American intern and later full-time sports reporter. He urged me not to take the *Examiner* job until he had a chance to counter. Well, I was so shocked I got an offer at 24 to work in California for the paper of the legendary William Randolph Hearst (combined with that Tony Bennett thing), I never gave Schottelkotte a chance to counter.

He wasn't pleased . . . for years.

I began at the *Examiner* covering the 1980 Giants of Dave Bristol, the first manager of the Big Red Machine, and courtesy of his instant temper, I discovered two things: why he was fired by the Reds after the 1969 season, and why the team became legendary afterward with the kinder, gentler Sparky Anderson. I also had some Oakland A's assignments with the brilliant yet bombastic Billy Martin as their manager. Then I covered the Oakland Raiders before I evolved into a feature writer jumping between the hottest team between the Raiders and the Bill Walsh 49ers of Joe Montana and Ronnie Lott. Finally, in 1983, I was named just the third

African American sports columnist in the history of major newspapers, which meant I had the ability to write my opinion on anything.

I quickly discovered during my first year with the *Examiner* that the 1980 Giants weren't the Reds of the 1970s. Those Giants dropped six of their opening seven games of the season, and at the end of April, they already were 8 games out of first place in the National League West with a 6-14 record. While the tensions in the Reds' clubhouse were mostly quiet, the ones surrounding the Giants were as visible as the Golden Gate Bridge on a fog-less day, and Bristol's confrontational personality had much to do with that.

After my opening year at the *Examiner*, I had three huge memories. In July of 1980, I took a road trip to Cincinnati, which was my first time back to the city since I left for San Francisco before the start of the baseball season. Nearly everybody responded with joy when I moved around Riverfront Stadium for the opener of a weekend series between the Giants and Reds: security guards, clubhouse workers, Reds players, and team officials, the elevator guy as well as the kindly elderly gentleman making sandwiches in the dining room. They treated me as if I were Dorothy returning to Kansas at the end of The Wizard of Oz, except I wasn't coming back to stay. The Giants did the bizarre for them with a sweep of the series, but the Reds as defending NL West champions had no Pete Rose, no Joe Morgan, no Tony Perez, and no Sparky Anderson, so I had no emotions one way or the other.

Long before that, I completed my transition from fan to journalist, and here was the biggest thing during my return to Cincinnati that summer: Those weren't my Reds, and they certainly weren't my Big Red Machine.

Another one of my huge memories of 1980 involved the Oakland Raiders of Jim Plunkett, Lester Hayes, and John Matuszek. It was my first season covering an NFL team. In fact, I was the first African American ever to cover an NFL team as a regular beat for a major newspaper. During training camp in Santa Rosa, California, Raiders owner Al Davis demonstrated his mysterious ways by walking toward me from the distance. We hadn't met at that point, but I was told by a

Raiders insider that the best way to get along with "Mr. Davis" was to let him speak to you instead of the other way around. I followed those orders. When he slid next to me, he just smacked his gum for another minute or so before saying, "Young man. We're gonna win the Super Bowl," and then he left for the other side of the field.

The Raiders indeed won the Super Bowl, and I covered it. Which tied into my other huge memory of 1980, which happened two months before. I went to my first World Series. *Examiner* sports editor Charles "Coop" Cooper was so pleased with my Giants coverage for the season that he asked me to cover something I first followed in October of 1968 on my transistor radio at Benjamin Harrison Elementary School in South Bend, Indiana. Back then, I heard the Detroit Tigers defeat the St. Louis Cardinals.

Wait. Did Coop really give me such a premier assignment over all those other guys in the Examiner sports department?

Uh-oh.

I accepted, of course, but I wasn't naïve. As I envisioned, more than a few of my colleagues weren't pleased with Coop's decision. Even though nobody told me directly, I heard it in the tone of their voices, and I always saw it in their eyes. To them, here was some 24-year-old Black kid who never covered Major League Baseball before as a full-time beat until now, and who was new to the *Examiner* dominated by veteran writers, and who (fill in the blank while adding a bunch of expletives along the way), and he was off to cover one of the two premier sporting events in North America (followed by more expletives).

I knew I couldn't mess up, and I knew I couldn't do less than great, but I also knew this was destiny calling. The 1980 World Series involved the Kansas City Royals versus the Philadelphia Phillies with my guy Pete Rose in his second year with the Phillies. During the day before the World Series in Philadelphia, Rose was surrounded by journalists from around the globe at his locker in the home clubhouse. As I approached the masses, Rose sat on his stool, but he still saw me between legs, arms, and cameras in his way, and he stood up, reached for my hand and said with his sparkling eyes, "How's it going, Terry? They sent you all the way over here from San Francisco?" Then he looked around, then pointed at me, "I remember this young man when he worked in Cincinnati, and he used to cover me for the *Enquirer*."

My guy.

I did see Rose earlier that summer when the Phillies came to San Francisco, so he knew I was at the *Examiner*. But this was the World Series, and despite such a gigantic presence of heavyweight journalists at his cubicle, he didn't do what other megastars would have done in that situation, ranging from acknowledging me with a nod to acting as if I didn't exist.

During my life as a professional journalist, Joe Morgan was another Pete Rose, starting with my stay in San Francisco. Like Rose, Morgan respected our past together with the Big Red Machine, and like Rose, he rewarded it. After the Giants fired Dave Bristol before the 1981 season, they hired Baseball Hall of Famer Frank Robinson, who had spent 1975 as the first African American manager in the Major Leagues when he took over the Cleveland Indians. This time, with the Giants, Robinson was the first African American manager in the history of the National League, and Morgan was among the players he wanted in his clubhouse to change the atmosphere around a team that finished 17 games out of first place in 1980.

Morgan was two years removed from his eight seasons of splendor with the Reds, and he had spent the previous year reunited with the Houston Astros franchise that launched his career from 1963 to 1971. That was before baseball's greatest trade ever that sent the speedy infielder with the impressive glove and the powerful bat to the Reds before the 1972 season. He left the Reds as a free agent to spend 1980 with the Astros, but even though he mentored the young Houston squad to the NL West title, he clashed with manager Bill Virdon, and he wanted out.

With encouragement from Robinson, Morgan signed a two-year deal as a free agent before the 1981 season with the Giants, but that first year was baseball's goofy split season due to a players' strike canceling 38 percent of the schedule.

The Giants didn't experience the full Joe Morgan Effect until 1982, when he pumped new life into his bat, glove, arm, and legs while also becoming the unofficial second manager in the clubhouse. Whether his audience involved teammates, reporters, Giants officials, or even Robinson and his tough-guy reputation, Morgan had no problem giving his opinion, and he did so bluntly. After all, who would dare to stop him? He had his Baseball Hall of Fame credentials with the Big Red Machine to back him up.

Morgan and I spoke often.

Actually, we spoke more than that, and our conversations were about everything surrounding the Giants, baseball, and the planet.

"You understand where I'm coming from, because you've been with me a long time," Morgan used to tell me during our sessions at his locker, in the dugout, over lunch on road trips, or through the telephone lines. I could expect four things from any Joe Morgan conversation: (1) revelations, (2) passion, (3) my notebook overflowing with quotes, and (4) language that would make grandmothers blush.

During the early summer of 1982, *Examiner* sports editor Charles Cooper called me into his office and said, "I don't want you to be blindsided by something. So I just want to let you know that the White players on the Giants are telling other writers that you only talk to the Black players, Joe Morgan in particular. I suspect these writers are telling me these things because they are jealous that Morgan is giving you so many scoops."

I appreciated Coop's honesty along with his wisdom. As he and I discussed, if I only spoke to Black players on the Giants, why were there numerous examples to the contrary, including a 3,000-word profile I did that month for the *Examiner* Sunday Magazine on Giants third baseman Darrell Evans, and he was as white as a baseball? Coop said, "All these Bay Area newspapers have White writers who mostly just talk to White players, which makes the whole thing ridiculous. I wouldn't worry about it. I just wanted to let you know."

Such was life as a Black pioneer in journalism.

During the early 1980s, it was still just Larry Whiteside of the *Boston Globe* and me as the only African Americans doing anything of significance involving Major League Baseball for major metropolitan newspapers.

The most important work of my career happened in the spring of 1982, spurred by Joe Morgan, who grew up in nearby Oakland. So did Frank Robinson, along with other future Black Major League stars of their era such as Willie Stargell and Curt Flood. That's why Morgan encouraged me to do a piece for the *Examiner* on why he and other prominent Black baseball players were convinced Major League Baseball was phasing African Americans from the playing field and other areas of the sport. Hank Aaron told me the same thing, and he worked for the Braves back then as baseball's only African American executive for a team. In addition, Hank, Joe, and others told me baseball had a quota system.

That was for starters.

With the backing of Coop, I did a month-long study that spring of 1982 on everything Morgan told me, and he was among the key figures in what became an award-winning series of five days, and nothing was off the record. I discovered that since Jackie Robinson broke the color barrier on April 15, 1947, the number of American-born Black players in the game had dropped from a peak in the late 1970s of around 27 percent to 19 percent by the spring of 1982. "If you're not looking for them, you're not going to find them," Morgan told me, saying that was the bottom line of a sport that my research showed had 568 full-time scouts overall, but only 15 of them were Black, and only full-time scouts can sign players. Fourteen of the 26 Major League teams had no full-time Black scouts.

Morgan also blasted Major League Baseball, not only for having just Aaron as the only Black executive in the game, but for having few Black people in general. "I confronted Reds president Dick Wagner about not having one Black face in the entire Reds offices. I said, 'They don't have any black people in Cincinnati who can answer the switchboard or type or know how to be secretaries?'" said Morgan, shaking his head in the spring of 1982. Then he added, giving his dire prediction for the game he loved, "This is where baseball is headed. By the next century, the number of Blacks in the game will be less than 10 percent."

He was prophetic.

More than two decades into the 21st century, the number of African American players on Major League rosters was barely 6% and dropping.

In general, Morgan kept me updated on the pulse of the 1982 Giants, and they nearly expired for the season after dropping 13 1/2 games from the NL West lead on July 30. Then they used a lot of Morgan both on and off the field to surge into contention with a September of mostly non-stop winning. The man who Reds manager Sparky Anderson told me was the most gifted cog of the Big Red Machine went from 39 years old to at least a decade younger. For the season, Morgan hit .289, which was 18 points above his career average, and he punctuated his two-year stay with the Giants by mashing one of the most famous home runs in franchise history.

First, there was the battle for the 1982 NL West title between the Giants, the Braves, and the Dodgers, but after all three were in contention inside the final week of the season, the Giants were eliminated with one game left. The Dodgers had to win in San Francisco against their archrivals on that final day to reach the playoffs over the Braves.

I was there when Morgan sent endless screams throughout Candlestick Park in the bottom of the seventh inning with a three-run homer off Dodgers' relief ace Terry Forster for the lead, and the Dodgers couldn't overcome it. After the game, I entered the visiting clubhouse with the rest of the reporters, and Forster wasn't his usual tough-guy self. He sat in the middle of the clubhouse in a chair, sobbing uncontrollably with his head bowed.

Morgan did that.

He left the Giants to spend the next season in Philadelphia, where his 1983 Phillies reached the World Series with a reunion of former Big Red Machine stars Tony Perez and Pete Rose. For me, it was a sad reunion, and not just because the Baltimore Orioles flattened the ancient Phillies in five games. Seven of the Phillies' eight regular starters were 30 years or older, including 42-year-old Rose and 40-year-old Morgan, and 41-year-old Perez played 91 games as Rose's backup at first base. My Reds guys were past their prime, although Rose would have a brief yet splendid second act as Reds player/manager, and Morgan would become the second-oldest player to homer during a World Series (a few months younger than Enos Slaughter) after his blast in Game 1 for the Phillies against the Orioles.

Even so, Morgan spent a forgettable 1984 season with the Oakland A's, and then he retired as a player after that, but he left to became one of TV's all-time best baseball analysts after working 25 years with either ESPN, ABC, or NBC.

We kept in contact throughout those decades, and our conversations never remained less than stimulating, with Morgan always remaining Morgan.

"Hey, man. If Willie was hitting under these conditions now, he'd have 800 home runs," said Morgan, shaking his head during one of our conversations in April 2000, referring to Willie Mays who finished his career after the 1973 season with 660. "Hank Aaron would have at least 150 more than his 755. Nobody gets knocked down anymore by pitchers, so you can imagine what Frank Robinson would do. I know people will say, 'Well, he's just living in the past.' The fact is that I can be objective, because I played against Aaron, Mays, and those guys, and I constantly see the great players of today. And the great players now would be good players then, and the great players then would be great players now."

Joe and I continued those kinds of baseball conversations, but our most frequent talks involved what I exposed during my 1982 series for the *San Francisco Examiner* on Blacks and baseball. Morgan was among those who continued to mention through the years that the decline of African Americans in the sport was more by design than for sociological reasons. The popularity of basketball and football in urban communities? Overdone, Morgan said, especially since he always countered with this: Basketball and football also were growing in popularity among Whites and other ethnic groups. "It's not just a Black thing," Morgan said, fuming over that and other excuses given for the decline of African Americans in baseball.

Those excuses mostly came (1) from Major League officials who often treated the matter by wringing their hands or by delivering token gestures and (2) from media folks who preferred skimming the surface of the issue instead of going deeper – deeper like my 1982 series for the *Examiner*, which featured a lot of Joe Morgan.

In April 2013, with the decline of African Americans in baseball continuing, along with those excuses from Major League Baseball and much of the media, Morgan was as exasperated as I'd ever heard him.

"It's not a dramatic drop like people keep saying. As you and I have been talking about for more than 30 years, this has been going on for a long time, and all of sudden people are acting like this is a surprise when they know better," said Morgan over the phone from his home in Danville, California, about 30 miles east of San Francisco.

At the time, around 8% of Major League players were African American, heading to below 6% over the decade after that.

"You have a better chance of getting to the Major Leagues if you're in Cuba than if you're an African American in an urban community," Morgan said, speaking nearly nonstop, and I wasn't complaining. "If you look at it, you'll see that's true. The urban kid doesn't get an opportunity to prove he can play in the Major Leagues. That's because the African American guys all have to be 5-tool players. They all have to look the same, which is 6-foot-4 and run like a deer. What happened to the Joe Morgans, like the White guys who get picked? They're not 6-4 and run like a deer, but there's a place for them. If you're a Black Joe Morgan right now, you would last a year in the Major Leagues, and then you're gone. But you have the White guys like that, and they're around for 10 years hitting around .190 or .200 all of their life. The Blacks guys are all specimens, because they have to be.

"It's always been like that. When I first got to the big leagues in 1963, one of the African American players told me, 'Joe, you look at all the benches, there's no African American guys sitting on those benches. They're either playing or they're out of here.' Even right now in the

Major Leagues. How many Black utility guys are on teams? They won't take those guys. They can't start every day, but they can contribute from the bench."

Morgan paused, which the garrulous Morgan rarely did. Since he ranked among the most emotional players I've ever covered in any sport, I imagined over the phone that his eyes were flashing with anger or filled with tears when he continued by saying, "Being blunt with you Terence, I have to tell you this: I am no longer fighting these battles. My wife asked me, 'Why do you have to be the one to say something all the time?' I've gotten to the point where, as you can see, I'm more frustrated and angry. I just said it's time for me to move on, but I don't say it to the guys, because I don't want to dishearten anybody.

"These things out there involving the lack of opportunities for Blacks in baseball, well, I'm not going to be in the forefront anymore. I fought this thing for 30 years or so, and it's time for me to relax and enjoy my life. But I got angry all over again, because I went with Hank Aaron two nights ago to watch the premiere of the Jackie Robinson movie called '42.' You get angry, because Jackie broke the color barrier as a player, but he also wanted to be a manager, and he wasn't given that opportunity. So what's going on in baseball with the lack of opportunities for Blacks isn't something that just started."

When our April 2013 conversation finally ended, so did Joe Morgan as another Jackie Robinson, at least in a highly public way.

He slid into the shadows.

Then, during the summer of 2015, which was five years after he left broadcasting to become a special adviser for the Reds, I looked at my TV screen. I saw Morgan leaving the dugout in Cincinnati at Great American Ball Park during one of those periodic celebrations by the franchise for the Big Red Machine, which was my Big Red Machine.

I gasped. The man who stole more than 50 bases in a season for the Reds five times struggled to reach the field with his cane leading the way.

Morgan suffered from Myelodysplastic syndrome, and it turned into leukemia, but he sounded like Joe when he sent a letter to me and other Baseball Hall of Fame voters during the fall of 2017. He said of

Cooperstown, "If steroid users get in, it will divide and diminish the Hall, something we couldn't bear." He was a first-ballot Baseball Hall of Fame class member of 1990, and he talked of how he had "been approached by many Hall of Fame members telling me we needed to do something to speak out about the possibility of steroid users entering the Hall of Fame. It's gotten to the point where Hall of Famers are saying that if steroid users get in, they'll no longer come to Cooperstown for induction ceremonies or other events. Some feel they can't share a stage with players who did steroids."

Morgan couldn't do it. He willed himself to greatness on primarily sweat, and he used his slight frame of 5-foot-7 and 160 pounds to become a defensive whiz at second base, a prolific base stealer and a clutch hitter with surprising pop for the Big Red Machine. As a result, he believed those who juiced in the game were insulting himself and others. He felt he had to reenter the public arena to explain as much, but he returned only for a moment. He wasn't doing well. By the fall of 2020, he was diagnosed with a non-specified polyneuropathy before dying in his northern California home on Oct. 11, 2020.

As soon as I heard the news, I headed for my bookshelf to pull out Morgan's memoir called "Joe Morgan: A Life In Baseball." Here was what Joe wrote on the inside cover: *"To Terence Moore. We have been fighting some of these battles for a long time. Enjoy! Joe Morgan #8."*

As for #14 – otherwise known as Pete Rose – my conversations through the decades weren't as heavy as those with #8, but they were riveting nonetheless, especially since #14 and I had that connection for the ages.

In 1983, when I worked for the *San Francisco Examiner*, and when the 43-year-old Rose reunited with 41-year-old Tony Perez and 40-year-old Morgan in Philadelphia, those Phillies came to Candlestick Park that August. It was a month after the Reds fired president and general manager Dick Wagner. At the time, Wagner was the most despised person in Cincinnati sports history after he swung a wrecking ball against the Big Red Machine. He axed Sparky Anderson after the 1978 season, and since he couldn't care less about free agency, he allowed Morgan to leave after the 1979 season and Rose to do the same the previous year. He later dealt Ken Griffey to the New York Yankees after the 1981 season, and he traded George Foster to the New York Mets in February 1982.

By the fall of 1983 – seven years after the back-to-back World Series championships – the only members of the Great Eight starting lineup remaining with the Reds were Dave Concepcion and Johnny Bench, and Bench was retiring.

I asked Rose around the batting cage at Candlestick Park during that afternoon in August of 1983: What if the old gang had remained together in Cincinnati from its heyday of the 1970s through the time we were speaking?

"There would have to be some changes, because a lot of us play the same position these days, like Tony Perez and myself," said Rose, pointing across the way to "Doggie," the favorite player among his Reds teammates. Then Rose looked toward Gary Redus, a Reds outfielder in his second Major League season and added, "I'm sure they'd be able to find the right combination and maybe put a guy like Redus in the outfield with Foster and Griffey. You have to have the right mixture of young guys and experience anyway. It can't be one way or the other. Right now the Reds are suffering because they're too young. If management would have made only a few changes through the years, the team would be competitive."

Instead, the 1983 Reds were headed for a last-place finish in the National League West for a second consecutive year, and the franchise that used to challenge the Los Angeles Dodgers for baseball's best attendance sat near the bottom of the NL.

Soon after Rose gave me his thoughts on Wagner's moves involving the Reds since the late 1970s, I called Sparky Anderson on a road trip with his Detroit Tigers.

I was surprised by Sparky's response.

No, I was floored.

The former Reds manager expounded on what he told me the year before around the pool in Oakland, California, and I wanted to cover my ears.

"You could have kept those guys together after those championships in 1975 and 1976, and they still wouldn't have won," said Anderson over the phone, referring to my Big Red Machine as I wondered if I dialed the wrong number. "It was over. They found out it didn't mean as much anymore. After we beat the Yankees in the 1976 World Series, I was more interested in the football season than thinking about next year. You grind it out for so long, and then you finally have no more grinding left. It happens to all great teams. That's why I think the Pittsburgh Steelers and the Montreal Canadiens were the greatest teams in professional sports history. They did it year after year. And those guys with the Reds did it for two years, which was outstanding, but they couldn't go anymore. They reached their peak."

Et tu, Sparky? No way I just heard that. With you and Pete and Joe and Tony, along with the rest of my Big Red Machine around through the mid-1980s, you guys would have remained as significant as anybody in the game. The defending world champion Cardinals of speedsters Willie McGee, David Green, and the Smiths (Ozzie and Lonnie) aren't a dynasty nor is anybody else in the game, and who's to say the Reds couldn't have gone from The Team of the '70s to the Team of the '80s?

I believed Pete more than Sparky.

Then again, I wasn't going against my all-time favorite baseball player who never forgot my name from Day One.

The only time I frowned at the sight of Pete was in May of 1984 when he came to San Francisco wearing the cartoonish uniform of the Montreal Expos. After he joined Perez and Morgan to help the Wheeze Kids of the 1983 Phillies (as opposed to the Whiz Kids of the 1950 Phillies) win a National League pennant, Rose didn't want his playing time sliced in Philadelphia, so he signed a one-year deal with the Expos, which didn't make sense. We talked in the visiting clubhouse at Candlestick Park during his Montreal stint about his milestone of collecting his 4,000th career hit the year before. But I kept thinking to myself – as I stood near his locker, seeing a pudgier Pete across his body – time to give it up, my friend, and his batting average was trending toward finishing 30, 40, 50 points below his career average.

I just couldn't stop cringing over those Expos uniforms. They were straight from the minds of something like a 3-year-old just messing around with crayons. The baseball gods were trying to tell Charlie Hustle something, and if their message wasn't for him to quit playing, then it was for him to get out of those ridiculous threads.

Bob Howsam came to the rescue.

Little did I know then that nearly a quarter of a century later, this architect of the Big Red Machine would tell me everything about *everything*, and he generally told the media nothing worth mentioning.

Anyway, Howsam agreed to leave retirement during the summer of 1983 to serve as Reds general manager again for two years, just two years, and then he said adamantly that he would return to the leisurely life he was enjoying with his wife after leaving the first time following the 1977 season. He replaced Dick Wagner, his former right-handed man whom the Reds fired for overall incompetence and the ability to alienate most folks around him. Except for the Tony Perez fiasco after the 1976 season to puncture the team's heart, Howsam had a splendid feel for making the Reds better and their fans happy.

He nailed it again in August 1984.

Not only did Howsam get Rose out of that Expos uniform, but he brought the hometown baseball hero back to Cincinnati in a trade that sent obscure infielder Tom Lawless to Montreal, and Howsam named Rose player-manager.

Just like that, Rose looked better, and he hit better with a .365 average during the 26 games he played for the Reds as opposed to .259 in 95 games with the Expos.

As the baseball gods would have it, Rose came to San Francisco in September of 1984 during his second month in charge of the Reds, and I chatted with him in the visiting dugout at Candlestick Park. Since somebody snapped a photo, I was blessed with yet another Terry-Pete moment captured for posterity. Earlier, I sat with Rose in the visiting manager's office when he put his name on the lineup card in the second slot at first base. It worked. He went 3-for-5 that Tuesday night of Sept. 4, and his Reds won 8-3 over the Giants.

That was just a preview of Rose's mystical run toward Ty Cobb's all-time career hits record.

I left the *San Francisco Examiner* at the start of 1985 to take a sports columnist job with the *Atlanta Journal-Constitution*, and I later had a dream assignment. Starting on Friday, Sept. 6, in Chicago, I was going to follow Rose until he surpassed Cobb's mark, either that weekend at Wrigley Field, or surely after the Reds returned to Cincinnati that Monday to begin a 10-game homestand against the San Diego Padres, Los Angeles Dodgers, and San Francisco Giants. He started that Cubs series with 4,187 career hits to trail Cobb by four. Rose held massive press conferences before each of those games in Chicago, and despite it all, he still made eye contact with me as if we were in a one-on-one setting.

That Sunday, with Rose chipping away enough against Cubs pitching to sit a hit away from tying Cobb's record, I spoke with Reds shortstop Dave Concepcion, among my favorite Big Red Machine guys to interview during my *Cincinnati Enquirer* days. He occasionally gave me one of those soul handshakes from the 1960s before declaring himself a "brother," as in African American. We chatted during Reds batting practice at Wrigley Field, and he frowned, saying as he studied the stands, "Looks like it's going to be packed. I can remember when Pete spiked Ernie Banks on a play here a long time ago, and they had to have police protection for Pete after the game. This can be a rough place, especially on a hot day."

The temperature rose steadily from the mid-80s, and Concepcion glanced some more at the crowd before adding, "That's why I think it might be a riot when Pete does what he has to do today. If he gets a hit, he has to take himself out of the game."

Yeah, but this was my guy Pete Rose, which meant he stayed in the game. He wasn't going anywhere after he ripped a single to right field in the fifth inning to tie the 57-year-old record of Tyrus Ramond Cobb, and for maybe the first time ever, Wrigley Field fans went bonkers for a baseball player not wearing a Cubs uniform. Of all people, they were celebrating Pete Rose, now the people's choice, even for the Bleacher Bums.

After a two-hour rain delay, Rose batted in the top of the ninth with a chance to break Cobb's record, and some of those same folks who used to spend previous seasons hurling bottles, coins, and other stuff at Rose in the outfield were likely among those standing as one chanting, "Let's go Pete" at the top of their lungs. It was surrealistic, especially since I saw more of the traditional Bleacher Bums (as in not good) toward opponents during my decade coming to Wrigley Field as either a fan or a reporter.

Nevertheless, Rose struck out, but not on purpose.

The baseball gods just wanted Charlie Hustle to break the record in Cincinnati, where he was born on April 14, 1941. Where he played baseball as a kid on Bold Face Park, just a bend around the Ohio River from downtown Cincinnati. Where he played as a youth in the Knothole League – just like I did. Where growing up, he attended Reds games at Crosley Field – 6.7 miles away from his house – just like I did.

And where on Wednesday, Sept. 11, 1985, on the most beautiful fall night you'll ever see along the Ohio River, he was back in Riverfront Stadium.

And I was there.

Of course I was, and since I was now an established journalist in a Riverfront Stadium press box filled with them, I used every bit of my strength to resist the urge to resurrect my time as a fan at The Water Pipe in Milwaukee when Rose wasted little time in the bottom of the first inning, sending a 2-2 pitch from Eric Show of the San Diego Padres into left-center field for a single.

It was the Ty-breaking 4,192nd hit of Rose's career, and as he received a seven-minute standing ovation, he used his white batting glove as tissue paper at first base.

"I've never seen him cry before. Never, never, never," Tony Perez told me, and Perez was back with the Reds that season as a reserve player. Rose eventually sobbed on the shoulder of Tommy Helms, his first base coach standing nearby and the original second baseman of the Big Red Machine in the early 1970s. Rose said he kept imagining his father, Harry, looking down from heaven at the lovefest for the prodigal son, and at one point while standing on first in the midst of the cheering, Rose pointed toward the sky.

The game ended at 10:07 p.m., but between postgame interviews and Rose's first meal since breakfast at a downtown restaurant, he said he didn't reach home until 4 a.m. He didn't sleep then. In fact, he never headed to bed, because he was off to Riverfront Coliseum to tape the nationally televised Phil Donahue Show, and I also was there. More than 6,000 folks stood inside while chanting, "Pete, Pete, Pete," and that was 30 minutes before the taping. When Rose took the stage, he received a two-minute standing ovation, and then the man of the moment said with a look of surprise, "All I got was a little base hit."

Exactly a week after Rose broke Cobb's record, he and the Reds came to Atlanta, where I was in my first year with the *Atlanta Journal-Constitution*, and I knew what I had to do. I had to have baseball's recently crowned hits leader sign my mounted poster of his younger self. I bought that one and a Hank Aaron one at the same time during my early teenage years, and even though I placed them on walls of my various homes over the years and of dorm rooms around Miami University in Oxford, Ohio, I kept both posters in pristine condition.

I got to Atlanta-Fulton County Stadium earlier than early on that September afternoon, and Rose was already there, sitting in the visiting manager's office, greeting me with his sparkling eyes. I placed the poster on his desk, and he stood up and hovered over it like a father viewing his newborn for the first time. "Do you want to sell it?" he said, and I quickly said no. Not even my guy Pete Rose was getting my Pete Rose poster, and after he grabbed a black marker, he signed it, "Pete Rose, 9-18-85."

It was a another Terry-Pete moment designed by the baseball gods, but I had several more to go before his death at 83 on Sept. 30, 2024. For instance: In late February 1989, I was still a columnist for the *Atlanta Journal-Constitution*, and I took a break from visiting the Braves at their spring training site in West Palm Beach, Florida, to drive up toward the middle of the state to visit my Aunt Lorene and Uncle Holmes at their long-time home in Plant City. It just so happened the Reds had moved their spring training site from Tampa to Plant City the year before, and it was two blocks from the front lawn of my aunt and uncle.

Ah, those baseball gods never sleep.

I walked over to visit Rose, because there was a report that he had just arrived back in town from flying to New York for a visit to the commissioner's office.

Something about gambling.

When I asked Rose about it, he eased from the chair in his office at the Reds' training facility and closed the door. "Terry, I did go to New York, but it had nothing to do with what they say it was about," said Rose, staring at me without blinking, suggesting with his body language that I should switch topics to the Reds' chances for the 1989 pennant, Plant City's annual strawberry festival, or anything involving my Big Red Machine. But I needed to remain the reporter, and I asked the same question in a different way. *So you're saying your discussion with the commissioner had nothing to do with gambling?*

"No," said Rose, which wasn't true. In New York, he joined two of his lawyers for a session with Baseball Commissioner Peter Ueberroth and National League president Bart Giamatti, Ueberroth's successor soon afterward. During that meeting, the two baseball officials mentioned allegations of Rose betting on baseball games. He always admitted to gambling on horse racing and other sports, but he claimed that was it.

Like everybody else, Rose knew the sin of all sins among Major Leaguers since the 1919 Black Sox Scandal was betting on baseball, period. So he told me, "No," about whether those baseball officials asked him about his gambling habits. But by April of 1989, the IRS seized betting slips carrying his name and fingerprints. Then in early May, baseball released a 225-page summary of his baseball gambling habits called the "Dowd Report" by John Dowd. Either the highlight or the lowlight of the report involved a day-by-day rundown of Rose's 1987 betting that included 52 Reds games. He retired as an active player in November 1986, but he remained with the Reds as manager until late August of 1989.

Throughout the summer, the Rose gambling revelations kept coming, and then I got word like everybody else on the morning of Thursday, Aug. 24, 1989, that Bart Giamatti used his first official act as commissioner to place Rose on baseball's ineligible list. That was a fancy way of saying Peter Edward Rose got a lifetime ban. Even though he could appeal the decision in a year, his hopes of a reprieve ranged between slim and forget about it.

I was in Chicago for the *Atlanta Journal-Constitution* when I discovered Rose planned his own press conference that morning at Riverfront Stadium, and I got the OK from the paper to rush for a flight out of O'Hare Field for Cincinnati. I arrived at the ballpark early enough for a front-row seat in a conference room on the ground level. With national TV cameras rolling live from all the major networks, Rose walked past me to the nearby podium. The following year, he wrote one of his several memoirs, and for that one called, "Pete Rose: My Story," I stood in a bookstore, flipping through the pages. When I got to the photo section, the last one showed me prominently at that Riverfront Stadium press conference in August of 1989. I was just a few feet away from Rose, who stared into cameras to his right. He said a lot of things, but the main thing he said that morning was, "I did not bet on baseball."

That remained Rose's mantra through his five months in 1990 in a federal prison for falsifying his income tax returns, and he continued his mantra the following year when the Baseball Hall of Fame board of directors voted unanimously to keep him – and anyone else on baseball's ineligible list – off future ballots. The 1991 ballot would have been his first year of eligibility for Cooperstown, and get this: That was the second year I voted for Baseball Hall of Famers as a 10-plus year member of the Baseball Writers' Association of America (BBWAA), so I would have had the chance to vote for my guy Pete Rose.

I would have declined. I was still perturbed that Rose had lied to me that he didn't meet with the commissioner about gambling when he did. Mostly, he refused to say for years that he gambled on baseball when his fingerprints on betting slips said otherwise. The primary qualifications listed for voters on Hall of Fame ballots say you must consider the "character" and the "integrity" of the player, which meant betting on baseball was one thing, but refusing to admit it was worse since it clearly showed a lack of "character" and of "integrity."

With Rose on baseball's permanently banned list, he never appeared on one of my BBWAA's ballots, but if he did, I eventually would have voted for him.

I began to change my mind before the start of the 21st century, and it went back to something from the previous one. I was there (of course, I was) to experience the emotional moment for Rose and his fans in Atlanta before Game 2 of the 1999 World Series between the Braves and the Yankees. He was chosen by a panel of experts as an outfielder for the Major League Baseball All-Century Team, and the Turner Field crowd roared the loudest for baseball's permanently banned career hits leader when the players were introduced. I could feel myself moving from "no way" to "maybe" regarding Rose in the Hall of Fame.

OK, he did have all those hits, and he did treat each game as if it were Game 7 of the World Series, and he did tell me during the 1980s that he played in more winning games than any professional athlete in history, and unlike others, he didn't use steroids, which enhanced a guy's playing ability.

And then something else happened.

In June 2004, Rose sort of came clean. He did so in yet another book, and this one was called "My Prison Without Bars." Beyond that, he expounded on his admissions about gambling through national TV appearances, and even though baseball investigator John Dowd and others disputed some of his gambling claims, Rose's candidacy for Cooperstown finally was just fine with me. I couldn't care less about the tawdry stuff in Dowd's report involving Rose and his sex life, because "tawdry" could have been the middle name of many folks either already in the Baseball Hall of Fame or on the way.

My redemptive thoughts for Rose continued after a *Cincinnati Enquirer* reporter wrote in September 2010 that Rose cried before some of his Big Red Machine teammates during a 25th anniversary celebration of his record-breaking 4,192nd hit at a casino in Lawrenceburg, Indiana, across the river from Cincinnati. According to the reporter, Rose told the crowd that he "disrespected baseball," which he did, but despite his many attempts to get out of the game's slammer by confessing his sins in public (well, at least some of them), all the subsequent baseball commissioners said no. That included Bud Selig, who oversaw the game from 1998 to 2015. I knew Selig through Hank Aaron, a close friend of mine, and Aaron was pals with Selig from Aaron's time in Milwaukee with the Braves from the early 1950s to the mid-1960s. Selig told me on several occasions he had no plans of ever reinstating Rose. I didn't know Rob Manfred who followed Selig, but Manfred also heard Rose's requests through the years, and he also yawned before moving on with the rest of his life.

Not coincidently, eight months after Rose died, Manfred removed Rose and others from baseball's permanently banned list. That made Rose eligible for Hall of Fame election through one of the special veteran committees of the game.

I was peeved.

It should have happened when my guy was living.

When I worked for MLB.com in the 2010s, I wanted Rose's expertise for columns here and there, and I occasionally phoned him in Las Vegas, where he signed autographs at various casinos. He also made a yearly trip to Cooperstown during Induction Weekend for Baseball Hall of Famers to sign autographs on Main Street as a reminder to everybody that the all-time hits leader was without a bronzed plaque in the famous building down the street.

Then came that fall of 2015, when Pete Rose spent an afternoon and evening in Oxford, Ohio, where I graduated from Miami University and served as a visiting professor in the journalism department. We hadn't seen each other in a while, and after he finished his chat with a group of students before his big event later that day, we took a photo together (see the back cover of this book).

Of course, we did.

"I've got something to show you," I told Rose as he eased into a smile, even before I completed the search on my cell phone. It was the black-and-white photo from May of 1978 when he sat in the corner of the dugout at Riverfront Stadium with his bowl haircut, and I stood nearby with an Afro conducting my first interview ever as a professional sports journalist while working for *The Cincinnati Enquirer*. In that photo, I was just eight days removed from my college graduation up the road from the ballpark, and I kept trying not to shake too much before my all-time favorite baseball player and the leader of my Big Red Machine.

As Rose enlarged the photo on my I-Phone with his fingers, his smile grew as he studied the younger and slimmer version of himself, and then with his sparkling eyes, he looked at me, saying, "So, Terry. We both have come a long way, haven't we?"

Yes, indeed.

CHAPTER 11

The Call

This was among the greatest flukes of my life. Somehow, when Antonio Davis lost his mind in January of 2006 while playing for the New York Knicks and sprinted into the stands at the United Center in Chicago toward what he said was an intoxicated fan, it led me to Bob Howsam, the architect of the Big Red Machine, and he told me everything.

I mean, *everything*.

According to Mary Brennaman, who spent 46 years – 1974 through 2019 – as the Baseball Hall of Fame announcer for the Cincinnati Reds, "70 percent" of what Howsam told me in January of 2006 had never been uttered before in public by the usually tight-lipped Reds official, but for me, he revealed sensational things, wonderful things, incredible things, and disturbing things regarding the greatest team in the history of Major League Baseball.

As I listened to Howsam for the first time in nearly two decades, my jaw dropped. That was either before or after my eyes bulged and my heart raced like crazy when he discussed:

- the firing of manager Sparky Anderson by his "overbearing" right-hand man who succeeded him as the Reds' primary decision maker
- Pete Rose and his flirtation with death through gambling
- the particulars on why trading Tony Perez "was the worst mistake I ever made in baseball"
- how he nearly made a deal that might have kept The Trade of Joe Morgan from happening

- the inside story on how he got George Foster by accident

Oh, and so much more.

Until I began research for this book, I forgot I conducted that Howsam interview way back in January of 2006, and then I remembered I saved the recording. I searched through nearly a dugout full of boxes in my Atlanta basement before I found it.

Wow.

I heard Howsam keep going and going and going, delivering those revelations throughout our 75-minute phone call, but except for the original reason I called (Antonio Davis), I never wrote about his Big Red Machine remarks. I was an *Atlanta Journal-Constitution* columnist at the time, and Reds talk didn't fit my Braves country audience. Even so, I said to myself, *I'm sure I can deliver Howsam's words to the public in a future capacity, so I'll just save the recording.*

That *future capacity* manifested itself through this book, and here was the wonderfully bizarre part of this: Prior to my telephone conversation with Howsam, we had never met. When I was an intern at *The Cincinnati Enquirer* in 1977, which was his last season before he retired as general manager of the Reds after a decade of excellence (well, minus the Tony Perez blunder), I saw Howsam only a few times, and that was from a distance at Riverfront Stadium in Cincinnati. Even though he left retirement during the summer of 1983 to resume his old GM role after the Reds fired Dick Wagner, his successor and former right-hand man, he stressed his return was temporary. He said he would stay for two years – exactly two years – before resuming his life with Arizona sunshine, and he did just that. He thrilled Reds fans by bringing Rose back to Cincinnati as player-manager during the fall of 1984, but his legacy came during his first stint with the Reds.

Which brought me to Howsam in January of 2006.

Our conversation happened days after Antonio Davis made national headlines after he said he saw his wife getting attacked physically and verbally in Chicago by a spectator whom Davis claimed was more than a bit tipsy during his Knicks' road game against the Bulls. He decided to race into the crowd, but the NBA wasn't amused. He was suspended five games, and as an *Atlanta Journal-Constitution* columnist at the time, I wanted to write about the absurdity of Davis's actions, especially since I believed it could trigger an epidemic of players throughout sports doing the same.

In the past, crowds were nastier than that Chicago situation, but opposing players resisted dashing into the stands. I thought of October 1973 when my Big Red Machine lost the fifth and decisive game of the National League Championship Series at New York's Shea Stadium, and the Reds traveling party was attacked behind the visitors' dugout by Mets fans. I remembered Howsam was among the potential victims, and I had an idea.

Where is Bob Howsam, and would he talk about October of 1973? Would he talk about anything since I remember his mostly reclusive reputation with the media?

Somehow, I tracked down the 87-year-old former sports executive living in a retirement home in Sun City, Arizona, with his wife, Janet. After some opening chitchat – about how I followed the Reds religiously during the late 1960s and throughout the 1970s, and about how I owned strong ties to southwestern Ohio, and about how I used to work for *The Cincinnati Enquirer* doing Reds coverage, and about how I always was fascinated with the inner workings of the Big Red Machine – he opened up about everything with little prompting.

First, there was Antonio Davis, the impetus for my call to Howsam, who was an accomplished sports executive and entrepreneur beyond his couple of stints with the Reds. We discussed the implications of the Davis explosion on the current sports environment, and then we returned to that near riot at Shea Stadium in October of 1973. After the Mets clinched a trip that day to the World Series as heavy underdogs, a growing mob in the stands forced Howsam and other members of the Reds entourage to scramble from their seats toward the railing near the visitors' dugout, and with help from Reds players, they jumped into the dugout for safety.

Howsam still fumed over the memory.

"The thing that really disturbed us was that there were some policemen in the dugout, three or four New York policemen, and we asked them to protect our people, and you know what they said?" Howsam asked before he responded quickly to his own question. "They said, 'We're here to protect the bats.' That's exactly what they said. That's when our players came out of the dugout to help our people get out of the stands. Anyway, we got the people out, and we put them into our bus, and when we got out of the stadium, we had a bunch of kids, maybe high school kids, trying to tip the bus over. So that was our experience. I'm just telling you.

"I wrote a letter to the mayor of New York, and he was very popular there," Howsam continued, referring to John Lindsay. "I wrote him a letter and called it, 'My darkest day of baseball,' and I also wrote a letter to the president of the Mets about it, and Lindsay didn't even answer, and, of course, I pointed out what his police had said about protecting the bats rather than protecting the people. I've never had a great feeling toward New York since then."

Howsam was just warming up. Triggered by those 1973 NLCS horrors for the Reds' traveling party at Shea Stadium, he said some of his baseball peers wanted every Major League stadium to add a separate area only for wives and family members, basically to create their own little world during games. He said he was against it. He thought about his days owning a Minor League franchise in Colorado from the late 1940s through the early 1960s before he later served as the founder of the Denver Broncos and a co-founder of the American Football League. "I've seen teams have a section like that during those Minor League days, and the wives began screaming at each other," Howsam said, chuckling. "So you have to watch that. We had places for the wives, but we were very careful who we sat together. Let's put it that way."

Then the fun began. I wanted to ask Howsam about my Big Red Machine, but where to start, and how to stop? We returned to January of 1967 when he came to the Reds from the Cardinals after building three pennant-winning teams during the 1960s in St. Louis, including two world champions. I wanted to jump to The Trade with the Reds when he stunned the senses after the 1971 season by shipping the right side of the Big Red Machine (first baseman Lee May and Tommy Helms) to the Houston Astros for players who would help fuel the Reds through the rest of the decade (pitcher Jack Billingham, center fielder Cesar Geronimo, infielder Denis Menke, utility player Ed Armbrister, and second baseman Joe Morgan).

Instead, Howsam delivered the first of his many revelations when he said he tried to make a significant move after the Reds were crushed in the 1970 World Series by the "maturity and the veteran players" of the Baltimore Orioles.

"We were a very fine young team at that time, but we didn't have any maturity, so after we lost to the Orioles, I tried to get an older first baseman who I felt had been into the World Series," said Howsam, referring to Ron Fairly who was in World Series play for the Dodgers in 1959, 1963, 1965, and 1966. The left-handed thrower and hitter fluctuated between first base and the outfield during his dozen years with the Dodgers, but he was mostly at first for the Montreal Expos in 1970 when Howsam said he contemplated bringing the 32-year-old veteran to Cincinnati. I thought about this later: *If Howsam would have traded for Fairly, a line-drive hitter with limited power, what would have happened to Lee May, the Big Bopper from Birmingham, since they both played first?*

That was Bob Howsam, though. So if he acquired Ron Fairly before the 1971 season, he wasn't thinking about checkers for the Big Red Machine.

He had a chess move in there somewhere.

Even before Howsam left St. Louis for Cincinnati in January 1967, he reached baseball genius status with the Cardinals. Take his Orlando Cepeda trade, which made sense only to himself, especially since Cepeda damaged his knee so badly with the San Francisco Giants that doctors told the first baseman to retire. Howsam ignored those medical reports weeks into the 1966 season, and he swapped Cardinals reliever Ray Sadecki for Cepeda. That first year in St. Louis, Cepeda won NL Comeback Player of the Year honors, and the next year, he was named NL Most Valuable Player while leading the Cardinals to a world championship.

Ron Fairly could have been the Reds' Orlando Cepeda, or maybe Howsam could have suffered his only major flop besides the Tony Perez fiasco. But here's what we knew for sure: With Lee May gone before the 1972 season, the Reds made several chess moves. They switched Tony Perez from third to first to replace May after Joe Morgan and those other pieces arrived from Houston, and then there was more juggling by manager Sparky Anderson. Before long, the Reds recovered from their 1971 drop to fourth place in the National League West to reach the 1972 World Series against the Oakland A's, and even though they lost in seven games, it was an improvement over the 1970 Orioles smashing the Big Red Machine in five games.

"They beat us pretty good, Baltimore, as you know, but then in 1972 when we played the Oakland club, I thought that was when we were coming into our own, and I thought we had a good chance to beat them," said Howsam, preparing for another revelation. This one involved George Foster, the 1977 NL Most Valuable Player for the Reds, who also grabbed two league home run titles and made five trips to the All-Star Game. When Howsam traded nothing worth mentioning to the Giants for Foster after the start of the 1971 season, Foster was barely a fourth outfielder in San Francisco after he spent the three previous years in the Giants' farm system. According to Howsam, Foster was easy to overlook back then, because that was exactly what Howsam did until he studied him closely during an entire Minor League game.

"Quite frankly, Foster hadn't played a lot of baseball, and he was down at AAA ball in Phoenix for the Giants, and I'll never forget I went out there to look at another guy, a center fielder by the name of Williams, but after watching the game, I thought I wanted to get George Foster," said Howsam, who wasn't referring to the Bernie Williams who later starred for the New York Yankees. That other Bernie Williams never made it out of the Minor Leagues while George Foster became the left fielder for the Great Eight starting lineup of the Big Red Machine.

"Yes," Howsam said on the other end of the phone, where I could envision him puffing out his chest for just a moment, "that was a good trade, and it worked out very well."

Yes, it did. The same went for the Cesar Geronimo portion of the Reds' trade with the Astros before the 1972 season. He went from barely playing during his three years in Houston to becoming an everyday contributor in Cincinnati. In addition, this was another one of those chess moves for Howsam and the Reds. Whereas the Astros kept Geronimo at the corner positions in the outfield, the Reds figured they could switch the left-handed hitter and thrower from mostly right field in 1972 to center field for the rest of the decade.

The man called "The Chief" by his Reds teammates won four consecutive Gold Gloves through 1977, which was no surprise to Howsam for an interesting reason. "You know, since you're a baseball fan, I'm going to tell you something that people didn't realize,' Howsam said, with a little chuckle. "A normal person has a stride of about 7 ½ feet, and Geronimo had one of 9 feet, so every time he took a step, he was already a foot and a half farther than the normal person would be, and he had that outstanding arm. So I used to watch Geromino glide along out there in the outfield to make it so easy for George Foster (in left) and Ken Griffey (in right) fielding their positions because he did it all. Geronimo was one of the finest ballplayers, and he didn't get as much credit as he deserved. But when you're on a team like that where everybody is just about a star, or two or three stars, it's tough to get it."

From there, Howsam rattled off the names of the Great Eight – catcher Johnny Bench, first baseman Tony Perez, second baseman Joe Morgan, shortstop Dave Concepcion, third baseman Pete Rose, left fielder George Foster, center fielder Cesar Geronimo, and right fielder Ken Griffey Sr. Then he mentioned a game he invented years before, and he said he still played it after he grabs his remote at his retirement home during the Major League season.

He laughed, saying, "What I do now when I watch a ballgame, quite frankly, I compare them (on the screen to the Great Eight), and I ask, 'Would I like that particular player?' I wonder if he could replace anybody on the Big Red Machine. In all the time I've done that, I don't think I've seen hardly anybody who could do that in all of the times I've watched. We had a wonderful squad. I've always said that you don't win unless your team is balanced, and that includes all the different areas of fielding, running, and throwing. The one thing I learned from (Branch

Rickey, the Baseball Hall of Fame executive who signed Jackie Robinson and who became one of Howsam's mentors) was the same thing I learned from George Weiss, who was the general manager of the New York Yankees (during the late 1940s through the 1950s, producing the likes of Mickey Mantle, Yogi Berra, and Whitey Ford). Balance your ballclub.

"Both of them did it differently. Rickey did it through his own eyesight, and Weiss did it through his scouts, and those were good lessons for me since I had the opportunity to work with both of them. I used all those things I learned from them, and I tied them into what I thought, and it worked. You have to have a little luck to go with it, but as Mr. Rickey told me, 'Luck is the residue of hard work,' and that's the truth when you come right down to it. With the Big Red Machine, we had great fans, too. We had it all at that time. A good stadium to watch a ballgame in and different things. When you get to my age, memories have so much to do with enjoying life, and the nice thing about it, the memories that you remember are the good memories."

That was mostly true on this day for Howsam, laughing again while thinking about "one of the nicest things to happen to me." For decades, stretching back to his time with his Minor League team in Colorado during the late 1940s, he had this self-imposed rule for himself when it came to his manager, coaches, and players: Stay away from the clubhouse. That didn't change during his Big Red Machine days until he was approached one day during the early 1970s by Joe Morgan and Johnny Bench. As Howsam remembered it: "They came up to me and said, 'You know, you never come down to our dressing room, and I said, 'Well, I look at your dressing room as your second home. In other words, you're away from home, so the dressing room becomes your home. That's where you get your mail. That's where you answer letters. That's where you really work with the other players.'"

Howsam didn't want to let that memory go. Those words from Morgan and Bench back then were huge in his mind. Finally, he added with a hint of authoritarianism in his voice, "As you know, we never let our players play cards or things of that nature (within the team environment). But Morgan and Bench said, 'We'd like to have you come down.' So I said, 'OK, I'll come down and visit, but then I'll go back upstairs to the office."

Even with that endorsement from Morgan and Bench, Howsam said he never entered the Reds' "dressing room" without first calling Sparky Anderson, and he said the manager always said yes, and he added the players never shunned the boss of their boss. "I didn't want them to think that I was looking to hear this or that, or trying to find out other things," Howsam said. "So I would go down when that time was agreed upon, and I would go around to all of the dressing areas, and if I thought somebody wasn't doing as well as he could, I might give him a needle, and then just walk on. I'll never forget that somebody was having a back problem, and I had a lot of exercises on back problems, so I got down on the floor and showed him what exercises he could use. I also used to always go into the trainer's room, and if somebody was in there, I'd give them a jab. I did that every day, and that was my visit, and I just appreciated them wanting me to come instead of saying, 'I wish that sonavagun wasn't always around.' Those were good memories."

After Howsam mentioned that Sparky was retired in Thousand Oaks, California, and that he spoke to the former Reds manager "every three weeks," I told Howsam I wanted to get back to his thoughts on Sparky, but I wanted to start with Dave Bristol who proceeded Sparky as manager. I told Howsam that I wrote for the *San Francisco Examiner* when Bristol managed the San Francisco Giants. I mentioned that Bristol always thought that he shouldn't have been fired by Howsam after the 1969 season and that he was convinced that he would have done exactly what Sparky did with the Big Red Machine during the 1970s by producing two world championships, four National League pennants, and five division titles.

"I wouldn't have fired Dave if I thought he could do what Sparky did," Howsam said. "You know managers, quite frankly, reach their peak, even in the Minor Leagues. It was the same way with Bristol, to me, at least. He had some of those guys in the Minor Leagues like Perez and others, but the thing was, I never will ever feel I did wrong with Dave Bristol.

He got to the place where he was not going to advance our club any further, and that's why I let him go, and I know Dave never did like that. I'm sorry that he didn't, but you have to do what you think is right, and the day that a general manager doesn't do what he thinks he should do is the day that a general manager is not going to be a good general manager."

Then came Sparky.

Howsam chuckled, saying, "I don't know if you know, but I hired Sparky (for our Minor League system) when I was still with the St. Louis Cardinals. I asked the vice president of the Dodgers who was a good friend of mine – and I respected the Dodgers very much, because they were such a good organization, and I think they did things right, fundamentally and all of the different things. Anyway, I asked this vice president if he knew anybody who could be a manager for us in A ball. He said no, but the next day he called, and he said, 'Hey, do you know that little second baseman who played in (Class A) Pueblo (Colorado)?' And I said, 'Yeah, I remember him. He couldn't hit, but he was a feisty guy.' And my friend with the Dodgers said, 'He's not in baseball anymore, and he's selling cars in a used-car lot out here in Los Angeles.'

"So I called Chief Bender (Sheldon "Chief" Bender who was Howsam's top baseball mind in St. Louis and Cincinnati), and I said I wanted him to check out Sparky Anderson to see if he would manage our A club with the Cardinals, and Chief said, 'Oh, you don't want him. He's always getting after the umpires, and he's always in trouble.' I told Chief, 'Well, I want him. I think his recommendation from my friend with the Dodgers is of such strength that I think he'll be a good manager.'"

Later, when Howsam ran the Reds, he needed Bristol's replacement during the winter of 1969, and he remembered Anderson, who went from winning pennants consistently during his four years as a Minor League manager in the Cardinals and the Reds organizations to spending 1969 as the third-base coach during the first year of the San Diego Padres. After that season, the California Angels hired Sparky for their coaching staff, but Howsam had something better for the 35-year-old George Anderson who got his nickname due to his fiery reputation.

"One time as a manager in the Minor Leagues, Sparky got into a wrestling match with an umpire, and I just read that recently, but the reason why I hired him is because, in all of our meetings, he was a person you felt had something special when it came to handling ballplayers, and he had very good work habits as all of our people did," said Howsam, referring to his observations in the yearly sessions he conducted with managers, coaches, and officials throughout the Reds organization. "Sparky stood out. He wasn't afraid to speak up in a crowd, and I always told my people, 'I didn't hire you to be yes people. I can get all of the yes people that I want. Say your piece, but once we decide in this room what we're going to do, don't ever let me hear anybody walk out of this room and second guess what we've done in that office.' We never had a bit of problem."

Howsam laughed before he mentioned the headline on the front page of the *Cincinnati* (and he always pronounced the city as "Cincinnatuh") *Post* after he hired Anderson as Reds manager, and the gigantic letters screamed: "Sparky Who?"

Folks discovered Sparky's worth in a hurry.

Which made this ridiculous: After the Reds finished second for two consecutive years through 1978 following back-to-back world championships, Howsam's successor, Dick Wagner, did the unthinkable, at least when it came to those of us who worshipped the Big Red Machine and its dynamic leader. He fired Anderson in November of 1978 for the vaguest of reasons. They ranged in public comments or through general whispers from "Sparky was just a push-button manager" to "anybody can finish second when the Reds are all about winning titles" to Sparky refused to follow Wagner's edict to make changes in his coaching staff to Wagner was secretly working with either the devil or the Dodgers, which was the same thing for those of who hugged the Big Red Machine.

When Wagner whacked Sparky, Howsam was finishing his first year of retirement, and he said he was blindsided as much as everybody else.

"Well, Dick worked for me, and he was an extremely outstanding guy to have working with you. The problem it turned out for Dick, you know, it's a difference between having responsibility at the top and having responsibility at your job," Howsam said. "He was outstanding as far as a second man helping me and doing things and coming in with information and keeping me informed about what was going on all the time. He was a very good reader of things. Your job is now different, quite frankly, than it used to be (when you weren't) general manager. To me, there are no general managers in baseball anymore. To be a general manager, you have to take and oversee a whole stadium, the operation, even the ground crew. You have to see about the concessions. You have to have a hand in everything. You're not doing the things, but you want reports on them, to make sure they're going right, and you might make a suggestion on something, and you have people who can carry out those responsibilities. But when you gave Dick the responsibility of yes or no, he then became, I guess, too overbearing. He wanted to force things."

Howsam paused, then he said, "See, when Sparky was fired, Sparky thought I had something to do with it, because (Reds owner Louis Nippert) had me as his consultant to represent him at the league meetings and everything. Sparky didn't realize that I had no involvement with his firing until I sat down and really visited with him about it. But Dick called me about it (before Sparky was fired), and he said, 'What do you think about changing the manager?' and I said, 'Well, the only thing I'm going to say, Dick, is that you and your manager have to get along,' and I said, 'If you can't, then you're not a good team.'"

After a little chuckle, Howsam said, "And, by gosh, he got rid of Sparky, and I was told that John McNamara was flying in from managing in winter ball. I didn't even know he was going to be hired. I hardly even knew him, but Sparky always felt there for a while that I had something to do with it, but I did not at all."

I told Howsam I was in *The Cincinnati Enquirer* newsroom that day in November of 1978 when we were told "Sparky is gone," and I mentioned it felt like a nuclear bomb had exploded throughout southwestern Ohio. Howsam said, "Well, it surprised everybody. In fact, when Dick worked under me, he used to say every once in a while, 'You know, you should get rid of one of the coaches to show them that they're just not here and having a job.' He always felt you had to do something like that to make people realize that he was running the show, and, of course, that got him in trouble."

OK, about Tony Perez. As ruthless as Wagner was, he had nothing to do with the Reds doing the absurd after they swept the Yankees during the 1976 World Series following their seven-game squeaker the previous year over the Boston Red Sox. With Howsam leading the way, the Reds dropped coal into our stockings as Big Red Machine fans nine days before Christmas when they shipped Perez, his clutch bat, and his irreplaceable leadership to the Montreal Expos for pitchers Woodie Fryman and Dale Murray. The Reds also threw reliever Will McEnany into the deal, but the horror of it all involved Perez, the most universally loved player in the clubhouse.

With all due respect, Mr. Howsam.
What in the name of lunacy was that all about?

"This, I admit, was a terrible mistake, the worst mistake I ever really made in baseball, and I think it cost the Reds being in the 1977 World Series, where we might have won three in a row," said Howsam, without hesitation over the phone. He kept going and going, almost as a way of cleansing his soul from his Big Red Machine sin.

"I really feel that way, because the thing that Perez had that, frankly, I underestimated but I knew was there was the chemistry in the clubhouse," Howsam continued. "It was a tremendously important piece to our clubhouse, and that's because Perez wasn't afraid to stand up and grab a guy by the collar and say what was needed to be said to him, you know. But the reason he was traded, quite frankly, is because Danny Driessen and Tony were going to compete for the job at first base, and Perez came to me, well, he said he wanted to play regularly. Because I had so much respect for Perez and his family, I wanted to help him, and instead of doing what I should have done – and this is the only time that I ever second-guessed myself – and I should have said, 'Well, Tony. You're a part of this team, and you and Driessen are just going to have to fight it out, and whoever doesn't win it is going to have to sit on the bench.'

"I really think the two of them would have forced each other to play very well. One could run really well and was a fairly good hitter. Perez was a great RBI man. Oh, boy. If that would have been done with the two of them in competition, I really believe we would have gone into the World Series in 1977, but, anyway, feeling like I did, I looked around, and I saw where he could play regularly at Montreal, and I traded him to Montreal, and it was a terrible trade. It could have cost us a pennant and a world championship. I even said it to the papers, because it was the truth, and the truth is always the best thing to say."

After another pause, Howsam searched for the right words, and then he found them: "You know, sometimes you think you're getting older and wiser, but that was stupid me."

He laughed.

"Do you remember Big Klu?" said Howsam, easing into a different subject, and I said, "Yes," because his reference was to Ted Kluszewski, the beloved slugger of the Reds during the 1950s before he eventually became the batting coach of the Big Red Machine. Klu and I spoke occasionally when I worked for the *Enquirer*, but the conversations weren't long. There wasn't much reason to speak to the batting coach back then when Rose, Bench, Morgan, and the rest of The Great Eight were their own batting coaches during the season.

Howsam laughed again, saying of Kluszewski, "Don't get him mad. I used to get so tickled in meetings, because they would tell these Polish jokes, and the hair in the back of his neck would kind of stand up. But I'll tell you what. He was a fine fella, and to show what can happen with fans, and then I'll get off my soap box, Big Klu came to me and said he had sugar diabetes. When he told me that, I said to myself that I was going to take that information and think how I can help him, so he can have meals on time, because when you're flying with a Major League team, you're in the air a lot of times when you should be eating or doing things.

"So I decided to make him the roving batting coach for the Minor Leagues. That gave him the chance to eat when he wanted to, schedule when he wanted to, visit his wife when he wanted to. It really worked well, but the fans suddenly thought I was getting rid of him. It made me feel bad, because people didn't realize we were trying to help him rather than hurt him."

I had the feeling Howsam could talk to me through the rest of the day, and I wouldn't have minded, especially since it was like listening to one of those narrators for Turner Classic movies, sitting in a comfortable chair, smoking a pipe, and wearing a cardigan sweater, while filling in the background of a story that you thought you pretty much knew. But I also realized Howsam was nearly 90 years old, and he also lived in a retirement complex, so I kept thinking that either a senior activity was close at hand or an afternoon nap.

Goodness knows, I couldn't end my discussion with the grand poohbah of my Big Red Machine without asking about my guy Pete Rose, the Cincinnati native, the sparkplug of those Reds teams, and the owner of more hits than anybody in baseball. During this period in January 2006, he was heading into his 17th Major League season on the game's permanently ineligible list, and his Cooperstown plaque remained a fantasy, but he had confessed his gambling sins (somewhat) by then in one of his books and through various television outlets.

Did you see any of this Pete Rose stuff coming, or was it a surprise to you as it was to me and to everybody else?

"Well, Pete Rose, of course, he was (allowed to leave the Reds as a free agent after the 1978 season) by Dick to Philadelphia, and actually, the police report as I understand it now was that he owed $30,000 to gamblers in Cincinnati, and the police were supposed to have said that if he doesn't pay up, then they'll find him in the Ohio River when he gets out of baseball," said Howsam, without emotion as I nearly dropped the phone on the other end of his words.

Howsam continued by saying, "I knew Pete gambled on horses. A couple of our people owned tracks like (Yankees owner) George Steinbrenner did at that time, the Galbreaths (of John Galbreath who owned the Pirates) did at that time, and the Baltimore owner owned a track. So they weren't going to say you couldn't go to a track, you know. But no. I didn't know about (Rose gambling on baseball), and if I had, I wouldn't have had him in Cincinnati. It's too bad, and I've been asked about this, and I don't back up at all. Anybody who gambles on baseball should never be in the Hall of Fame. I feel that strongly, because there has to be rules, and you have to abide by them.

"As you know, walking from our dugout to our dressing room at Riverfront, right on the door as you go into the dressing room was the commissioner's bulletin right there telling you what would happen to you. We also used to have the FBI come and talk to our players before spring training, and we used to read that commissioner's thing both in Spanish and English, so there was no misunderstanding what were the rules."

I told Howsam I was a Baseball Hall of Fame voter, and I mentioned how I gradually moved over the years toward supporting his entry into Cooperstown someday. Howsam said, "Well, I feel bad about Rose, because we have such fine Reds players in the Hall of Fame. I would have liked to have seen him in there, but because of what he did, I say nobody who gambles on the game of baseball or takes steroids should be in the Baseball Hall of Fame."

We chatted some more about Cooperstown, and then I told Howsam the truth, and that was, I couldn't think of a more enjoyable conversation I ever had during my decades as a professional sports journalist. I didn't tell him this: During my days at The Water Pipe in Milwaukee, I never was within several Johnny Bench blasts of my wildest dreams of thinking I might have this kind of exchange more than 30 years later with the Big Red Machine's designer.

Thank you, sir.

This was a great honor.

"OK," said Bob Howsam, delivering another one of those chuckles that comes from a man living in peace with his decisions. "So nice to talk to you, and you have a very good day."

When Howsam died two years later at 89, it was after a very good life.

Epilogue

For the longest time, I hadn't a clue who waved me over from the on-deck circle to the edge of the home dugout. It was July 11, 2025, at Truist Park in Atlanta for All-Star Game Weekend. As always, baseball's Mid-Summer Classic featured several events – such as this game between historically Black colleges and universities – and the events attracted the Who's Who and the Who Used To Be. So, this moment ranked among my worst fears as a journalist whose professional career spanned jobs in the Midwest, West, and South, eight different U.S. presidents, and multiple sports.

People change over a half century.

Athletes really change.

"You're still working?" said the voice, softly then loudly while repeating the question. That's when I turned around to see somebody I didn't recognize while fearing it was somebody I should know.

The voice kept talking, and I placed my memory into overdrive in search of a name. He knew me, and that didn't help, especially since he spoke with authority about our past. Then, in nearly a flash, his worn face above a body more fit for a grandfather of yore – as opposed to a three-time baseball All-Star who used to challenge outrunning the wind – became 10, 30, 50 years younger.

This was Ken Griffey Sr., who once was a prominent player as the right fielder for The Great Eight, the nickname given to the everyday players for the Cincinnati Reds dynasty that became the Big Red Machine. He and the Machine's other cogs were my obsession as a youth during the 1970s before I covered them as a writer for *The Cincinnati Enquirer*.

That's why even the older (the much, much, much older) Griffey triggered something. Suddenly, I was 13 years old again, enjoying the greenest of green grass on the floor of that enchanted place called Crosley Field in Cincinnati. But then I was across town along the Ohio River at Riverfront Stadium during the late 1970s, and there was still magic, but I had to purge much of it from my soul while turning from fan to journalist.

I had great training. It went back to high school in Milwaukee under Mary Griesbach, my journalism teacher who was way ahead of her time teaching ethics in the business at that level. It also didn't hurt that she invited Bill Dwyre, the no-nonsense sports editor of the *Milwaukee Journal*, to speak to one of our classes my sophomore year. I latched onto Dwyre's philosophies as a hardliner for journalistic principles quickly and forever.

Once at Miami University in Oxford, Ohio, I discovered quickly I was in the right place, even beyond the solid writing back then of *The Miami Student*, the oldest college newspaper west of the Alleghenies. We were huge on journalistic ethics, even to the point that the Miami athletics director often blasted me for refusing to operate a rah-rah section when I became sports editor.

No question, I had more than a few feelings surface inside from fan days while covering my Big Red Machine, but I mostly kept the hero worshiping in check. Deadlines will do that to you. So will the realization in a flash that Joe Morgan curses as much as he blinks his eyes and that Johnny Bench wishes Pete Rose was stuck on the other side of Mars.

No matter what, I remained a Rose guy, but don't get me wrong. I was stunned, crushed, and then ticked in February 1989 when I discovered he lied to me in his office as Reds player-manager during the team's spring training in Plant City, Florida. It was the same day he returned from meeting with Baseball Commissioner A. Bartlett Giamatti in New York.

After Rose closed the door, I asked him if the rumors were true about him huddling with Giamatti about gambling.

Rose said it wasn't about gambling.

The meeting was about gambling.

As a Baseball Hall of Fame voter, my stance for the longest time was to say no to Rose for Cooperstown, but I never put my actions where my words were. Since he was given a lifetime ban by baseball, he never appeared on our ballots as members of the Baseball Writers' Association of America.

Then Rose confessed. Sort of. That's when I changed my stance to pull for Rose to make the Baseball Hall of Fame by any means necessary, preferably before his death. Of all people, how could I not forgive the guy with more hits than anybody in the game's history, the guy who gave me all of those thrills as a player for my Big Red Machine, the guy who signed that poster I've had since I was 12, the guy who never forgot my name after I briefly met him on Friday, May 14, 1976, in the home clubhouse at Riverfront Stadium.

"You know, last fall, we were all there together in Franklin, Tennessee at a sports memorabilia show, and it was the day before Pete died," said Griffey, referring to Rose, who had the eternal love of most of his teammates. They included Tony Perez, George Foster, Dave Concepcion, and Griffey. Little did they know back then on Sunday, Sept. 29, 2024 that they were huddling around their old leadoff hitter in a wheelchair for a final photo.

Griffey and I switched to the good ole days, which were all things involving My Big Red Machine with Baseball Hall of Famers or near ones at every position. Led by colorful Baseball Hall of Fame manager Sparky Anderson, those Reds of Johnny, Joe, Pete, Tony, Ken, and the other Machine cogs were invincible, or so we remembered, which brought us back to the present.

After Griffey revealed that he really was a grandfather these days by introducing me to three of his grandsons nearby, he mentioned his aches and pains. He was a prostate cancer survivor, and through the decades, he suffered knee and back issues. Then he went around the horn describing the health (or the lack thereof) of the other Great Eight members.

He said Concepcion had lung replacement surgery after years of chain smoking, including between innings before playing brilliant shortstop and ripping line drives from the plate. He mentioned the heart bypass surgery for Foster, the left fielder who was the slugger among sluggers with his black bat. He mourned the deaths of Rose and Morgan, the superb second baseman when he wasn't flashing his clutch gene with his bat and his legs. He said starting pitcher Don Gullett and super reliever Pedro Borbon also were deceased.

He added a Machine member beyond The Great Eight was in a wheelchair, and he gave equally grim reports on others.

"About the only ones doing well are Cesar Geronimo and Tony Perez," said Griffey of Geronimo, a four-time Gold Glove winner in center field, and Cesar swung a quietly effective bat at the end of the order. As for Perez, he was the RBI master while playing efficiently at first base, but more strikingly, he was everybody's favorite human being.

Before Griffey continued, I said, "What you are saying is jarring, but you know what? We're all getting older."

Griffey nodded, and then he flashed that grin I first saw when he was 25, but now he was 75. Just like that, I heard the closing lines moving through my subconscious of a Firefall song called "Younger."

Gonna try to lose a pound or two
Gonna sit back and admire the view
Gonna memorize a Dylan song
Fix all the things that I've done wrong
   I'll appreciate the friends I've got
Maybe give true love another shot
   When I get younger
When I get younger
When I get younger
When I get younger

When I get younger, I'm going to remember my parents never got old, never stopped encouraging my brothers and me, never ceased trying to make us better at everything. In particular, they gave me the template for becoming a trailblazing sports columnist. Their Jackie Robinson lives helped me develop a reputation for toughness yet fairness while operating with a skin thicker than the belts dad used during our adolescence when we disobeyed.

Those times were few.

As I told my parents often as the years became decades, my brothers and I quickly discovered the truth: They always were right.

They always were proud, too.

There rarely was a moment Mom didn't approach somebody at random during a public setting and point to me. "Do you recognize that face?" she would say, grinning, daring the person to shake their head. "That's my son, and he's on TV. You've probably seen him, so take another look. He's also on Wikipedia. Just Google Terence Moore."

Dad took an early retirement from AT&T at 55 in 1987, because he said work was getting in the way of his golf game. He was part of golf clubs in each of the cities we lived (South Bend, Cincinnati, Chicago, and Milwaukee), and he made sure his fellow members knew my every move as a journalist.

Dad died at 84 in October 2016 in Brownsburg, Indiana, just outside Indianapolis, where my parents moved in 2004 after 32 years in Milwaukee. We brought Mom back to Cincinnati, where my brother Dennis continued to live with his wife and family. Mom loved Cincinnati like the rest of us. She never missed watching a Reds game on television, and her favorite player at her death at 88 was Elly De La Cruz. She called or texted me after his every move of significance.

With apologies to poet T.S. Eliot, April isn't the cruelest month, or at least it wasn't compared to September 2024.

My mom died on the 20th.

My guy Pete Rose died 10 days later.

Acknowledgments

So many times through the decades, I've told stories involving my love affair with the Big Red Machine to relatives and to friends, especially to those who enjoy baseball or storytelling about anything. They've listened before saying, "Well, you need to write a book."

Dexter McCloud and Milton Warden were among those who pushed me from talking to typing. Milt also shot the photo on the hardcover wraparound of me holding my two previous books.

Thanks, guys.

Thanks also to the many Cincinnati Enquirer decision makers who gave me the chance to write about the Machine and other high-profile subjects straight from college.

I also wish to thank Fred Reeder Jr., a professor at my alma mater of Miami (Ohio) University.

Starting in 2014, Fred and I spent six years combining to teach journalism at Miami. While I flew between my home in Atlanta and campus in Oxford, Ohio, he operated from Miami. He has been nominated for the Outstanding Professor award multiple years. Even more, he has been a diehard Cincinnati Reds fan since he moved as a 1-year-old with his family to Cincinnati suburb Mount Healthy in 1972.

Oh, and guess where the Samuel Moore family lived when we moved from South Bend, Indiana to Cincinnati in 1968?

Mount Healthy.

So Fred was the definitive person to proofread this book.

www.ingramcontent.com/pod-product-compliance
Lightning Source LLC
LaVergne TN
LVHW091541201025
823870LV00007B/83